who do they think they are?

new literacies

AND DIGITAL EPISTEMOLOGIES

Colin Lankshear, Michele Knobel,
and Michael Peters
General Editors

Vol. 40

PETER LANG
New York • Washington, D.C./Baltimore • Bern
Frankfurt • Berlin • Brussels • Vienna • Oxford

connie morrison

who do they think they are?

teenage girls & their avatars in spaces of social online communication

PETER LANG
New York • Washington, D.C./Baltimore • Bern
Frankfurt • Berlin • Brussels • Vienna • Oxford

Library of Congress Cataloging-in-Publication Data

Morrison, Connie (Connie M.)
Who do they think they are?: teenage girls and their avatars
in spaces of social online communication / Connie Morrison.
p. cm.
Includes bibliographical references and index.
1. Internet and teenagers—Psychological aspects.
2. Identity (Psychology) in adolescence. 3. Teenage girls—Psychology.
4. Avatars (Computer graphics)—Psychological aspects.
5. Online social networks—Psychological aspects. I. Title.
HQ799.2.I5M67 302.23'1—dc22 2009018331
ISBN 978-1-4331-0552-4
ISSN 1523-9543

Bibliographic information published by **Die Deutsche Nationalbibliothek**.
Die Deutsche Nationalbibliothek lists this publication in the "Deutsche
Nationalbibliografie"; detailed bibliographic data is available
on the Internet at http://dnb.d-nb.de/.

FSC
Mixed Sources
Product group from well-managed
forests, controlled sources and
recycled wood or fiber

Cert no. SCS-COC-002464
www.fsc.org
©1996 Forest Stewardship Council

The paper in this book meets the guidelines for permanence and durability
of the Committee on Production Guidelines for Book Longevity
of the Council of Library Resources.

29 Broadway, 18th floor, New York, NY 10006
www.peterlang.com

Printed in the United States of America

Table of Contents

Acknowledgements

This book was written while juggling the final stages of my doctoral studies, teaching at Memorial University's Faculty of Education and being a mom to my three daughters. While these separate directions in my life might appear to be at odds with each other – in reality, they have served to ground, give perspective and motivate each other. I couldn't exist any other way.

What is presented here is a version of my doctoral work. It is a look at how creating a cartoon self image can also be understood as visual autobiography. It's about girlhood identity and the social implications of online representation.

It was Dr. Ursula Kelly, my doctoral supervisor, mentor and friend who first encouraged me to submit a proposal for this book. Those who know Ursula will know how profoundly she changes lives and how her support can inspire hope and possibility. Her careful and thoughtful guidance has made this journey possible.

Even though writing a book and a thesis simultaneously is a little out of the ordinary, Colin Lankshear and Michele Knobel believed it could be done. They helped me to transform my dissertation language into something more approachable. For their unwavering support and advice through the writing and revision of this book, I am both grateful and indebted.

I thank Kathryn Currin for her careful reading of the manuscript. Kat proves that it is possible for teachers to learn from their former students.

Sophie Appel at Peter Lang has provided production support and an endless amount of patience from the beginning. I am deeply appreciative that she has been my guide through the creation of this book.

I must also acknowledge the ten girls who informed my research. They willingly let me into their lives and gave of themselves. For their contributions, their honesty and their passion, I am eternally grateful.

And finally I wish to acknowledge my beautiful family. Neal, you have been unwavering with your support. And Lauren, Claire and Sophie – you teach me; and you bring me joy every single day.

Chapter One

Introduction

Evolution of a Question

One morning in the spring of 2008, an interview on a TV network morning show caught my attention. British photojournalist Robbie Cooper was promoting his new book, *Alter Ego,* by providing a "gallery of portraits" to look at the physical relationship between gaming avatars and their creators. As Cooper explored the relationships between the virtual and real-life identity of online gamers who had assumed alternative personas as a condition of the games they played, the graphics behind him displayed split screen images of the 3D monster warriors beside images of the actual people who had created them. While compiling his collection, Cooper found that, initially, individuals seem to create online personas under the guise of anonymity, and that the identities of online characters tend to be "less ordinary" than individuals are in reality. Cooper revealed that he had deliberately set out to find someone who played a "fat avatar," but his search was unsuccessful. With this admission, I stopped dead in my tracks. No fat avatars. This chance encounter with Cooper's interview and his observation made me wonder about the online world and virtual identities.

At around that same time, my oldest daughter, Lauren, made an avatar for my Rogers Yahoo account. A headshot of the avatar appears as a personal icon each time I log on. It is embedded in my toolbar and it appears alongside any blog posting I make from that account. It can appear in full body, and it can also be changed to reflect the season, a special occasion or any mood. Lauren had great fun representing me in this two-dimensional cartoon form, and when she was finished I confess that the avatar she had created surprised me. It looked younger, slimmer and was dressed in funky clothes that bear little resemblance to anything in my real-life closet. I questioned what it might look like if I had created it, and that made me wonder about the considerations individuals must make when they create these avatars.

In the meantime, the phrase "no fat avatars" was haunting me. I wondered if avatars existed in an infinite range of size and shape, and I admit that I had not given it much thought before having heard the interview. In the case of Cooper's book, gaming avatars had been intentionally created to be "alter egos" for use in competitive on-line spaces. Implied in his title was that these avatars were not intended to be "realistic egos" or even "stylized egos"; instead, these "egos" were designed to be alternatives — but alternative to what? Reality? As I began to research the literature on avatars, I found that Angela Thomas (2007) had also observed only thin avatars in her study in *Second Life*. Like Cooper's avatars, her study examined explorations in fantasy and role play in a number of online contexts. The avatars from both Cooper's collection and Thomas' research had not been created as deliberate representations of their creators. *If* it was true that no fat avatars exist in these contexts, I wondered why not? In such examples, avatars are three-dimensional and interactive. They are designed to be communicative and possess social and cultural qualities that allow them to interact with others in specific virtual online spaces. Their close association to virtual worlds of fantasy made it easier (only slightly) for me to accept that only thin avatars might exist. Perhaps, stylized and alternative forms of visual representation hold no expectation that the avatar should look like the person who created it (even though Cooper's work demonstrates that many do bear striking similarities). Given the media culture's preoccupation with thinness, it is likely inconceivable for those who create the avatar programs to even offer a body option that is not thin. After all, as we have learned from Bridget Jones movies (tongue planted firmly in cheek), being a "hefty" size eight is akin to giving up on life, love, and all things worth possessing. In ideal worlds such as *Second Life,* and in competitive online spaces such as *World of Warcraft*, perhaps the message is that individuals should choose ideal bodies. That, however, is another research project.

In the case of the Rogers Yahoo avatar creator, there are many options available to personalize avatars in terms of skin color, hair color, hairstyle, clothing, accessories, and even backgrounds. Considering the places that these avatars are visible, it seems that an avatar is, at best, *supposed* to look like the creator, and, at least, be a close enough likeness that it would be recognized as a stylized version of its creator. What might happen if this deliberately representative kind of avatar could not accurately represent the creator for some reason? These musings raised further questions regarding how avatars might (or might not) contribute to the meaning of identity and representation in the online and digital spaces in which they appear.

As I mulled over these questions, my teenage daughter set up an account on the online social networking site, Facebook, so that she could communicate with her friends. In the process of setting up her account and choosing her profile picture, I wondered what would it mean if she and her friends were to use avatars to represent themselves instead of photos. Would they choose avatars of the alter ego variety, or would they stick with something more deliberately representative? With a generation of teenage Facebook users who share bits of their life with hundreds of "friends" at a time, what would it mean if they represented themselves with one of these always and apparently forever thin avatars? Surely an avatar can tell a story about its creator, I thought. However, such stories might be difficult or even be impossible to tell given the limited choices within the websites that enable avatar creation. What, then is the connection between avatars and identity, and what does the act of deliberately representing oneself with an avatar say metaphorically about how teenaged girls see themselves in a social, communicative context?

Out of the convergence of a chance encounter with the Cooper interview, the creation of an avatar in an email account and the questions that emerged from watching my daughter pick a profile picture for her Facebook page, a central question evolved: *Who do they think they are?* Not a question that can be answered easily or quickly, it conjures key notions of identity and representation. Within academic discourse, the notion of girlhood identity has been given a great deal of consideration. As one might expect, asking a group of teenaged girls to consider who they are might elicit complex, conflicted and sometimes even contrary responses. Within cyberspace, teenaged girls have ever-evolving opportunities to construct identity in both realistically conceived and alternative forms, which themselves evoke considerations no less conflicted or complex. As a result, this book looks at what happened when a group of ten Canadian teenage girls, ages thirteen to seventeen, came together as case study participants and first created avatars to represent who they think they are, then joined an online forum to consider the choices they made during the creation of their avatars.

My engagement with youth culture and youth cultural acts is intended to be inherently pedagogical. When we think about the rapid growth in popularity of social networking sites like Facebook and MySpace as well as the popularity of programs that allow avatar construction, these online social networking spaces become important cultural locations where youth identities are constructed and shared. So it makes sense to spend time working with youth in ways that help us understand how and why they do what they do on these sites. Not only are they important locations because of how identity is represented there, but they are also important because of their vast popularity as sites of identity construction. A BBC Online report, from February 6, 2009, indicates that worldwide membership on Facebook had grown to 110 million just five years after Harvard student, Mark Zuckerberg, formed the site to keep track of social events on his own campus. What does it mean when new social discursive practices become mainstream as taken-for-granted methods of socialization and communication?

By August 2008, comScore Inc. (which describes itself as "a global Internet information provider to which leading companies turn for consumer behavior insight that drives successful marketing, sales and trading strategies") reported that in June 2008, Facebook had 132,105,000 unique visitors to its site. And while the use of social networking sites like Facebook and MySpace have started to level off in North America (with a growth of only nine percent in 2008) their global user base is still expanding significantly. Use of Facebook in regions like Asia/Pacific and Middle/East Africa have increased by over 400%, and use in Latin America has increased over 1055% in the last year. The implications for this research, then, is that notions of identity and representation are, at the very least, considerations that each of these users must make when posting profile pictures — pictures which in essence will say, "this is who I am" to their network of friends.

Citing University of Toronto sociology professor Barry Wellman, Proudfoot (2009) argues "technology enables people to connect more through informal channels such as the grassroots mobilization that helped propel Barack Obama into the White House. If anything, the Internet has encouraged regular contact with a wider, looser web of acquaintances than before." New literacy practices, or spaces to enact these practices, might provide transformative opportunities for educators and students, but they are not without their challenges. With this wider, looser web of acquaintances has come a new way for individuals to represent themselves in these discursive spaces. Coiro et al. (2008) ask, "How do people encode, receive and negotiate meanings in current technological conjunctive" (p. 14)? Having millions of individuals connected to more acquaintances than ever before gives added weight to the considerations around how these individuals will choose to construct their identity online. If the potential exists for individuals to represent themselves in their social networks using a deliberately constructed cartoon image, the questions that guide this study, (namely, who do they think they are? and who do they want others to think they are?), might have broader social implications than can be learned from a group of teenaged girls.

As a site of identity construction, and since all of the participants in my case study chose to create their avatars using the flash based WeeWorld.com site, the site itself demands some attention. However, since much discussion and analysis will be given to this site and the choices available to the participants of this study in coming chapters, I will provide only a basic overview of the website and its designed purpose at this time.

It is also necessarily to be clear, up front, that the WeeMee avatars created by this group of girls were *not* of the alter ego variety. Nor were they three-dimensional or interactive. However, in spite of the apparently pared-down, two-dimensional cartoon nature, the constructions of these avatars let us consider notions like identity, representation, audience and purpose. By constructing avatars initially designed to be used for playful, social and communicative purposes in places like email signatures, in text messaging, with blog postings and on social networking sites, the girls provide an opportunity to examine how their avatars were constructed, not to mention the manner by which they did or did not represent their creators. The fact that these avatars are used by youth as a means of digital identity construction makes them subject to serious social and cultural examination.

According to the company information posted on the WeeWorld.com website WeeMees are

> personalized digital identities, which reflect their owners' looks, hairstyle, fashion sense, pets, pastimes, passions, pursuits, sports, tastes, and even emotions. WeeMees can travel with their owners across their entire digital lives, from IM and applications through to emails, blogs, forums and social networking communities, as well as onto cell phones, where they can be used as picture messages, wallpaper and even as a visual Caller ID. (WeeWorld.com)

Business Wire.com (2009) reported that WeeWorld is "the world's first and most extensive multiplatform visual identity with more than 10 million WeeMees in more than 39 countries around the world." The intent behind its US launch in 2006 was to "create, update and maintain a consistent, personalized visual identity throughout the creator's entire online mobile life." It is a deliberate attempt to tap into the increased richness within the visual capacity of online environments and mobile technology. What WeeMee offers individuals is an opportunity to personalize online and offline expressions as they are able to create a "personalized identity that travels throughout their digital world." WeeMees partnered with many of the world's biggest Internet and mobile technology companies. MSN, Skype, Vodafone, and Motorola are just a few. In a partnership with AOL, WeeWorld allows AIM users to build WeeMees and select backgrounds for free. The WeeWorld.com site claims that there are WeeMees born every few seconds using this application. Through AIM, which is the largest instant messaging community in the United States, users in Canada and the United Kingdom can also enhance their instant messaging experience by adding animated WeeMees to their applications.

Windows Live Messenger also boasts hosting 14 Million WeeMees since March 2005. Using their site, WeeMees can be built for free; however, if they want their friends to see it and to share emotions while chatting, it will cost an average of 3 euros.

Skype has also developed a partnership with WeeWorld since 2005. Since then, nearly 450,000 WeeMees have been made and can be viewed while texting and instant messaging within buddy lists. WeeMees are available on Skype in the USA, UK, Germany, France, The Netherlands and Poland. WeeMees are also available on SkypeOne which allows virtual global access.

Much attention has been given to new literacy practices with youth who have carved out alternative spaces as acts of rebellion or as forms of resistance to popular culture's hegemonic intention. Those youth with both access to and expertise in new and evolving modes of digital expression have become the subjects of academic study as they represent a promise of what is possible. For Gee (2003), *affinity spaces* can exist within a digital realm where youth engagement with a technology is often viewed as a means of group belonging and agency. Such youth are native to a Web 2.0 reality. They cannot conceive of a world without Google, and they create blogs, web pages, fan fictions, and video remixes with a comfort that seems second only to breathing. However, for others (for a number of reasons ranging from access and opportunity to competence and desire), engagement with digital technology is far less innovative. In such cases, a "first mindset" (Lankshear and Knobel, 2006) puts old established practices in the hands of users of new technologies for whom "new technologies [are] simply more recent forms of established tools, rather than as constitutive elements of new ways of doing things and new ways of being" (p. 54). But even in what has evolved into more mainstream spaces such as email, text messaging and engagement in social networking sites, there remains an opportunity to explore identity construction through the vehicle of avatar creation. Such an exploration not only provides a pedagogical opportunity for educators to learn *from* youth as they explore with new ways to construct their online identity(ics), but in so doing, these avatars might provide an opportunity to critically examine a new way of being in the world. These avatars, with all their built-in intention to be created in the likeness of their creators, say, "this is who I am," and in doing so speak volumes without ever having to rely on the academically privileged written word.

The participants in my case study were certainly comfortable navigating online spaces, to a degree. Their engagements were limited to common practices of email and text attachment, texting and instant messaging, and participation in social networking sites. None of the girls had created a blog or contributed to a wiki or even a fanfiction. So, while the avatars that will be examined here may not constitute the newest of the "technical stuff" in ontological terms (Lankshear and Knobel, 2006), in these contexts, and with these girls, the creation of an avatar, in any form, was indeed new "technical stuff."

The goal of this book is to contribute to and participate in academic discourse in new literacies, critical media studies, youth pedagogy, girlhood identity, and autobiography, particularly in its visual form. At the intersection of these scholarly discourses is an underwritten understanding that the visual and the image provide significant pedagogical opportunities that have yet to be embraced or exploited within English language arts curricula. Even though foundational curricular documents provide a space for the inclusion of new literacies, my past experience as a teacher, and now as one who educates teachers and teacher candidates, suggests that traditional print literacies continue to be privileged in local English classrooms. Lankshear and Knobel (2006) advise strongly against the temptation for educators to cling to technology only to use it in place of old and tired literacies. The temptation to put old wine in new bottles, as they say, is something I try to avoid, though it is sometimes hard to resist the temptation of a good glass of wine in whatever way it is presented! While the battle to include new literacies appears to be won, at least within academic discourses, what I have seen when I observe interns and when I review provincial standardized public examinations suggests otherwise. For me, this book represents an opportunity to join in on a conversation based on my own research findings and offer suggestions for those daring enough to cross the conventional boundary of what gets considered literacy to join a growing movement toward a broader and more inclusive conceptual framework.

This book explores a new literacy practice that teenage girls have used or could use in their everyday online, social communicative practices. It rests at the intersection of new literacies, girlhood identity, youth pedagogy, critical media studies, and visual autobiography. Also, it is premised on the understanding that as youth create social relationships in and through popular cultural or social texts, they do so while negotiating complex and often conflicted notions of desire and fantasy. The idea behind creating a personalized identity by constructing an avatar is not something I can take credit for — I wish it were. Instead, making an avatar that looks like a mini, cartoon version of its creator is the expressed (and advertised) intent of the WeeWorld.com site. Millions of WeeMee avatars have already been created, which means that millions of individuals have made visual statements that say; *this is who I am*, *this is who I would like to be*, or *this is who I would like others to think I am*. From this perspective the representation of identity with an avatar is not just a metaphorical expression, it is a deliberate and intentional personalized statement of identity.

Because I wanted to learn more about the social practices that shape identity in teenage girls, I deliberately turned to the participants to guide me through what they thought were the important aspects of their identity in such digital spaces. Overwhelmingly, the girls wrote about identity and representation as they relate to categories of appearance and activity. In other words, they told me that, for them, identity was tied intimately to what they looked like and what they did (and, in some cases, what they hoped to do). Appearance meant both how they looked physically and how they presented and represented themselves to the world and in the world, in terms of what they wear. While this might not seem like a big deal on the surface, Stern (2007) reminds us that adolescence is a period when "people develop and construct identity and, notably, negotiate feelings of confusion as they straddle childhood and what most would consider some 'adult' concerns" (p.

2). While some may not consider choosing the right shirt or the right hairstyle to be an "adult" concern, these decisions were paramount for the girls in this study as they considered what options would best allow their avatars to most accurately represent them.

This book is also premised on an understanding that new literacy practices include multimodal forms of representation. To that end, my study deliberately positions the construction of avatars within the realm of new literacy practice (Kress, 2003; New London Group, 1996), as it is situated within the youth social networking practice of instant communication, poly-synchronous communication and social networking communities such as Facebook, blogs, instant messaging, and email. I will look at the process (and product) of creating a personalized avatar by using a frame that recognizes it as a form of autobiography in the sense that it is designed to be a mini, cartoon personal identity. A playful and communicative discursive practice gets a serious ideological analysis that looks at how teenage girls narrate themselves in their social spaces as they struggle and strive to belong.

Virtual Is Real

While Agger (2004) argues that the Internet opens up new, more public communities through which and with which one may author oneself, I put forward that often too much is made of the difference between online worlds and offline worlds. Valentine and Holloway (2002) suggest that the "virtual" and "real" worlds of youth are mutually constituted. They explain that industrial technology transformed Western society in the nineteenth century to the point that the two are now mutually constituted. In a similar fashion, it is impossible to discuss youth culture as being separated from engagement with digital and mobile technologies. To that end, I do not attempt to make a distinction between online and offline behavior as two separate and discrete realities. I find such discourses to be problematic. Rather, I have accepted, as do Valentine and Holloway, that online spaces are "used, encountered and interpreted within the context of young people's off-line everyday lives" (p. 305). Put another way, particularly for those who are native to a digitally enabled world, engagement online is simply part of living in an everyday existence. Consider that adults from the baby boomer era do not differentiate between a pre-television era and a post-television era when they discuss how they function in the world, because television has been part of our reality for decades. However, for those a few generations earlier (or currently in less economically privileged locations globally), this would not have been the case. It would be impossible to deny that the presence of television has changed how we understand others and ourselves within public and popular discourses; it shapes how we relate, create and perform our identity. Yet, we do not talk of our engagement with television as separate from our worlds without it. The technology of television has wiggled into our popular and everyday discourses to the point where we are culturally immersed in it, with it, and through it. To speak of our engagement with television as separate from our lives without television would seem ridiculous. I argue that for many youth today, life online is simply the way they live and the way they socialize. These youth have not known a world without the Internet; it is simply part of their world.

Avatars Appearing Everywhere

In January 2009, the *Globe and Mail* reported that avatars, which describes as "characters or personas standing in for real people" (Hartley, 2009) are beginning to enjoy a more mainstream acceptance. As social networking sites like Facebook and MySpace work out copyright and compatibility issues with one another, we might expect a rapid take-up of these virtual identities in the near future. As with so much related to popular culture, the reason behind this mainstream take-up seems tied to market forces. More plainly, companies have figured out that they can make real money from people who buy things for their virtual identities and their virtual spaces. In line with the findings from Robbie Cooper's exploration into gaming avatars, in April 2007 Matt Jackson reported in *The Boston Globe* that avatars tend to be more adventurous than their real life creators in that creators will try on identities in a virtual environment that might be more risky and perhaps more revealing than what individuals will be in real life. Consistent with research by Kelly, Pomerantz & Currie (2005), as well as with Gee (2004), the notion of trying on alternative identities provides an opportunity for real people to experiment, push boundaries, gain confidence, and explore from the protective comfort of a virtual, alter ego persona. Jackson (2007) reported that for some, an avatar is an extension of their offline selves. In other cases, the avatars are designed to be whimsical and fanciful, likely because of their application and participation in the massively popular multi-user graphic virtual realities (GVRs), such as *Second Life*.

The academic literature on avatar research focuses strongly on their construction within GVRs, and I will draw briefly from this literature as a way to situate my discussion as separate from it in the way a distant cousin might be related but not really from the same cultural world. My research focuses on the intentionally autobiographical nature of avatars. Given the social repercussions implied in a discursive practice that co-authors identity in partnership with the producers of such avatar-making programs, I have focused on literature which intersects at points of relevance and interest with my own research in terms of the limits and possibilities of identity construction. I have not drawn on literature that explores the nature of avatars as alter egos or avatars within gaming practices. Quite simply, the avatars constructed for my case study were not intended to be alter egos nor were they intended for interactive social purposes such as the 3-dimensional experiences in *Second Life*, or other forms of online gaming.

Kang and Yang (2006) conducted a study in Korea to examine how avatars used in the context of Instant Messaging (IM) were different from those constructed for use in Internet Relay Chat (IRC) versions of computer-mediated communication (CMC). Their study is limited to avatar use in Korea, where, admittedly, the discursive practices and engagement with avatars is generally more mainstream than it is within North America, and specifically more so than the population that I studied. Their work describes IM as "social software" used between people with prior relationships (as in MSN), as opposed to IRC, which tends to be used by people who have never met in real life. Kang and Yang explain that following the collapse of the Internet bubble in 2000, a company called Sayclub introduced avatar services in Korea. Since that time, the avatar market has grown steadily. In 2001, the avatar market in Korea yielded approximately 24 billion dollars. By 2004, that figure has risen to 180 billion dollars. "In 2001, avatars were selected as one of the 10 most popular products in Korea" (p. 1174).

The degree of anonymity allowed and sought in IM and IRC applications yielded the greatest difference in the degree of creativity and imagination exhibited in the avatars in Kang and Yang's (2006) study. Because of the fundamental differences in their use, Kang and Yang's findings suggest that avatars used in IM applications tend to have more realistic features than the avatars used in IRC contexts which often include expressions of imaginary identities (having fairy wings, for example). The authors found that "the primary purpose of using an avatar is to build and reveal an identity for the sake of satisfactory communication in cyberspace" (p. 1180). In fact, they argue, "an avatar represents a user's self-identity and desire for self-disclosure" (p. 1173). The notion of using an avatar to build and reveal identity bears significance to my study in so far as these constructed self-representations deliberately "reveal" or deliberately disclose aspects of self-identity in a similar way that the construction of an autobiographical avatar intends to deliberately reveal and disclose aspects of the self. Kang and Yang suggest that there is a limit, however, to which users will reveal who they are or who they want others to think they are. "Users want their identity within a virtual community to replace their physical body and to control the degree to which they disclose themselves over the computer" (pp. 1173-1174).

A decade ago, Beth Kolko (1999) examined how avatars were used to represent virtual bodies in multi-user graphic virtual realities (GVRs) like *Second Life*. Debunking the once-popular belief that viewed the physical self and the online self as separate and distinct entities, Kolko argues that the design of an avatar affects the possibilities for its communication inside virtual worlds. She explains that early scholarly work on computer-mediated communications (CMC) focused on "the fluidity of on-line identity, developing a kind of mediated electronic body that resulted in certain inconsistencies between the virtual and physical self" (p. 177). Identity play allowed experimentation, empathetic identifications, virtual border crossings, and a sense of the non-unitary nature of identity. These explorations in "mediated" and "disappearing" bodies online were "laudable goals of innovative communication strategies that would help assuage all manner of discrimination in interpersonal communication" (p. 177). In other words, the absence of a physical body to mark a user's gender, race, or age would liberate the user to "exist in the realm of ideas" (p. 177). She argues that until her study, the question of how gendered bodies (represented in avatar form) affect communication patterns had been largely ignored. Her argument is premised on the belief that GVRs cannot be understood apart from their technological capabilities. "How physical bodies can be represented in electronic spaces ultimately reveals how gendered bodies come to affect gendered voices" (Kolko, 1999, p. 179).

In the case of her research, avatars in GVRs are designed to communicate with one another. Not so in my study. In my research the avatars are representation of real people who are communicating with one another, making them more akin to users in IM environments. However, what is consistent with both studies is that elements of gender, for example, are not within the sole control of the users creating the avatars. Drawing on Kress and van Leeuwen (1996), she argues that the author of an avatar is masked behind the producer of the program that allows its construction. This relationship gives over power to the designers of the avatar-making program in terms of what can or cannot be represented. By limiting the possibilities of how the avatar can be created there is a "denial of agency encompassed by this dynamic" (p. 184). This denial of agency, or the limit to agency, is something that factors heavily in my own research.

Kolko also draws on Kress & van Leeuwen's (1996) notion that social interactions and social relations can be *encoded* in pictures and images. Their argument links language's semiotic code to the way that images or pictures can be transported and thereby considered within larger socially constructed (D)discourses. (For a more detailed discussion of (D)discourse, please see chapter two.)

Avatar work conducted by Kafai, Fields and Cook (2007) provides some parallels with my research in terms of the semiotic considerations behind avatar construction and manufactured virtual identities. However, it also differs in a few fundamental ways. The authors address avatars within the context of the online world, *Second Life*. They draw from Shirley Turkle's (1995, 2005) claims that computers are not only work tools but also provide a vehicle for self-exploration and identity play in what can be described as a form of "identity workshop." The authors describe avatars that are "not ephemeral and spurious creations: players spend considerable time selecting and customizing them and then interacting with others online" (p. 31). Recognizing the teenage years as a critical time for the development of identity, Kafai et al. examined teens within the context of a "tween" virtual world, Whyville.net (a large scale multi-user GVR environment with over 1.5 million registered players), as they interact with others as part of their social discursive practice. In Whyville, avatars can be customized within a limited two-dimensional framework. Their existence as deliberate and conscious constructions ties them to notions of an "identity playground." Quite simply, the discursive practices associated with teens in Whyville are closely associated to play.

Given the purposeful and deliberately autobiographical intent behind my study's avatars, I align my research more closely with Turkle's notion of an "identity workshop" but also acknowledge the important contribution of the playful nature of this new literacy practice as demonstrated by Kafai et al. Drawing from Goffman's (1959) work on face-work, the authors understand that identities are negotiated and validated in everyday face-to-face settings where encounters are akin to "staged" performances. Online environments such as Whyville merely provide a cyber stage where teens have the ability to "represent themselves, or perform via their avatar creations" (Kafai et al., 2007, p. 32). From this perspective, avatars are potentially seen as agency-making vehicles within the conflicted and complex social networks.

The study examines how the "resources, constraints, and agency" were negotiated as participants created their avatars in this social online space, beginning with an examination of the degree of "expressiveness" afforded to their research participants. Kafai et al. (2007) looked at how the number and variety of options available to construct avatar faces affected how the participants were able to claim agency in their creations. Within Whyville, a participant's avatar evolves to become more complex as participation on the site increases. For example, a "newbie" might appear as a simple smile face, whereas a seasoned user might appear in full body with an individualized style in terms of clothing, hair and facial expression. Acquiring a facial part from the 30,000 options available involves first earning a good salary in Whyville so that shopping options are available.

Finally, the study explores how the social constraints within the online community impacted a user's sense of agency. Using an analysis of the actual avatars, group interviews and email postings in the online newspaper *The Whyville Times*, Kafai et al. (2007) found that some participants expressed that they "had more than one reason for making a particular look, or some youth changed their looks periodically" (p. 32). In fact, on Whyville.net individuals often created *multiple* selves. Rather than an exercise in multiple identity per se, this practice was connected to the economic flexibility that could arise when multiple bank accounts could be created (allowing for participants to have multiple opportunities to collect more "clams" for their accounts).

Overall, Kafai et al. (2007) found that appearance was extremely important for those in Whyville because it allowed participants to make friends and flirt with members of the opposite sex. In what appears strikingly similar to the messages inherent in popular culture in general and the commercial beauty industry in particular, one young participant observed, "looking 'good' is a way of demonstrating social status and more likely to get people to talk to you" (p. 33). While it was never explicitly stated in their work, relationships examined within this study were implicitly heteronormative. In the study by Kafai et al. (2007) participants listed six reasons for constructing their avatars as they did. These were (1) aesthetic considerations, (2) to make it like their "real" self, (3) to affiliate with someone or something, (4) to demonstrate something they cannot have in real life, (5) to align with or against a popular trend, (6) or to provide a deliberate disguise. In some cases, teens in their study made deliberate attempts to construct their avatars to appear like themselves, though this was not the intention of the study. These categories relate closely to my own findings, as several bear a remarkable similarity to the reasons cited by my case study participants as being important considerations in their own avatar construction.

The Chapters to Follow

Chapter two begins with the epistemological perspectives that provide the theoretical frame and ground this examination of autobiographical avatar creations. Concepts central to this exploration are defined and followed by a brief rendering of the implications for the findings. Finally, as a way to position my understandings and interpretations, I will situate my role as researcher within this project.

Chapter three begins by briefly introducing each of the girls in this study, and then briefly outlines the process by which this study was conducted. I will then explain how the WeeWorld.com site works in terms of avatar production, and then situate avatar construction within the larger theoretical framework of new literacy and autobiography scholarship. I will take a brief look at the limitless and/or limiting choices the girls faced when attempting to construct their avatars.

Chapter four provides a brief glimpse into the constructed identities of the ten girls who participated in this study by introducing readers to the avatars that the girls created in their likeness. This introduction will provide a frame for the upcoming analysis of how they were constructed. Considering the limitations of the avatar creation programs, the girls demonstrate how they are active participants and collaborators in their own identity representation, even though at times their avatars do not or cannot tell the stories they first want to tell. Teachable moments are briefly highlighted as they arise, and questions are posed around how comfortable the girls are with their avatars as virtual representations. Following the introduction of the girls and their avatars, I will discuss the practical importance of understanding avatars and the manner by which online identity is constructed.

In chapter five, I consider how virtual space becomes a laboratory for performativity and identity construction, not to mention nearly constant reinvention. Issues of appearance, ability and gender help to frame an examination of what happens when the girls feel free to represent who they are in a seemingly limitless fashion only to learn that their options are limited by the language and rules of the site being used. By looking critically at the choices involved in the production of autobiographical avatars, this chapter will examine what happens when the girls are not always able to construct their avatars the way they want to.

In chapter six, the manner by which the girls struggle to represent themselves accurately against the challenges of limited choice is examined. Even though the avatar creation site used by girls in this study is, for the most part, free and available in the public domain, it also has a significant commercial component. WeeWorld.com includes a thinly veiled branding component that tempts users to purchase items for their avatars, and it appears to be adding more commercial content on a constant basis. Notions of gender become salient as options like figure skates with pink laces provide a touchstone for issues of representation. And the serious issue of being judged based on appearances (in several forms of representation) is explored. In the case of the five older girls, attention focused on the real-life social implications of being judged, not only on their real physical appearances, but how such judgments impacted the way they represent themselves in their online social spaces.

In chapter seven, the fluid representation and constant renegotiation of identity is examined within a cultural context of sharing and surveillance. Not only do the girls not seem to be affronted by the evolution of this sharing and surveillance culture, they seem eager to embrace it and seek out literacy practices that allow their images to be snapped up, uploaded and shared in cyberspace. The purpose and context of Facebook profile pictures are considered as the girls discuss what photographs and avatars can do in this space. Finally, the girls' words help me to consider the pedagogical implications of getting teenaged girls to slow down and represent who they think they are.

Finally, in chapter eight, I will argue how this form of new literacy contributes to a body of knowledge that provides guidance to educators and researchers interested in the semiotics of identity in an increasingly visual world. More specifically, I will offer an argument for introducing the playful new literacy practice of avatar design into the secondary English language arts classroom. Such everyday literacy practices could be, and even should be, considered as part of an English language arts curriculum that combines an expanded notion of multimodal literacy with the desired curricular outcomes in personal and critical communication across a wide range of media texts. Hall (1999) has demonstrated that power and privilege play an important role in the construction of social knowledge within the discourses of cultural studies. To that end, it would seem that the critical reflection made possible with autobiographical writing in its print form, or as argued here, in a visual form of representation, presents an opportunity for educators and students to explore notions of identity, representation and the construction of social knowledge. More specifically, this chapter will examine how allowing youth to narrate their identity in the world and to the world provides an opportunity for them to claim individual agency and to create the vital political space they seek. I will suggest a form of visual writing that connects macro notions around identity and representation with intensely personal micro considerations of autobiography, and I suggest that it can be done without writing a word.

Chapter Two

Avatars, Identity and Autobiography: A Theoretical Perspective

I want to be clear: I do not believe in grand narratives, nor do I hold any convoluted notion that the girls who participated in my study speak for and/or represent all girls in all places. What this book offers instead is a recounting of a simple case study in which ten teenage girls in a particular place and at a particular time created avatars intended to represent who they are. Perhaps more accurately, it describes who they *were* at the time. Their stories, which are written through the creation of their avatars, contribute to a growing understanding that addresses notions of identity and representation in social online spaces. However, before I can ask for these avatars to be read in ways other than through the dominant social lens, I must first acknowledge that such texts are also social practices infused by notions of race, gender, class and ability (Berlak, 2004; Bloustien, 2003; Boler, 2004; Houston, 2004; Luke, 2002). Seen this way, creating a visual representation of a physical self for use in a communicative and social environment is much more than a rhetorical act. It also has significant consequences for how notions of the body, gender, race and ability can be represented. The accuracy of a deliberately accurate avatar creation as a form of representation also has a profound impact on the kinds of conversations that might occur in the intersection between culture and power when visual representations of self are integrated into social spaces. How does power operate through the production and consumption of these avatars? If individual agency is understood to be assertively participating in and/or resisting culture (Pomerantz, 2006), then how are competing discourses taken up, challenged, contested or refused?

Perhaps even more important, however, are the considerations around how these commercially-laden sites work to shape knowledge and how youth learn to understand identity in and through these spaces. It is also, therefore, with a cultural studies frame that this research examines the construction of identity, subjectivity and knowledge production, specifically as it pertains to appearance and social relationships. Kelly (1997) reminds us that "Once the innocence of language is undone" (p. 20), creating an avatar for use as an email signature or on a Facebook profile page becomes not only a semi-public act of identity construction, but it also allows for an "articulation of the political nature of text and meaning" (p. 20).

Recalling once again my poststructural frame, and drawing from scholarship on autobiography in education by Graham (1991) and Kelly (1997), the exploration of identity is tied closely to notions of self-consciousness. Here, identity is closely associated with its social construction. Not only do we contribute to and participate in our social and cultural worlds, these worlds, most broadly conceived, also participate in us. Put another way, we are constructed by and constituted in our socially discursive practices. From this perspective, autobiography is positioned as a form of constructed self-representation. The visual, purposeful, self-representation provides audiences with insight into what Kelly (1997) calls the "will to truth." More simply put, we cannot possibly render visible every detail about our stories; besides being limited by an encoded language that tries but fails to capture minute details of experience, thought and emotion, the complex and often conflicted process by which a story is rendered visible necessitates that some details become salient while others remain forgotten, omitted, hidden or denied. At once recognizing the profound limits of both language and the telling of our stories, Berlin (1992) chooses to refer to autobiographical stories in terms of autobiographical fragments. In a sense, the avatars created for this study might be most accurately described in a similar way — as autobiographical fragments.

Broadly speaking, poststructuralist theory calls for a de-centering of the human subject and acknowledges that we all inhabit various and multiple "subject positions" which are constituted by discourse. This frame also prevents me from assuming that the same questions asked of the participants today would yield the same responses they did only a few months ago. However, an analysis of these visually constructed identities requires that I first step back and provide a theoretical frame for my assumptions. Key concepts that will follow as they relate to the analysis of these avatars will also help to position the discursive practice of creating virtual identity within a realm of new literacy. Finally, I will turn briefly to my own biases as a researcher as a way to position the examination of what is lost and/or what is gained by creating an image of self in cyberspace.

Epistemological Perspectives

Poststructuralism

Peters and Burbules (2004) offer an understanding of poststructuralism as a philosophical response to the social scientific pretentiousness of structuralism; it is in its broadest sense, a rewriting of structuralism. Generally, poststructuralism includes three main tenets: the primacy of theory, the de-centering of the subject, and the fundamental importance of the reader (Bush, 1995). Giroux (1994) pulls apart these tenets more carefully by explaining that three main forces destabilize not only Marxist economic narratives but also material causality and Cartesian grand narratives. First, he understands history not only as formative in the creation of individual and collective identity, but more so, it is the reading and re-writing of history that contribute to knowledge production. Second, Giroux also acknowledges Freud's contribution to understanding how the unconscious is appropriated in order to provide direction through identity self-formation. The idea is that factors playing on the unconscious can never be completely known. And third, the notion that identity is always constructed (as is language), as "contingent, shifting and deferred" (p. 113). Put in more simple terms, our knowledge is always positioned socially, historically, and economically, and knowledge is constantly shifting. Knowledge then is a construct just as history is understood as a construct. Giroux also reminds us that poststructuralism is more than critiquing Marxist materialism, as well as the Cartesian concept of the unified subject, and the Enlightenment notion of foundationalism. In fact, poststructuralism "reasserts the importance of language as a mode of representation that constitutes rather than merely expresses what counts as reality" (p. 112). I will return to the place that language occupies in poststructuralist thinking shortly.

Discourse

Since poststructuralists resist the modernist, scientific pretensions of structuralism and claims of "truth," "objectivity," and "progress," they are also poised to critique theorizing of media "reading," "writing," teaching, TV, visual arts, plastic arts, film and electronic communication. Poststructuralism understands that language and discourse are not neutral and are not natural modes of communication; rather, they are entangled within power relation, as well as social and historical phenomena. That is, the way we speak and act is tainted by discursive practice as well as by social and power relationships. As such, there is an inherent instability in meanings — specifically in terms like race, gender and sex. If we think about our own existence and the forces that regulate who we are, how we behave and what we know, it might be fair to say that our discursive practices are quite different from those of another person in another global location or even another person at another historical time. Who I am as an East Coast Canadian woman in 2009 is likely markedly different from a woman living in Afghanistan in 2009. How we both use language to communicate who we are and what we know will also be markedly different because our experiences are historically, socially and culturally situated.

Blake, Smeyers, Smith, and Standish (1998) remind us that for the poststructuralist, discourse is "a unit of analysis in epistemology" or "a collection of statements (including knowledge or validity claims) generated at a variety of times and places, in both speech and writing, and which hangs together according to certain principles as a unitary collection of statements" (p. 14). Discourses are therefore sites of conflict where conceptual and epistemological possibilities and the cultural practices that inform them are recombined, reiterated, and refurbished. One of the fundamental claims of poststructuralism is that subjectivity is constructed within discourse; as such, it is unstable, multiple, contingent, and constitutive of the self. We are constructed not only by what we say, but also by what others say about us — perhaps more importantly, we cannot be constructed *unless* we have engaged in or have been engaged by discourse. There is no predetermined subjectivity or transcendental ego outside discourse. Put another way, if I do exist, it is because I have engaged in and been engaged by public discourse: more to the point, my identity within a hegemonic ethos of consumer democracy has been shaped and decided for me. It is important to note that subjectivity is a constructed matter and does not mean that agency is no more than a function of shifting signifiers (Giroux, 1994). This notion becomes infinitely complex when we consider the messages we receive from popular culture, what they say about our desires, our fears, and our ways of being in the world.

The de-centering of the subject

According to Merleau-Ponty, meaning comes from our concentrated attention to our embodiment as a means to create aesthetic meaning (Palermo, 2002). That is, "in perceiving something, what we see is performed or constituted by our sensing body and at the same time, the process of a product we undergo" (p. 4). A *chasm* is created in the crossover from embodiment to perception. The chasm represents the shift of meaning intrinsic to the dialogue between teacher and student, artist and observer, incarnate human and world.

While poststructuralists reject the binary oppositions of structuralist thought, they prefer a form of language that is non-hierarchal and indeterminate. The subject is understood as the *effect* of culture as opposed to the origin. From this perspective, subjectivity is more likely to reproduce uncertainties than to resolve them. As an alternative to the Enlightenment's Cartesian logic, where consciousness existed without condition (I think, therefore I am), where the subject was "unified, autonomous, [and] self-present" (Berlin, 1992, p. 18), language is no more than the *instrument* to communicate about the world. However, if our consciousness is borrowed from the "Other," the world is differentiated by language. In this context, truth and knowledge both exist at the level of the signifier. What we believe is not a personal conviction, rather it is what our culture allows, or it is shaped by the experiences we have had.

The existence of the human "subject" or "self" as conceived by humanism is called into question by poststructuralists on the grounds that, according to traditional belief, the individual is endowed with purposefulness, initiative and singular will. For the poststructuralist, however, human subjectivity is more likely to convey the influences of "unconscious mainstream ideologies" (Bush, 1995), which manifest in and from cultural constructs.

The poststructuralist notion of destabilization, or *de-centering* of the author, is relevant to this book—specifically as the system of (visual) language is conceived. By allowing the reader to become the focal point, poststructuralism places the reader at the center of the interpretation. When an avatar is read or interpreted, for example, the notion of a singular, objective meaning is denied. Not only can an avatar mean one thing to its creator and another to someone who views it, the avatar possesses multiple and even conflicting meanings and interpretations. Methods of "deconstruction" uncover a chain of signifiers which may at first appear to evoke a singular meaning from the text, but upon further examination might uncover signifiers that appear to contradict themselves and hence "deconstruct" meaning. Bush (1995) explains that in the most extreme forms of deconstruction, meanings are impossible to determine; therefore, any claim to understand a text is an illusionary "effect."

The notion that *difference* (or *differance* which means both to differ and to defer) is the linguistic limit of the subject (Peters and Burbules, 2004) demonstrates Derrida's understanding of "the root of all our positional concepts marking our language" (p. 69). Derrida also questioned the way speech is privileged as falsely sentimental, pure, innocent, and natural when it also works to classify and differentiate. He criticizes Saussure and Levi-Strauss as being phono-centric, arguing that their attention to linguistics gave primacy to speech. His intent was not to revise the hierarchy of structuralist binary oppositions in language but to show how speech has inherently negative qualities—just as does writing.

Power

In order to discuss the role of power in the rejection of binary oppositions within language, it is necessary that I first return briefly to the structuralist traditions of linguists: Ferdinand de Saussure and Roland Jacobson. In what has become his seminal linguistic triad, Saussure sought to explore the nature of *signs*, which he understood as having two features. These signs gain meaning through their relationships to each other rather than through their relationship to something outside language. The s*ign* is broken into *signifier*, which often takes form as a written or spoken word, sound, or visual appearance of word/phrase/image, and the *signified,* which can be understood as a concept, or representation, or meaning. As Saussure understood it, if things/objects/concepts named by language already existed or pre-existed outside language, then exact translations would be possible across languages—but they do not. Since humans are creatures of difference, the relationship between signifier and signified is arbitrary. Put another way, there are no givens in a language that is based on differential (though not entirely disordered) meanings. The differences found in *signifieds* were understood to exist interrelated in complex structures (hence structuralism). Using an overly simplistic example, the differential pair mother/father relates to the pair, male/female, and even to the pair parent/child (Blake et al., 1998). To learn a language is to understand the complex structures of signifieds that exist within it. The structuralist argument follows that communication between subjects would not be possible between private language systems unless some common ground could be found. Poststructuralists took Saussure's linguistic triad another step by expressing an interest in the *origins* of the relationships to the word (particularly as they relate to power and the unconscious), by demonstrating that meanings *are* unstable, and that language and discourse *are not* neutral, nor are they natural modes of communication.

The turn from structuralism to poststructuralism occurs in Foucault (Peters, 1996; Peters and Burbules, 2004). While he continues to hold onto structuralist emphasis on language and discourse, Foucault employs methods of archaeology to dig up historical conditions and genealogy to expose hegemonic theories that serve to subjugate and discipline the individual (Palermo, 2002). Mahon (1992) explains that Foucault's quest for the origins of truth was not in the Nietzschian sense where "origins" meant the "locale of something's primordial truth, essence, or original identity." Instead of pursuing these "metaphysical fictions," the genealogist, according to Foucault, was charged with cultivating the "disparate details, events, and accidents found at any beginning" (p. 8). What Foucault brings to poststructuralism here is a notion that truth is relative, not relational. Peters (1996) reminds us that Foucault's genealogy of modern power radically de-centered the epistemic privilege of the Cartesian notion of the "centered" subject, and it denies "the humanist ideal of rational, autonomous and responsible self" (p. 7). For Foucault, discourse becomes the location to explore language's political power and the site where the subject is also created. He demonstrates that power is constituted within language, especially illuminated in relationships between teacher and students.

Another of Foucault's notions—*discursive formations*—is helpful here as it provides an explanation for how individuals have been created and sustained by power structures. Discursive formations insist that historians cannot accurately access the past—they can only record how they experienced it and how they understood it. Quinn (2003) also supports Foucault's belief that history needs to be more than a recording of a linear progression as new knowledges attach themselves to old ones. While examining the patterns of power or force that make certain thoughts and actions possible, Quinn explains that there is an inherent challenge for researchers who can only rely on the voice of historians as having witnessed and recorded a partial version of the story and never the entire truth.

Returning for a moment to the poststructuralist notion of the primacy of language in knowledge formation, and that nothing exists outside of language, Giroux (1994) clarifies Foucault's insight regarding how non-discursive forces extend their own weight on social and material forces. These forces can only be understood within language and discourse. "In this respect, power does not exist outside of language but is seen as an attribute of discourse in its capacity as a signifying practice to actually construct reality" (p. 113). The central assumption of Foucault is that any form of critical agency, then, must be aware of how power and authority are secured through language.

The significance of poststructuralism to this research is in how it is connected more broadly to education. As a philosophical reaction to the 1950s-1960s trans-disciplinary "mega-paradigm" of structuralism, poststructuralism challenges the epistemological claims from the social sciences that have been based on a centrality of language and scientific analysis of human social and cultural existence. As attention has shifted from "individualism to subjectivity, from text to discursive practices, and from signifier to signifying practices" (Kelly, 1997, p. 19), poststructuralism aims to challenge or disrupt, and trouble or destabilize foundational assumptions within all modes of Western discourse and discursive practice. This inherently oppositional and/or adversarial stance places poststructuralists in positions that criticize established institutional and often taken-for-granted discursive practices. To that end, this research is premised on the poststructural understanding that the manner by which teenage girls choose to represent themselves visually considering body type, facial expression, dress, accessories, and background will be influenced by, but not limited to, family, peers, institutional practices, and media (Bloustien, 2003; Driscoll, 2003; Hall, 1999; Kincheloe, 2005; McRobbie, 2005; Stack and Kelly, 2006; Valentine and Holloway, 2002).

Cultural Studies

In addition to using a poststructuralist framework, a cultural studies frame also allows for the avatars created for this study to be examined against larger cultural ideologies like racism, patriarchy, and the division of social class. The intent of cultural studies generally might be aligned with critical pedagogy in its commitment to a greater transformative educational project, particularly as it relates to the lives of the subjugated, marginalized, or oppressed. The influence of poststructuralist thought provides cultural studies an interest in how individuals read particular "common sense" discourses and discursive practices. Notions of class, gender, race, history, and resistance are examined as they occupy (or are occupied in) the space between individual agency and cultural reproduction.

Pedagogy in cultural studies requires a positioning of knowledge within social, historical, and economic contexts. To that effect, this examination of cultural studies requires a similar positioning. In what follows, I turn to Simon During (1999) to provide direction and provide context through this brief historical survey, which traces the socio-political influences of a discipline that would eventually challenge the traditional imperialist values of the West. Notions of class divisions and youth sub-culture guide an exploration of the evolution of cultural studies as an international movement, which has as its many foci, an attention to various forms of feminisms, race, popular culture, and the politics of identity. It also influences the manner that educational research is conceptualized and conducted today. During (1999) cautions that while cultural studies examines contemporary culture, its exact definition is problematic since it lacks well-defined methodology or clearly differentiated fields of inquiry. However, it is difficult to remove the genesis and subsequent evolution of cultural studies from the cultural criticism that evolved from Marxist thought. Of the influential Marxist thinkers who bear relevance to later theories in cultural studies, particular notice must be given to the German Marxist Walter Benjamin, who placed hope in the emerging art forms of film and radio to redefine the artistic domain in broader terms for wider audiences. Antonio Gramsci, the Italian Marxist whose *Prison Notebooks* criticized literature for being elitist while calling for a broad working-class take-up of culture, was also a central influence. By suggesting that intellectuals be regarded politically, he broke ground for many thinkers like Giroux who draw from his views as foundational to the notion of cultural politics. Gramsci is also important for his contribution of the notion of *hegemony*, which can be defined as the dominance of one political class over another.

Evolving out of adult literacy programs of the 1930s and 1940s and emerging in the United Kingdom in the 1950s, cultural studies sought to examine elements of culture through methods of "subjectivity" *in relation* (Foucault, 1999) to individual lives, as opposed to with the "objectivitism" that had been popular within scientific and positivist research (Willinsky, 1998). Richard Hoggart's (1957) *The Uses of Literacy* provided guidance for work going on in adult literacy programs as he expressed concern for established academic boundaries, structures of power, and linking literature to the real-life experiences of working class adults. Here, Hoggart positioned education as a tool of empowerment (Giroux, 1994). Meanwhile, Raymond Williams' (1958) *Culture and Society, 1780–1950*, dealt with the separation of culture (implied high culture), and society (the whole way of life). Williams makes it clear that the driving force behind cultural studies is a pedagogy centered on the exploration of how power is constituted within historical, social and political contexts (Giroux, 1994). Together, these founding publications by Hoggart and Williams provided the genesis of cultural studies. Their collective understanding of pedagogy as a critical and even transformative practice would lend itself to further explorations around knowledge and identity formation within various cultural sites—this, of course, includes school.

Prior to the 1950s, During (1999) reminds us that Great Britain had embraced Leavisism as a way to distribute and appreciate literary knowledge broadly. By insisting on a literary canon of predominantly white male authors and literature that avoided any risky experimentation, this practice attempted to ensure that the "moral sensibility" of readers would be fostered. However, as mass culture developed and increased in popularity, this moral sensibility was threatened. Hoggart and Williams had both come from working-class Britain and were initially able to reconcile the existence of the rich canon of texts alongside contemporary mass culture. Coinciding with the disappearance of working class life, the pair joined with Stuart Hall and founded the Centre for Contemporary Cultural Studies at Birmingham in 1964.

During (1999) explains that along with increased immigration and a narrowing financial gap between the working class and blue-collar workers, income became available for consumer goods. Among other things, a commodified higher education became available to a portion of the working class, thereby diminishing "locally produced and often long-standing cultural forms" (p. 40). A version of culture created at a distance began to demand attention. Among those attending to these forms with consideration that had previously been reserved only for the literary canon were Stuart Hall and Paddy Whannel, as they critiqued the hegemonic of effects culture. The proletariat culture of the past began to fracture, and politics that had once aligned itself with the working class began to diminish in importance; with that, cultural studies began to explore the political power and function of culture. By the 1970s, notions of "culture" and "hegemony" were linked as descriptors of "domination" and "consent."

By the 1970s, Louis Althusser's theory of individuals as constructs of ideology created the illusion of life with the nuclear family as "natural," "unique" and "free." Because this ideology enabled people to make sense of the world and their place within it, During (1999) explains that it was easy to accept. Althusser understood that the various media forms disseminated discourses or "signifying practices," particularly of and about dominant social values. The recognition that these signifying practices are internalized lead to their take-up in methods of semiotic analysis. However, Althusser's theory was not able to withstand criticism for being too theoretical, not scientific enough, and not attentive enough to individual practices. Another semiotic concept, namely "polysemy" or the multiple meanings created by a signifier, began to gain popularity. With this notion, the process of cultural production was recognized as being something that is negotiated through conflicting and multiple "hybridizations." These concepts were then applied in three key texts: Paul Willis's, *Learning to Labour*; David Morley's *"Nationwide" Audience;* and Tony Jefferson's, *Resistance Through Rituals.*

By the late 1970s French theorists Pierre Bourdieu, Michel de Certeau, and Michel Foucault brought their influential theories to cultural studies, thereby sending it in a new direction. They recognized hierarchal "fields" of belonging, where individuals' signifying roles were defined, directed, and structured. During (1999) explains that in the more rationalized fields, like schools, the ways an individual could belong or be "self-formed" or "self-governed" were directed authoritatively from above. However, individuals also had the capacity to make the choices to affect the way they were regarded within these constantly shifting fields. For these theorists, it made no sense to study subjects in isolation because they are all related; that is, recalling Foucault, all knowledge is relational.

During (1999) explains that with the emergence of the new rights in both Britain and the United States (at the hands of Thatcher and Reagan), any social-democratic power bloc that had previously been gaining momentum was temporarily abandoned. Market-driven forces were seen as regulators of social structures, and traditional values and sameness were promoted as a way to safeguard notions of national unity and the seemingly contradictory notion of a grand narrative. Stuart Hall (1988) pointed to "popular knowledge" promoted through market-driven media as the tool used by Thatcherism to promote traditional values. However, this glorification of globalization brought with it yet another contradiction since the more global trade and commerce became, the more open certain countries like Britain and the United States needed to become in respect to countries and cultures from afar, thereby challenging their own constructions of national unity. As such, globalization is at once unifying and divisive.

The next shift in cultural studies theory came from de-centering feminist work that "began to affirm 'other' ways of life on their own terms" (During, 1999, p. 13). This celebration of "otherness" proved to be a powerful oppositional force against mono-culture-promoting governments of the time. Eventually, cultural studies absorbed what During calls the "radical wing of anthropology" as it had consumed sociology in Britain by becoming the voice for the marginalized. As the media industry globalised, the cultural industry concentrated itself to face the challenges and opportunities faced because of marketing and distribution. With this, the commercial popular culture became a site of celebration.

From its inception, cultural studies has been fueled by the notion that culture is pedagogical. Many (Dolby, 2003; Giroux, 1999, 1998, 1994; Kelly, 1997; Luke, 1997; Walkerdine, 1997), point to critical literacy practices within cultural studies as a means to identify the "process by which culture works to inform the readings of the world" (Kelly, 1997, p. 17). In more recent manifestations drawing on bell hooks (1994) and others, Kelly (1997) shows us how cultural studies focuses on the circuits of power within a frame of critical literacy by giving a nod to "feminist and poststructural politics of identity, desire and difference" (p. 72). For Giroux, Shumway, Smith, and Sosnoski, 2000), the work of cultural studies is to employ praxis-based pedagogy in the mobilization of critical resistance. The authors propel an argument for *resisting* intellectuals by drawing on but differing from Gramsci's understanding of intellectuals as "mediators, legitimators, and producers" of ideas and practices. They also distinguish between conservative status quo agents and radical organic intellectuals who also attempt to provide moral leadership for working class struggles. For Giroux et al., resisting intellectuals assume the "transformative critique of the conditions of oppression."

I turn briefly now to Cassella (1998) who provides a framework for the theoretical aspects of cultural studies. These include 1) the interdisciplinary nature of cultural studies, 2) how a discipline of cultural studies challenges hierarchies within culture, 3) how ethnography is criticized as a method, 4) the emphasis on concepts such as pleasure, desire, sexuality, and 5) its denial or distrust of behavioral world models.

Interdisciplinary approach

Cultural studies evolved as a trans-disciplinary/ interdisciplinary field with multiple directions (Giroux, 1998; Kelly, 1997; Morgan, 2000). Bolstered by the argument that fragmenting our scholarly pursuits into disciplines (history, sociology, anthropology, for example) only serves to fragment our knowledge, which thereby works against larger egalitarian principles of social justice and democratization. Giroux et al. (2000) are highly critical of work in the academy that remains fragmented by discipline or area of specialization, claiming that it only disables critique and further perpetuates the reproduction of dominant ideology with in culture. The individual disciplines attempt to contort themselves into models that were designed to fit scientific pursuits in as much as they are designed to create specialists, figures of authority, and professionals. However, by opting for a multidisciplinary approach, broader social issues can be explored from "unique perspectives and theoretical positions" (Kincheloe, 2005, p. 140). The intention to work *between* theories of cultural studies allows for a fuller picture of the world (McRobbie, 2005).

Challenging hierarchies

Cultural studies challenges notions of culture traditionally bound in Arnoldian or Leavisite binaries of high and low not just for the cultural value or worth but more importantly for how creation of individual and collective identity contributes to meaning making. This relates to not merely the new ideas brought to theory and research but also to the new topics of study. Cultural texts are understood to be tangible, reproducible (and usually commercially available) products and discursive practices such as weddings or graduations. As Cassella (1998) explains, they can be found abundantly anywhere that commercialization entertainment, education, and leisure come together.

Within school, a mandated curriculum is most often regulated by government standards through prescribed curricula and checked through standardized examinations. The refusal to acknowledge multimodal forms of literacy (Kress, 2003; Lankshear, Gee and Knobel, 1997) is an example of how power structures continue to work. Looking more specifically at the hierarchal structures behind literacy practices, Kelly (1997) points to the nearly two decades of calls for "cultural literacy" (which include rituals, traditions and objects) within a conservative political ethos as a frame to understand the impetus behind cultural studies. It is worth quoting her at length on this point:

> Culture here is not only selective, but elitist, not only closed but often openly hostile to unassimilable Others for, ultimately, culture here is a history of a particular notion of civilization spawned in the Enlightenment, fueled in schooling through Arnoldian and Leavisite English, the legacies of which much of the curriculum subject of English still enshrines, and reclaims in this usage. (p. 16)

For Kelly and others, literacy practices remain steeped in the notion that the canon represents the "gold standard" (Giroux et al., 1990) against which all works are considered. These staples are meant to provide a wealth of values to the point where their effects "humanize" in a manner complicit with "the economy which has produced that wealth for humanity." It is this very hierarchal ranking of symbolic cultural texts, within the canon, for example, that cultural studies is designed to question.

The limits of ethnography

In the 1960s, cultural studies emerged in the United Kingdom to examine contemporary culture through methods of subjectivity rather than with methods of scientific and positivist research. The intent is not to create absolute truths but rather to allow students to engage in the knowledge production process (Alvermann, 2000; Buckingham and Sefton-Green, 1994; Giroux, 1999; Stack and Kelly, 2006). Most often, those who work within the realm of cultural studies will conduct research that is ethnographic in nature. Drawing on Gilroy, Cassella (1998) notes that by fixating on specific locations (the classroom, for example) research methodology often fails to resonate more subtle transitions of culture's constitutive nature (Kelly, 1997).

Cassella (1998) points to a global focus on the local for providing context, which also reveals historical, economic, and cultural connections within the research. No longer limited to educational institutions, the scope of locations of "sites" has been broadened to include anywhere that education occurs; in effect, no site is out of bounds in whatever form.

Emphasis on concepts

Cultural studies understands that as we negotiate our place in the world we are guided not only by our pleasures, desires, fears and fascinations (Kelly, 1997; McRobbie, 1994), but these mediating factors are also shaped by modes of power and politics. Our desires reside within every day relationships (Kelly, 1997). To that end, Kelly reminds us that within the multiple forms of literacy practice, human desire is "manufactured, shaped, and regulated" to the point where the informing discourses "position students and teachers in ways that define—and, therefore, confine—sense and sensibility" (p. 10). These enacted disciplinary practices "regulate" and "domesticate" with a pedagogy designed to position students to "read and to write the world in specific ways" (p. 11). Cultural studies allows us to realize aspects of education as cultural practices. How meaning is negotiated, produced, circulated, and engaged becomes a critical, political and cultural process.

Kelly (1997) provides guidance through three key concepts that bear relevance to the analysis of autobiographical avatars, as it is instructive in the mobilization of social and individual identity within cultural studies. These terms are helpful as we negotiate notions of, but not limited to, racism, sexism, and ability in our society. *Engagement* refers to how discourses are engaged, negotiated, and transformed by individuals. *Affective investment* refers to the desires that propel our engagements. Finally, the *political terms of engagement* refer to the understanding that culture is flexible and often contradictory. By allowing an analysis and critique of how and where texts are engaged, what affective investments are involved, and how the political terms of engagement of these texts figure into their reading, we can begin to gain insight into the dynamics of popular culture. The intention is not to view these texts in order to see how they fail us, as Kelly notes, but rather and also to look for ways that they might allow for the possibility of empowerment.

Denial or distrust of behavioral models

Within a poststructuralist framework, the view that individuals are merely passive recipients of culture is challenged. Individuals are neither passive recipients of discursive practices, nor are they entirely free to make their own decisions. From this perspective, accelerated globalization of media which is promoted through commercial market forces can be regarded as, at once, unifying and divisive. Stuart Hall (1999) tells us that how we understand the world can be attributed to mental frameworks, or codes (Saussure). Mass media culture, for example, implicitly assumes (or encodes) society's dominant ideology, and its messages are designed to reproduce dominant ideologies. However, these representations also present a location for ideological struggle. For Hall, these messages may be read or decoded in three distinct ways. They may operate within the dominant ideology, which is also the *preferred reading,* and not question what is being represented. Depending on the social situations, other readers/viewers/listeners may apply a *negotiated code*—an alternate position that reflects an individual member's position and understanding. They may also promote an *oppositional code* in which they are critical of the dominant code being presented and reject its claims. It is in this oppositional reading that cultural studies finds itself at home.

Others (Buckingham and Sefton-Green, 1994; Dolby, 2003) suggest that audiences may also negotiate/resist or co-opt mass culture in a variety of ways. They hold that children do not necessarily absorb meaning and intent designed for them and that are not necessarily duped by the commercial strategies employed by the consumer market (Gunter, Oates and Blades, 2004). McRobbie (1994) argues that youth styles and preferences do more than promote subculture. Besides the small economic benefits and life-skills experience that come with the production and distribution of sub-cultural goods, elements such as music production, fashion, and hairstyles represent "intense activity of cultural production" (p. 161) which are central activities of cultural production and social transformation. Using similar examples, Kelly (1997) points to the manner in which youths mark their bodies through attire, tattooing, and piercing in the dual roles of cultural production and resistance.

From this perspective we are all simultaneously multimodal producers and consumers of culture—regardless of what gets produced or consumed. According to Hall (2000) everything is about context. It is impossible to separate understanding from how meaning is created. How we make meaning in our world depends on the language we use to externalize our meaning, and this depends on what we bring to the concept being represented. The very act of representing a concept is not fixed, but instead it is constitutive (a condition of its event) and unique to the people creating the meaning. Hall (1999) explains that the structuralist, semiotic, and poststructural influences on cultural studies include but are not limited to: the importance of language; how text and textuality both shape and silence meaning; heterogeneity and multiplicity of meaning (that textuality is in itself a site of power); and that identity is formed through the symbolic. Hall also acknowledges the challenge that cultural studies is a field that attempts to intervene in other theory. What happens when cultural studies requires the active participation of the other theoretical realms it is attempting to make a difference in? His response highlights an acknowledgment of the complex and often conflicting push and pull that is required. He states:

> Unless and until one respects the necessary displacement of culture, and yet is always irritated by its failure to reconcile itself with other questions that matter, with other questions that cannot and can never be fully covered by critical textuality in its elaborations, cultural studies as a project, and intervention, remains incomplete. (Hall, 1999, p. 106)

What exists is an enduring tension between the ever-irresolvable questions of theory and politics that holds cultural studies together. However, it is also this tension that "allows the one to irritate, bother and disturb the other, without insisting on some final theoretical closure" (Hall, 1999, p. 106).

Key Terms and Concepts

Avatar

Traditionally, in the world of cyberspace—if there can be any such thing as being traditional within a new and always-evolving digital technology—an avatar is understood to be a two or three-dimensional representation of an individual for use in a virtual online space. Three-dimensional avatars are often created and used in gaming applications or in multi-user graphic virtual realities (GVRs) such as *Second Life* (Cooper, 2007; Turkle, 2005, 1995). In such cases avatars are often created with the intention of being an alter ego of its author. In his book *Alter Ego*, Cooper provides a definition of an avatar as:

> a Sanskrit word originally referring to the visible forms adopted by Hindu gods to represent themselves in this, our lesser, mortal world. Online culture nicked the term to name the digital forms that represent us in virtual worlds, and if it gives us godlike feelings to inhabit them, that's not to say we're anymore immune to the seductions of these worlds than the ancient gods of myth were ever safe from ours. (Introduction)

In other cases, such as in my study, an avatar is a two-dimensional picture or icon for use as a kind of digital signature. This form of avatar is more often found embedded beside blog postings or as an email/texting signature. The avatars used in my study came exclusively from the WeeWorld site. These two-dimensional, line-drawn avatars are full-body, front-facing cartoons (except for the nose, which does not exist—apparently there is nothing to smell in cyberspace). These avatars can be designed by choosing from a bank of body options, hairstyles and colors, clothing options, and accessories. Once completed, they can be further personalized by placing them on a choice of backgrounds. (For a more detailed explanation of the production options within this site please see chapter four.) The central difference between my avatar research and the studies done by Cooper and others rests on the assumption that in the online gaming community, the game is the reason for the avatar to exist in the first place as it is the means through which individuals can engage in the online community. Likewise, studies involving *Second Life* avatars have found reasons for creating alter egos, or for expecting an element of identity shifting with and through these avatars (Thomas, 2007, 2004). However, in the case of this book two-dimensional avatars have been created as purposeful representations of self and as such were analyzed as autobiographical fragments.

Literacy/new literacies/everyday literacies

In order to situate my research within the scholarly literature on new literacies, it is first necessary to briefly discuss the manner by which the field of new literacies evolved to be separate and distinct from literacy studies. I look first to Colin Lankshear and Michele Knobel (2003, 2006) to guide me through this evolution, which essentially views the "new" as a sociocultural turn as well as an ontological and chronological shift. While concepts of literacy and its accompanying partner term "illiteracy" guide central educational policies in Canada and indeed worldwide, literacy as a term remains contested. Only a few decades ago, the term "literacy" replaced "reading" as a discourse within formal education practices. Prior to the 1970s, it referred to non-formal programs designed to enable adults to read and write in order to become "functional" within society's economic structure. Lankshear and Knobel (2003, 2006) trace the rise of literacy as an educational imperative to three factors. The first of these imperatives belongs to Paulo Freire's (1970) work with Brazilian and Chilean peasants. What Freire's work demonstrated was that literacy could provide a basis for radical approaches to education, which could then present a form of critical social praxis. His notion of "reading the word and the world" propelled the concept of literacy beyond traditional decoding models. Learning to decipher the alphabetic code provided a tool to enable groups to learn together in order to gain a kind of critical consciousness (what Freire calls *conscientization*). For Freire, literacy provided peasants with the opportunity to "perceive social, political, and economic contradictions, and to take action against the oppressive elements of reality" (1970, p. 17). A discourse of market globalization is the contemporary version of cultural and colonial imperialism, which constructs oppression as both natural and acceptable within the popular discourse. However, Freire rails against such a discourse by proposing a radical pedagogy of hope for the oppressed members of society. The concept of critical praxis (reflection and action) positions "illiteracy" as a consequence of a socially unjust system. While socially unjust arrangements have been created by human inaction, Freire argued that they could also be undone by human action. "To exist, humanly, is to name the world, to change it" (p. 69). In order to do the naming, however, the illiterate must become literate so as to understand the sources and systems of their social oppression.

The second factor cited by Lankshear and Knobel (2006, 2003) saw the development or invention of a notion of "illiteracy" among US adults in the early 1970s. This crisis was tied to changes in a post-industrial reality and a restructuring of a labor market, as well as its organizations and institutions. The crisis was felt in the UK, North America, Australia, and New Zealand. As a result, governments called for a new curriculum and pedagogical approaches to address areas of functional literacy.

The third factor can be drawn from a rise in consciousness about socio cultural perspectives as they relate to language study and social sciences. Lankshear and Knobel draw from work conducted by Gee (1996) which points to a number of conceptual and theoretical engagements with text that highlight this rise in consciousness. They are: Graff's (1979) revisionist history, Scribner and Cole's (1981) socio cultural approach to literacy which included the development of the concept of "practice" and drew heavily from Vygotsky and Lauria's notions of social cognition, Heath's (1983) notion that literacy included an embedded cultural context, and Street's (1984) anthropological approach which argues that literacy is rooted in socio historical contexts and carries the baggage of more than limited sign systems needed to decode letters and words. The forbearers of this shift, together with a more general epistemological shift toward cultural studies, combined to position literacy within a broader educational context.

Within the context of formal education, literacy became an industry in and of itself, attracting research attention, funding, and public focus. In response to increased funding opportunities, literacy achievement initiatives began to flourish. With that, the definition of what counts for literacy also expanded to include concepts such as (but not limited to) 'cultural literacy,' 'critical literacy,' and 'multiliteracy.' Within such a cultural literacy model, Hirsch (1987) proposed that literacy practices enable individuals to communicate with one another within a larger national cultural context.

Cope and Kalantzis (1999) approach a pedagogy for multiliteracies by acknowledging that technology combined with linguistic diversity are both important and interconnected threads in what counts toward literacy practice, especially within a society which values multiple forms of literacy. Operationally and culturally, the range of what gets considered knowledge is ever expanding for individuals who participate in society's rapidly changing work force. Critical engagement with and through the new technology-laden literacies is crucial. Knowing how to operate a technological system is only part of what is required to become literate in this new multi-literacy sense.

Gee (2000, 1996) understands that literacies cannot be separated from their socio cultural contexts, and they are always embedded in Discourse. There is a fundamental difference between Discourse (ways of being in the world that integrate identity), and discourse (with a lower case "d"), which reveals bits of language or uses of Discourse. Simply put, people read and write differently in different social spaces, so it makes sense to pay attention to not just what is said but, what is said and what is done. Lankshear and Knobel (2006) demonstrate the importance of considering sociocultural context as they provide a list of varying discourses with different perspectives including a youth zine, an online chat space, a school classroom, a feminist reading group, or a religious ceremony. They also explain that dealing with the vast amounts of information available through a socioculturally conceived form of literacy involves infinitely more than understanding how to operate a language system. They state, "The cultural and critical facets of knowledge integral to being literate are considerable" (p. 17). The notion of literacies as being "powerful" gained prominence through the work on sociocultural linguistics by Gee (1990). The authors explain that, for Gee, having a powerful literacy involves "having control, or fluent mastery" (p. 17) of how language is used within secondary Discourses. Lankshear and Knobel (2006) explain that according to Gee, Discourses integrate identities: "As individuals participate in Discourses they are identified and identifiable as members of socially meaningful groups or networks and players of socially meaningful roles" (p. 17). They explain that Gee believes we belong to only one primary Discourse, which shapes how we see and understand the world. This includes all of those with whom we interact in a face-to-face manner, and these groups are different in terms of social class and ethnicity. We are also shaped by secondary Discourses, which occur in places like schools, churches, sport clubs and community groups. Because there are multiple forms of language that may be engaged through these secondary Discourses, so too are there multiple forms of knowledge—hence, multiple literacies. "In all cases, however, being literate means being able to use the 'right' language in the 'right' ways within a Discourse" (p. 18). This is nearly the same as having a command of the operational and cultural elements of literacy.

Gee (1990) explains that new literacy studies have their origins in the collapse of the old contrast between oral culture and literate culture. New literacies evolved to imply a multiple set of social practices, which deny the binary logic of the Enlightenment's dichotomous thought. Rather than subscribing to long-held labels like literate versus illiterate, or civilized versus savage, Gee demonstrates how anthropologists like Ruth Benedict, Margaret Mead, and Levi-Strauss broke down previously held, narrowly conceived notions of what constitutes a primitive or civilized distinction. Gee highlights how, rather than just teach English, English teachers more accurately teach a set of dominant school-based socializing practices. He explains that "language and literacy acquisition are forms of socialization, in this case socialization into mainstream ways of using language in speech and print, mainstream ways of taking meaning, and of making sense of experience" (p. 67).

The pedagogical shift from traditional print-centered literacy to new literacy is also tied intricately to an engagement with technology and limited only by the technology that will hold it. Coiro, Knobel, Lankshear and Leu (2008) point to seminal work on the theoretical shift from literacy as it moves from the page to the screen in terms of text comprehension and composition of production. They tell us that as new heuristics appear to inform the multidisciplinary work within new literacy research, new perspectives also emerge. The main challenge is to pin down what it means to be literate in the twenty-first century. From multiple perspectives and multiple frames of disciplinarity, this is incredibly challenging. To invite everyone into the conversation is to broaden the parameters to the point where it is impossible to contain. By late 2005, one billion people had access to the Internet. Current estimates suggest that one half of the world's population will be on-line by 2012. While this points to the enormity of access, it also highlights a vast disparity among the world's population. (And while the issues connected to the disparity inherent in matters of global access to technology are not the primary focus of this book, I would be remiss not to acknowledge it as a significant matter worthy of its own deep inquiry.)

This challenge can be highlighted by the unprecedented scale and scope of change within technology and literacy over the last twenty years. Coiro et al. (2008) tell us "No previous technology for literacy permits the immediate dissemination of even newer technologies of literacy to every person on the Internet by connecting to a single link on a screen" (pp. 2-3). The authors acknowledge that literacy is no longer the static construct that it had been for nearly 500 years. It is more appropriately conceived as "a rapid and continuous process of change in the ways in which we read, write, view, listen, compose, and communicate information" (p. 5). Are new technologies merely tools to accomplish the same old literacy practices? Are the same social practices, including reading and writing, accomplished through the centuries?

The New London Group (1996) provides a definition and a vision for literacy that sees it splinter into different multi-literacy practices. In what has become a seminal piece, "Pedagogy of New Literacies" proposes a method of transformed practice which includes: situating student practice within the *lifeworlds* of student experiences; overt instruction to provide a systemic analysis of the design systems required to design and interpret texts; critical framing to understand the various and multiple social and cultural contexts of a particular text and; transformed practice which allows students to "re-practice" what they have learned—in this sense theory becomes reflective practice. For the New London Group, the term literacy is understood to include a "multiplicity of discourses" (p. 9), which extends the scope of literacy pedagogy to include diverse and plural notions of what it is to be literate. The New London Group understands that technology has influenced the type and manner by which texts are disseminated. Rather than embracing what Dewey called the "assimilatory function of schooling," The New London Group believes that education now seeks to work in reverse. Rather than embrace the outdated pedagogy that seeks to make "homogeneity out of difference" (p. 18), it now claims that in order to be relevant, pedagogies must recruit "different subjectivities, interests, intentions, commitments, and purposes" (p. 18).

Theorists have classified literacy into sub-genres such as computer literacy, electronic literacy, media literacy, and so on; however, Kress (2003) argues that doing so dilutes how we understand the categories of literacy, especially in its print form. While Kress argues that literacy implies a connection to writing, this implication is problematic given the nature of computer technology. In his earlier seminal work, Kress (2003) troubles the definition of literacy as the term used when we make messages using letters as the means of recording that message. This definition leaves us with the challenge of finding new terms for the uses of the different resources. However, Kress denies the logic behind labels such as visual literacy" for the use of the image, and "gestural literacy" for the use of the gesture, or "musical literacy" or "soundtrack literacy" for the use of sound other than speech (p. 23). For him, "literacy" is a term that is most closely associated with "writing." He explains:

> *Literacy* remains the term which refers to (the knowledge of) the use of the resource of writing. The combination of knowledge of the resource with knowledge of production and perhaps with that of dissemination would have a different name. That separates, what to me is essential, the *sense of what the resource is* and what its potentials are, from associated questions such as those of its *uses* and the issue of whatever skills are involved in using a resource in wider communicational frames. (p. 24)

Later, Kress (2005) provides a frame for an argument that redefines the way educators understand literacy by situating it within a shift from language to semiotics. In a broad sense, his argument asks students to focus their attention on the features and elements of language on the page. This semiotic would ask them to pay attention to everything on the page: font size, spacing, illustrations, layout, the type of paper, etc. This renewed attention to detail brings students back to a time of "practical criticism" where educators and students sought an understanding of language that is meaningful and profound. His argument is based on research that observed a divide in how curriculum is delivered. He found that literacy pedagogies still range widely from a traditional, authoritarian, and science-like attention to the texts prescribed by a national curriculum (in the United Kingdom, for example), to a constructivist, learner-centered model that permits contemporary, popular media texts to frame how students learn to understand themselves and the world they inhabit. However, he does acknowledge that despite the differences he observed, it seemed clear that "a battle had been won—a recognition of the value of culture other than elite culture" (p. 103).

Kress (2005) also observes that the opposition between different positions for the teaching of English can no longer be described as being between orality and literacy, because he believes the two offer vastly different "representational resources" (p. 103). Instead, he explains, the opposition that exists is more accurately described as being between "a resource which is relatively fluid and dynamic (say, speech, but also dance, maybe video and film) and the less fluid and less dynamic (maybe writing, still images, objects)—the spatially organized as against the temporally organized" (p. 103). Central to Kress's argument is that the boundaries that we use to define language must be redefined in the shift from linguistic to semiotic. Regarding language in a semiotic sense allows for what Kress sees as a deepened sense of what language is. It also has the ability to bring profound change. He recognizes that

> The dominant technology for dissemination at the moment is the screen, and it is influencing the book. It's important to think of the technology of writing or of visual representation as quite distinct from the technology of dissemination. The media, the screen, the book—will continue, but their relations to modes will change. (p. p. 104-105)

By presenting an argument for the inclusion of multimodal texts, as opposed to the strict and rigid adherence to texts in their "skeletal" print form, Kress (2005) also suggests that seeing texts as multimodal enables them to hold layers of meaning, each partial and incomplete, but nonetheless necessary to the contribution of the greater whole. This reconsideration of the boundaries which hold language within the English curriculum helps to frame avatar design within that same curriculum as a legitimate form of study. In what Kress argues is a return to practical criticism, the semiotic details of how something is represented gets taken even further to consider where elements fit historically. As educators did with the historical specificity and historical locations of words, Kress suggests that we now ask students to pay attention to the details—except this time, "the frame is set differently, much more widely" (p. 98).

In some locations, English has shifted from a canon-based curriculum to a discipline on the verge of becoming a curriculum that focuses on communication, as it has in South Africa (Kress, 2005). The shift to a semiotic version of English as opposed to one that is strictly of a linguistic frame represents a turn toward cultural studies in its acceptance of popular media texts and its willingness to hear the subjugated voices that had been silenced by traditional authoritarian and canon-based pedagogies. Besides recognizing the multimodal text as a legitimate form of meaning making within the English curriculum, Kress argues "one needs to see language as partial" (p. 97). By encouraging students to produce and create texts in multimodal forms, he encourages English teachers make room for genuine exploration.

The theoretical and methodological challenges of social semiotics of structuralist ideology and multimodality are the focus of Kress and van Leeuwen's (1996) critique of Barthes (1977), where the authors claim social semiotics are "the theoretical, analytical and descriptive branch of cultural studies" (p. 28). Together, Kress and van Leeuwen (2006) are prominent advocates of a social semiotic approach to reading and writing (as literacy). Their visual grammar focuses on how depicted elements combine to make visual statements; elements are combined to create meaningful wholes. They explain:

> Our approach to communication starts from a social base. In our view the meanings expressed by speakers, writers, printmakers, photographers, designers, painters, and

> sculptors are first and foremost social meanings, even though we acknowledge the effect and importance of individual differences. (p. 20)

They suggest that a "literate' person in the future will need to negotiate elements and layers of visual design such as those present on a Windows Operating System (1990). More generally, they point out that modes of visual communication are less attached to the domain of specialists than they are to public communication. As such, visual grammar describes the social resource accessible to a particular social group, as well, it provides a general grammar which, in our case, draws heavily from our Western culture and includes elements and rules that are culture specific (including, but not limited to the conventional paradigm for reading from left to right). Kress and van Leeuwen (2006) argue that there is not a universally understood form of visual grammar.

Their social semiotic theory of representation draws from a semiotic movement over the past 75 years or so. They explain that in Europe, three schools of semiotics brought ideas from linguistic traditions over to non-linguistic modes of communication. What the social semiotic theory provided was a vehicle to understand forms of deviation from standard forms of expression. In the 1930s and 1940s the Prague School brought linguistics to Russian Formalism. Here ideas such as 'foregrounding' were developed and applied to language, art, theater, cinema and costume. During the 1960s and 1970s, the Paris School combined Saussure's ideas on linguistics with painting, photography, fashion, and more. The resulting notion of "semiology" used the sign as a central concept. Combined with the signifier and the signified, it borrowed structuralist notions that are still used in many schools today despite the belief that these notions have been overtaken by poststructuralism. The third movement comes from critical linguistics generally, and from linguist Michael Halliday more specifically. Kress and Van Leeuween (1006) explain that Halliday sees grammar as less formal than how it has been traditionally conceived; rather, "grammar forms as resources for encoding interpretations of experience and forms of social (inter)action" (p. 1). In the late 1970s, as with any semiotic approach, the 'sign' is a central notion. Kress and van Leeuwen prefer to write about "sign-making.' While they do discuss "signifiers" (such as line and color) and "signifieds" (how meanings are made), they move beyond this approach to acknowledge how sign-makers have meanings which are "motivated…conjunctions of signifiers (forms) and signifieds (meanings)" (p. 8). For the pair, signs are never just arbitrary. In fact, the context under which the sign is constructed cannot be properly addressed without acknowledging the motivation used to create it and the act of producing analogies and classifications with it. In other words, "sign makers use the forms they consider apt for the expression of their meaning" (p. 8).

In his early work on new literacies, Street (1998, 1984) examines how new literacy practices might be legitimately viewed as *enabling* social practices as well as how they might be conceived within the ethos of reading and writing. At the extreme, Street suggests that traditional language constructs such as semantics, grammar, and lexicon are replaced by a broader system of semiotics. Drawing heavily on work in the traditions of ethnography of communication and semiotic linguistics, Street (1998) offers a call for educators:

> To take on the task of helping new generations to learn how to not take things at face value; to recognize when people are 'not talking straight'; to see grammar as a means of representing patterns of experience' and as helping them 'to build a mental picture of reality, to make sense of their experience of what goes on around them or inside them'; to be 'aware of the figurative devices that lie at the heart of discourse'; to recognize the rich variety of tropes, registers and language forms; to deploy to the full the metaphoric potential of language. (pp. 22-23)

By going beyond the skills-oriented pedagogies of the past, Street (1995) suggests a critical literacy perspective, which invites teachers to uncover the power dynamics present in our institutions. He asks that "all voices in our classrooms need to be allowed to be heard, regardless of preference of medium" (p. 7)

For Alan Luke (2007), new literacies represent an agency-creating opportunity as they provide occasions to mold, shape, reject, accept, and anticipate ideas. However with that opportunity, there must be a new form of educational imagination engaged by educators. Literacy in its most basic form is intrinsic to issues of social justice as we consider indigenous communities and those from lower socioeconomic locations. Because we live in a text-saturated culture and a multisemiotic universe, new literacies are necessary to allow children to move from the local to the global, from the known to the new. Luke explains that new literacies offer children a critical disposition and should be understood as a human right for those who believe that learning to read a text should involve an element of learned or constructive skepticism. Within a reality of Internet communication, technology is central to the concept of literacy within a global community. Luke explains that new literacies are not only the new basic but are also required to navigate the Internet just as the Internet is required to utilize new literacies. Questions related to text interpretation should ask: who wrote it, where did it come from, what is the intent of the text, what is missing, and what is it trying to do?

A playful new literacy

Premised on the understanding that new literacy practices include ever-evolving, multimodal forms of representation, my study deliberately positions the creation of autobiographical avatars as a new literacy practice (Lankshear and Knobel, 2006; 2003; Knobel, 1999). New literacy appears in many related guises like multi-literacy, media literacy, critical literacy, and critical media literacy. However, in all of these cases, as mentioned above, the "new" implies the sociocultural turn as well as the ontological and chronological shift. Drawing from Knobel, I understand the definition of literacy to move beyond a static decoding of print on a page to encompass multiple, and evolving practices in reading, writing, composing, viewing, listening, and communicating as legitimate forms of social knowledge. In 1999, Knobel's book *Everyday Literacies: Students, Discourses and Social Practices* adopted the term "everyday" literacies from Ludwig Wittgenstein's notion of "ordinary language, socially constituted meanings and forms of life" (p. 16). Knobel acknowledges that everyday literacy practices are those used to negotiate computer-mediated networks and other forms of technology and media that deliver information to those in postindustrial communities rapidly, easily, and continuously.

Such literacy practices are also readily accepted within the emerging field of new literacies as a valid and important form of social knowledge. For Lankshear and Knobel (2006) the term 'new' also carries an understanding that traditional practices have been reworked or remixed in some way. New literacy practices are those that use an insider mindset, or use a Web 2.0 orientation to invite collaboration and distribute expertise. They are constantly evolving and are limited only by imagination and the emerging technologies that hold them. While in some places a distinction is made between "everyday" and "new" literacy practices (new implying the relative freshness of the practice), I acknowledge that for the participants in my study, avatar design was introduced as a new literacy practice (though admittedly in many other online spaces it would not be considered new, but rather, an everyday literacy practice). When the girls made their second avatars near the end of the study, however, the process might be described more accurately as an everyday literacy. Following that reason, for the purpose of this book I use both terms, not to discredit or minimize the complexities implied within either definitions but to acknowledge the manner in which the term came to apply to the participants of my study as they progressed. In either case, new or everyday, avatar design was also positioned in the social realm of teenage girls, and for that reason it is positioned as a playful (though at times serious) literacy practice.

I use the term *playful*, again, not to diminish the seriousness of this literacy practice by equating it with something childlike or trivial but to position it, as does Bloustien (2003) as "deadly earnest." For Bloustien, play is "integral to all human activity throughout life; it is one of the fundamental ways in which all of us deal with uncertainty" (pp. 2-3). She explains that popular discourse within Western culture has separated "play" from "real work" thereby making it synonymous with escapism from institutional obligations. She argues that the work of understanding identity and the self within a turbulent culture has become an urgent matter, and that reliance on play might help make sense of our place within this culture.

Text, reading and writing

In Atlantic Canada, the *Foundation for the Atlantic Canada English Language Arts Curriculum* (1996) still guides provincial curricula in English. Similar foundational documents occur under different names in other locations across the country, but their intention is never all that different. This particular document guides schools in my area of the country, and its definition of text moves beyond a print-based definition more common under structuralist ideologies of the past to include "any language event: oral, written or visual" (p. 11). To that end, a text might be a music video, a poster, a song, a poem or a t-shirt, as long as it conveys meaning. Taking this notion one step further, this liberal and progressive pedagogy understands "reading" to include multiple forms of representation beyond merely print text and understands "text" to be anything from which meaning can be conveyed. It states:

> The term is an economical way of suggesting the similarity among many of the skills involved in 'reading' a film, interpreting a speech, or responding to an advertisement

> or a piece of journalism. The expanded concept of text takes into account the diverse range of texts with which we interact and from which we construct meaning. (p. 11)

Identity/Representation (in Cyberspace and Beyond)

In *Online identity,* Angela Thomas (2007) provides an argument that within virtual spaces the self-produced body is created/authored by using images and words from our social and discursive communities. She examines the online identity construction of several girls and in so doing finds that how young people construct their online identities within a social context is significant, specifically as it relates to issues of power and belonging. She found that identity markers such as race, gender, age, and personality "are strongly evident in virtual spaces" (p. 6), regardless of the discursive purpose of the online space. Thomas (2007) argues that one of the most important aspects regarding how identity is shaped online relates to the sense of community belonging. She acknowledges that youth have complex and social lives where "identities are fluid and are constructed through social and cultural experiences" (p. 38).

While the construction of avatars figures into her study as one of the multiple ways youth represented themselves in online spaces, online identity in Thomas' study was also tied to the ability to write. In fact, it was through a combination of the expression of writing and their chosen avatar that the youth "performed" their identity. To that end, children know that being literate means being powerful. "Literate behavior is also privileged as it sets up its own form of class system within the community" (p. 107). More plainly, she finds that "identity is shaped by desire and that desire is expressed through both language and image" (p. 182). Thomas (2007) draws heavily from Judith Butler's (1999) notion of performativity as "that aspect of discourse that has the capacity to produce what it names" (pp. 111-112) through repetition and recitation. Thomas explains that Butler (1999) views the body as "an imaginary construction, being fictional and therefore being capable of being rewritten and reinscribed" (p. 15). This notion is contradictory to much poststructural feminist work, which follows Foucault's claim that the body is "always and already" inscribed by discipline practices. Remember that for Foucault, subjectivity is tied up in notions of language or a variety of historical discourses. Discourses lead to various social practices, authorities, rules and regulations, fields of knowledge, and truths; therefore, discourses equal power/knowledge. Thomas (2007) claims:

> identity is a performance of fantasy and desire—a pursuit of being and becoming the image of this desire. In our lives, we perform our identities within the physical world, and this performance is constructed by numerous factors: the identity inscribed in our bodies such as gender, ethnicity and age; our individual personalities as evidenced through fashion sense, hairstyle and other bodily markings (tattoos, piercing, make-up); and out psychological make-up such as our mannerisms of walk and talk. (p. 5)

Recalling Cooper's (2006) observation regarding the gaming avatars, which played a pivotal role in initiating my study, Thomas (2007) also found that with girls online in a cyber world called the *Palace* there were also no fat avatars. In the *Palace*, youth interacted by using a choice of avatars which were limited and doll-like. In fact, many of the avatars were strongly sexualized representations that reproduced discourses of heterosexual sexuality and desire. Using Foucault's (1967, Online), notion of the mirror as a "heterotopia" (a placeless place where one can see oneself where on is not) Thomas (2007) points to the close editing involved in this form of public online representation when she cites one of her study's participants who explains her online persona as: "it's me, but minus the things I don't like about me" (p. 9). Thomas describes the avatars in her study as literally being rewritten or traced over by desire. Put another way, she explains the cyber body is "a clean fluidless body offered up as ideal" (p. 128). Athough Thomas found that gender swapping is commonly reported with respect to adult experiments online (Turkle, 1995, Bruckman, 1993), she found that children or youth are more likely to exaggerate their identity through gender performance. Butler (1997) calls this "hyperbolic exhibitions" of gender.

Thomas (2007) offers a feminist critique of the *Palace* for limiting the choice of avatars to be "complicit with patriarchal ideologies idealizing certain groups of girls: girls who have access to leisure time to spare for the playing out of their fantasies." Even though Thomas's study involves youth in a different online context than my study (her youth were engaged in interactive forms of online role playing and storytelling, and my participants are engaged in a visual authoring of the self), the principles around belonging to a community apply. What Thomas's study provides is a bridge between the avatar literature and the identity work associated with the (new/everyday) literacy practice of avatar design. "With ever new forms of community, children are participating in new forms of literacy, literacy is being transformed and is evolving with every new set of social practices" (Thomas, 2007, p. 182).

In an earlier work, "Digital Literacies and the Cybergirl," Thomas (2004) explores how teenaged girls use both language and image to construct a digital presence online. By "writing" their bodies, they write themselves. Her findings demonstrate how cyberbodies are encoded representations of fantasy and desire. "The body is self-produced through words and images within the social and discursive practices of the girls in the community. It exists within particular discourses of femininity, some of which conform to western ideals of beauty and girlhood; others reflect notions of resistance and rebellion" (p. 359). Thomas acknowledges that such writing of the self demands that individuals have a command of the digital literacies required to construct the self. This point is significant to my own findings, particularly as it relates to one girl who was marred by technological challenges.

Girlhood and Identity Making

At this time I will move more specifically to an exploration of research from the field of girlhood identity. I acknowledge that none of the studies explicitly addresses the intended and purposeful autobiographical identity that my study seeks to understand; therefore I draw from these pieces for their contributions to how teenage girls represent themselves within a complex and often conflicted social structure.

In her ethnographic study, Gerry Bloustien (2003) gave teenage girls video cameras and asked them to record their experiences. It is in the deliberate nature of self-representation examined here that provides guidance for my own study. Rather than giving my participants a video camera, my study attempts in another way to do what Bloustien aimed to accomplish. That is, Bloustien addresses the tangled nexus between a text and a lived experience in order to demonstrate how "subjectivity is negotiated, reflected upon and constituted through everyday social practices. Texts become a way of testing our limits, and through play ultimately enable the representation and the simultaneous constituting of the self" (p. 18). However, as Bloustien (2003) watches girls change through a highly personal and self-reflexive methodology, she finds that the texts they produce in their quest for meaning-making and identity-making, are *not* the authentic records of self that are often touted by other researchers.

Bloustien (2003) approached the ethnography of girl culture from a position that refuses to pathologize the fantasy and play in their constructed worlds. For her, the world of the teenage girls does not have to be described in terms of deception and confusion, addiction or delusion, ritual or resistance, as it often is presented within popular discourses. Instead, Bloustien understands girl culture to be nothing more than girl culture. The world of the teenage girl is one where meanings are made, changed, and remade; it is a place where identities are tried on and explored and refitted—it is a place where identities are transient, experimental, and shaped. This is significant in a society that works within fixed sets of social identities for youth as it seeks to define youth before they have a chance to define themselves. Society, particularly within commercialized popular culture, deceptively limits their choices, and in so doing defines young girls within limited parameters—often determined by hegemonic and consumptive practices. Bloustien (2003) choose participants between the ages of 15-18 because "in Western cultures, it is during these years that an individual is popularly recognised as moving from childhood to maturity and thus adulthood" (p. 6).

For Bloustien (2003), recent cultural studies research has tended to emphasize how texts are read and how "the role of consumer as producer of new meanings" manages to make meaning and develop a sense of identity "through the commodity in spite of social and material constraints" (p. 16). Moving away from Morley (1992), she argues that by defining social relations themselves as texts, the implication is that everything is "sayable" and thus everything can be read and interpreted. Bloustien argues that the question should be: "How do texts emerge from everyday life to become so meaningful? And in what ways can cultural texts...sometimes bridge the gap between the 'sayable' and the 'unsayable'" (p. 18)?

For Bloustien, the girls in her study were aware of "striking a pose" in front of the camera, both literally and figuratively as they engaged in the project of identity construction. They understood the self as an act in progress, and self-making itself as an active, purposeful process to be engaged. "They were attempting to pin down the ephemeral, the elusive, the fiction that became 'fact' only in the process of their fantasy" (p. 26). What Bloustien's research found was that the girls she studied were not keen to resist the hegemonic structures of a broader culture; rather, they were content to remain protected within these boundaries. The girls here found comfort and safety in remaining within the realm of what they knew.

Continuing with the notion of constructed girlhood, Catherine Driscoll (2002) states,

> Girlhood is made up and girls are brought into existence in statements and knowledge about girls, and some of the most widely shared or commonsensical knowledge about girls and feminine adolescence provides some of the clearest examples of how girls are constructed by changing ways of speaking about girls. (p. 5)

While traditionally puberty has defined the boundary between girlhood and womanhood, adolescence cannot be clearly marked by age or physical development. However, Driscoll argues that adolescence is and has been historically marked by gender—to speak of adolescence was to speak of boys, for example. What her book does is contribute to the literature on girlhood identity within popular culture and cultural theory, as it further positions feminine adolescents within theoretical discourses all their own. For Driscoll, the word "girls" implies "an idea of mobility preceding the fixity of womanhood and implying an unfinished process of personal development" (p. 47). This unfinished business and mobility echo themes of identity-in-progress stated by Bloustien (2003) and Thomas (2007).

Driscoll's work, specifically on body culture and body image, is helpful as it situates the discursive practices constituted in fashion, make-up, and self production within an ethos of feminine adolescence. Fashion provides not only "a range of already sanctioned codes for coherence and recognition" but also provides "a process of simultaneously producing, recording, and consuming the self" (p. 215). Fashion is understood to be mass-produced, and in that sense it represents something mainstream. It is rarely an expression of individuality, though it is always an expression of identity. "Fashion is both change and continuity, and ambiguity particularly associated with youth" (p. 246).

There is a collection of critical, feminist, and poststructuralist work by scholars Deirdre Kelly, Shauna Pomerantz, and Dawn Currie that either individually or collectively contribute to the notions of constructed identity, girlhood, and cyber culture that is worth exploring. I will briefly make note of some of their work as I highlight the points that are relevant to my own study.

Shauna Pomerantz (2006) contributes to the literature on girl culture specifically as it relates to the fashion choices the girls chose to use for their avatars in this study. In her chapter "'Did you see what she was wearing?' The Power and Politics of Schoolgirl Style" Pomerantz responds to a wave of news stories which sparked moral debates around girl fashion and a public discourse around the new "slut" look of bare midriffs, exposed bra straps, body piercings, exposed cleavage, and micro mini skirts. She highlights the complexity of schoolgirl style as a means to conceptualize and understand identity. She understands that style is a politically driven statement of identity and belonging, and that girls in schools enact it most passionately. "Inside the schools, overt and covert negotiations take place that are contingent upon the meanings that are created within its social world" (p. 189). Clothing for girls becomes a "social skin" and a form of "embodied subjectivity" which symbolize not only a manifestation of how girls see themselves but also how they want others to see them. "Style is a shifting and malleable text that enables girls to find each other, to form (dis)identifications, and to distinguish themselves, and how they want to be seen within the social world of the school" (p. 175).

Drawing on Stuart Hall's (1996) understanding of identity as constantly "in process" and something that is constitutive of discourse, identity is the "point of suture" between identity and discourse; it is "the structural constraints that shape us and the resulting subjecthood that enables us to shape ourselves. This suturing is made possible through agency" (p. 176). What Pomerantz found was that regardless of social or cultural group, girls were "routinely defined by style" (p. 177). This gives weight to the findings in my study where girls also used style to define their visual representations of self. She found that "style acted as a membrane of permeability, as a porous covering over the body that enabled girls to transfer something of themselves into the school's social world (subjectivity), while simultaneously enabling the school's social world to transfer something of itself into girls (discourse)" (p. 177).

Currie and Kelly (2006) conducted a study called *Girl Power* to explore notions of agency exhibited by girls as they negotiate the complex transition between girlhood and womanhood. The manner by which their study gave primacy to the girls in the study, rather than to the researchers, was the first of many ways this study influenced my own. Interpreting "meanness" as a product of girl's agency was an accidental direction for the researchers who did not anticipate the multiple discourses of female aggression that they found in the field. In short, Currie and Kelly "interpret meanness for what it tells us about the gendered nature of power in the highly competitive context of youth cultures" (p. 155). Conducted in Vancouver, the study used semi-structured interviews of twenty-nine preteen and teenage girls. The researchers draw from Connell (1987) to explain how gendered agency is considered against the complex constructions of self that stand against heteronormative versions of emphasized femininity. What they found is that within the boundaries of emphasized femininity, girls become the objects, not the subjects, of desire. In order to avoid the wrath of other girls' meanness one had to identify with an emphasized version of femininity within a gendered economy. If they did not, "meanness positions the 'other' in a peer hierarchy through a process that robs the 'othered' of control over defining 'who she is' and 'what she is all about'" (p. 162).

In another study, this time on skater girlhood and emphasized femininity, Kelly, Pomerantz and Currie (2005) explore the identity of skater girls and find that "some girls will resist emphasized femininity, either wholly or in part" (p. 130). In their study girls defined themselves as "alternative." In mine the girls described themselves as "unique." The description of being other than normative or mainstream might also be seen as resisting against the norm and claiming agency in their uniqueness. Claiming agency, however, is not without its contradictions. In fact, poststructuralist theorizing would dictate the impossibility of pinning down identity as in any way definitive—but, it also recognizes identity to be constantly shifting, conflicted, and in a virtual state of being contested. "Skater girlhood (as any girlhood) is always in process" (p. 130).

Kelly et al. (2005) found that "expressing one's unique personal style while adhering to particular group norms; disavowing fashion and popularity" (p. 145) provided an opportunity to tease out the subtle and often conflicting tensions that exist when girls connect to an alternative group. Even in the disavowing of an emphasized femininity, their rejection of popular culture's expectations brings the girls to a place where they identify with a highly hierarchal form of alternative girlhood identity that is skater girlhood. And even in this alternative location, there is structure.

Valentine and Holloway's (2002) study is titled "Cyberkids? Exploring Children's Identities and Social Networks in On-line and Off-line Worlds." In this study the pair employ an empirical study to examine how children's on-line worlds are affected by their off-line worlds and vice versa. Their research is significant to my own study as they find that the connection between "virtual" and "real" worlds is mutually constituted. They find that "boosters have uncritically celebrated on-line worlds as disembodied spaces, in contrast to the materiality of 'real-world' environments" (p. 304). While they note that online technology has been valorized for its ability to free users from the constraints of the body and for the ability to let youth create alternative identities through the kind of identity play noted above, they note a range of thinking regarding representations in virtual space—from those who believe that virtual environments negate the need for face-to-face socialization (Robins, 1995), to virtual spaces actually transcending everyday life (Doel and Clarke, 1999). They draw from Robins, who argues that the virtual represents a poor imitation of the real, thus making disembodied bodies "inauthentic" in contrast to real life ones. The accompanying moral panics see children disappearing into their cyber worlds, abandoning all need to socialize in person, and turning away from real life all together. What is significant to my own research is not so much the position of the supporters or debunkers of virtual worlds, but that both camps regard the "real" and the "virtual" as separate and perhaps discrete.

What Does This All Mean?

To have a potential cultural significance seems to be tied to a core adolescent preoccupation – that is, to belong (Bloustien, 2003; Clark, 2005; Dolby, 2003; Driscoll, 2002; Gee, 2003; Harris, 2003; Luke, 1997; Mazzarella and Pecora, 1999). What I have attempted to do is better understand the identity of teenage girls within an online context—a context that allows for the creation of a virtual identity and involves negotiating notions of gender, race, and ability, not to mention power, knowledge, and a sense of cultural locatedness. Seen this way, the negotiations involved in creating an avatar are not unlike the negotiations that occur in real life discursive practices. The questions: "who do I think I am?" and "who do I want others to think I am?" are challenging because there are no simple and straightforward answers. They are more challenging still when the responses to these questions are *written* with an image. Images are culturally encoded, as is written language. Where this becomes interesting is when we begin to tease out the metaphoric connection between the limits of these avatar creations and the limits of conventional forms of language. Kelly (1997) offers guidance for how a poststructuralist lens can critically reframe traditional literacy practices where "texts are fluid constructs, the permeable boundaries of which are continually negotiated in the intersection of knowledge, power, culture, and desire" (p. 20). When we begin to understand the options for online identity construction in this light, questions emerge regarding who are the real creators and authors of such identities.

There is no mistaking that images are pervasive in Western society, particularly where mass media is responsible for snatching up and colonizing public and private spaces. The pervasive dominance of the image within what Trend (2003) calls a new media studies movement suggests that educators engage with an amalgam of reader response and resistance theories, where practitioners concede that viewers use media in highly individualistic ways. If knowledge *is* derived from politically contrived versions of the truth, as Kincheloe (2005) reminds us from a critical constructivist frame, then in the absence of informed modes of meaning making, the "dominant power wielders" in schools tend to reinforce patriarchic, Eurocentric, racist, and homophobic practices. Even though our mass media culture implicitly assumes (or encodes) society's hegemonic ideology, these representations also present a location for ideological struggle. If educators understand that language and discourse are not neutral modes of communication but are entangled within power relations and social and historical phenomena, then they might see the way individuals act as tainted by discursive practice as well as by social and power relationships. For those in marginalized groups, new technologies and new literacies provide a means for individuals to find voice and claim agency (Kellner and Share, 2007). For members of society's dominant group, by contrast, such a new literacy practice "offers an opportunity to engage with the social realities that the majority of the world are expressing" (p. 9). It is the responsibility of cultural workers and educators to attempt to connect theory to practice (Giroux, 1999; Trend, 2003), and ultimately connect the macro with the micro (Livingstone, 1998; Morley, 1993). It is my hope that findings from this study will, in some small way, help do just that.

While creating autobiographical avatars may not be an activity one would expect to see sanctioned within traditional English language arts (ELA) curricula, this book hopes to demonstrate how this new literacy practice might be regarded as an activity that recognizes notions of personal development, citizenship and critical communication across a wide range of media texts that are common to many ELA curricula (Alvermann, 2002; Kist, 2000; Morgan, 2000; Nixon, 2002; Peim, 1993; Pirie, 1993; Street, 2005, 1998). More importantly it provides a pedagogical opportunity and a discursive space to critically examine the constructed nature of social knowledge as it bears on identity creation and allows for a space to openly discuss notions of race, class, gender, and ability (Giroux, 1999; Kalmer, 2001; Share, 2004; Trend, 2003). It would seem that the critical reflection made possible with autobiographical writing in this (or another) visual form of representation presents an opportunity for educators and students to explore the social construction of identity and belonging not only as it is "written" by teenage girls with their avatars, but also as teenage girls discover that popular culture has been written on them. However, it is with the end goal of creating what Dolby (2003) calls a "vital political space" in mind that position, this new literacy practice, and the critical analysis of it, within the realm of radical democratic practice (Giroux et al., 2000; Kellner and Share, 2007; McLaren, 2007).

It would be naive to assume that audiences accept mass media messages uncritically and without question—even youth audiences. It would also be impossible to fully address the infinite number of ways that audiences might negotiate/resist or co-opt mass culture (Dolby, 2003; McRobbie, 2005). Some argue that youth audiences are not necessarily duped by the "mythic" properties of the text (Barthes, 1989), or by the commercial strategies employed by the consumer market (Gunter, Oates and Blades, 2004). However, an entire industry exists based on the understanding that fads and styles marketed to youth will get picked up by youths, for whatever reason. To that end, I wanted to examine if and how the articulation of autobiographical avatars designed for this study might "buy in" to the commercial fads available within the avatar production process as they have with such vigor in Korea. As a pedagogical practice, it is my hope that examining the presence of the commercial and political influence of popular culture on how young people construct identity (and in some cases claim agency) will provide an opportunity for educators and students alike.

I am also interested to know if creating an avatar might become an act of political resistance (McRobbie, 2005; Fiske, 1992, 1989), or social conformity (Livingstone, 2002), or both, or more, or neither. And, in what way is agency enacted or shut down by the limitless and at times limiting possibilities available in avatar design of the self (Currie and Kelly, 2006)? When a girl is unable to find the options she wants, what choices will she make? By looking at what is missing from the avatars I have an opportunity to read into the silences or learn from what has been left out (Kumashiro, 2001; Tierney and Dilley, 1992). Obviously I am interested in what the girls' avatars look like; however, the heart of this examination is in the poststructural willingness to "interrogate the will to truth" (Kelly, 1997, p. 53). Put another way, and drawing from work in autobiography, examining the complex and often conflicted negotiations that occur during the construction process of these avatars, I might get closer to understanding how and why these girls represent themselves the way they do. As I have asked earlier, what stories about themselves will they tell? And which will they choose to keep to themselves?

Outing My Biases

Back in the 1980s, when I was a teenage girl, outside of school I spent a lot of my time in a rink. I was a competitive figure skater, and although I did not ever make it big I did get close enough to see first hand what making it big looked like. Figure skating shaped my identity growing up, not only with regard to who I was, but also how I looked. To my family, friends and acquaintances, I was Connie, the skater. Growing up I referred to myself as a skater. At that time, prior to the evolution of skateboard culture, the tag did not imply (at least in my small world) the same cultural code that it carries today (Kelly, Pomerantz and Currie, 2006). In a sport that depended (and still depends) on appearances and awarded as many points for "artistic impression" as it did for technical competence, attention to detail meant a chance at success. While the International Skating Union (ISU) has recently dropped the once familiar 6.0 grading system in figure skating and adopted a new, more nuanced scoring system that now divides the final score into many smaller categories, it is still reliant on elements of artistic impression. The statement that figure skating scores are currently based on a 50/50 split between technical requirements and artistic impression would not be entirely accurate—but it's not far from the truth either. During the 1980s, there was a period prior to 1987 where the artistic mark often broke a tie in total points, giving it the higher weight of the two scores. All this meant that planning a "look" for a competitive skater often meant working with a choreographer, a designer, a coach, and a sport psychologist. Originality and appearance were important, yet staying within the parameters of what was accepted was as well. Everything was considered, from music choice, dress design, and careful and purposeful choreography—even a haircut was an important nuance. In short, appearance and representation consumed the sport that defined me. Growing up, it is probably fair to say that defining who I was and how I appeared could not be removed from what I did. I remember cutting my long hair off when it was trendy for skaters to wear a bun because my coach, Wallace Diestelmeyer, told me it would make me look faster when I skated. I also remember wearing black spandex pants to a figure practice at the Canadian championships and that same coach being horrified that I had not brought a skirt. On the ice, individuality was rewarded but within strict limits. Off the ice, however, it was still important to fit in with the crowd.

The youth market was beginning to explode in the 1980s (Klein, 2002; Kenway and Bullen, 2001; Schor, 2003). MTV had only begun its evolution as a giant marketing machine, and teenagers were beginning to emerge as prey for hungry corporations. I share these stories as a way of positioning my bias as a researcher. In my youth, notions of style, appearance, and attention to detail shaped how I saw myself within a larger social group. I wondered if it would be the same with the group of girls in my study. Our worlds were so vastly different, after all.

What is it that the participants of the study will want to reveal about themselves through their avatars? What will they want to hold secret? How will they choose to visually represent themselves? And how will they decide? Following a theoretical positioning of avatar design within the realms of new literacy and autobiography in chapter three, I will provide a detailed description of the process by which the girls created their avatars, including a description of the website, WeeWorld.com, that rendered it possible to create these avatars. I will then introduce the ten girls who helped me to examine these questions.

Chapter Three

Making a WeeMee One Click at a Time

To begin, this chapter will look at the discursive practice of online identity and representation, as well as the form of this type of avatar construction, by situating them within the larger theoretical frameworks of new literacy scholarship and autobiography. Next, I will briefly explain the process by which this research was conducted, including a detailed look at the avatar creation web site, WeeWorld.com, and how it works, since this bears relevance to the semiotics of identity representation and notions of autobiography. As the site is examined for the possibility for nearly constant reinvention (Turkle, 1995), I will take a brief look at the apparently limitless and sometimes limiting choices the girls faced when they constructed their WeeMee avatars. Finally, I will briefly introduce the participants involved in the study.

Constructed Identity and Online Representation

Youth have complex and social lives (Thomas, 2007), which often blend offline and online worlds in a manner that does not distinguish between the two. Today's Western world teens have never known a world without cyberspace, where "identities are fluid and are constructed through social and cultural experiences" (p. 38). Thomas argues that one of the most important aspects regarding how identity is shaped online relates to the sense of belonging to a community. When this is viewed in regard to the sense of community and belonging to the community within the vast popularity of social networking sites like Facebook, the issue of online identity and representation takes on added significance. Representing oneself to the world is no longer a discursive practice that remains within a small tangible social circle.

Hypothetically, if a teen decided it might a good idea to dye her hair green for St. Patrick's day thirty years ago, chances are good that the only those in her immediate social circle would have been privy to her feeble attempt to have cultural relevance. If one of her friends had taken her picture that day she might have had a souvenir of the experiment; chances are also good that the event might have gone unnoticed. What is more, it is likely that for all but her closest circle of friends, the event would be forgotten. However, if a girl today dyed her hair green in a similar attempt to claim some cultural relevance, chances are far greater that either she or one of her friends will snap up her image and have it posted and tagged on her Facebook page in no time. The image would be shared online, and it would be nearly impossible to remove—the playful expression of identity becomes semi-public and immutable.

Thomas (2007) tells us "with ever new forms of community, children are participating in new forms of literacy, literacy is being transformed and is evolving with every new set of social practices" (p. 182). Within the Facebook community, new literacy practices involve posting and editing profile pictures that will represent members to their sometimes-vast social networks. With the evolving commercial nature of Facebook, the option to create one's cartoon likeness is among the many advertisements that now regularly beckon Facebook members from the banner that runs down the right-hand side of their homepage. The advertisement invites Facebook users to create an avatar for their profile picture. This advertisement depicts a picture of a doe-eyed brunette beside her strikingly accurate cartoon likeness, and when users click on the link they are taken to another page with the title makeacartoonyou.com. Here a split screen depicts female and male character choices in virtual rooms with virtual clothes closets. The cartoon images move about, changing their attire and hairstyles, thus showing potential users what might be possible in creating a cartoon self image. One more click and users are taken to the home page for Zwinky.com, a site described above as a choice that was considered but not used for the research project for its similarity to the WeeWorld site. It made little sense to give participants two options, which were virtually the same. The Zwinky site now, however, has more recently evolved to include avatars with more realistic, but also more sexualized body types; legs are visible, as are curves and cleavage on the female avatars, for example. These characteristics were not obvious only months ago.

Avatar Creation as New Literacy/Everyday Literacy

How do we know when a new literacy emerges? Coiro, Knobel, Lankshear and Leu (2008) tell us that "New literacies are identified with an epochal change in technologies and associated changes in social and cultural ways of doing things, ways of being, ways of viewing the world (worldviews), and so on" (p. 7). The ability to author oneself to the world—or at least to networks of hundreds of friends—has become a relatively new social practice for millions of individuals. Creating an avatar is no longer tied exclusively to belonging to an online virtual world, a Multi User Dungeon (MUD), or other such online gaming community. Individuals whose engagement with cyberspace is limited to web surfing and email communications can connect to a social networking network like Facebook and can now engage in the process of online identity creation that would not have been possible for them only a short time ago. To present and represent oneself in cartoon form with both the level of accuracy and fluidity that is possible today through these avatar programs would have been the exclusive domain of cartoon artists only a few decades ago. To have these programs deliberately marketed to youth today implies knowledge about what Thomas (2007) calls "the semiotics of identity" in this visual realm. The complex and often conflicting negotiations of fluid identity (re)construction are underwritten by the notion that "identity is shaped by desire and that desire is expressed through both language and image" (p. 182).

The definition of literacy is a contested one (Hagood, 2008). Some scholars argue that it belongs to only the process of reading and writing, but others ask: what kinds of reading and writing? Livingstone, Van Couvering and Thumin (2008) recall the argument between the Enlightenment thinking, which viewed literacy as a democratic vehicle designed to empower the masses and ordinary people, while more critical visions of schooling saw the project of literacy as the source of inequity, divisiveness and the promotion of an elite culture (Kellner, 2002; Willlinskky, 2000). Debates over literacy still, as always, seem to revolve around the questions of how and why the public will participate in society. As educators we know that the shift from traditional print-centered literacy to new literacy pedagogy is tied intricately to an engagement with technology and limited only by the technology that will hold it. Coiro, Knobel, Lankshear and Leu (2008) point to seminal work on the theoretical shift from literacy as it moves from page to the screen in terms of text comprehension and composition or production. "Literacy is no longer a static construct from the standpoint of its defining technology for the past 500 years, it has now come to mean a rapid and continuous process of change in the ways in which we read, write, view, listen, compose, and communicate information" (p. 5). More broadly, with definitions of literacy now including elements of popular culture (as I believe it should), a more expansive definition of text is called for. Street (2005, 1998) argues that literacy is rooted in sociohistorical contexts—with that, literacy carries the baggage of more than limited sign systems needed to decode letters and words.

As an alternative, new literacy practices might be legitimately viewed as social practices as well as be conceived within the ethos of reading and writing. If the definition of "text" can be understood as any language event that makes or creates meaning, and "language" can be understood in a semiotic sense, as Kress (2005) shows us, as one of many differently configured potential means to make meaning, then language can be understood more broadly. Also, as Kress notes, "that can bring a profound change" (p. 101). Lankshear and Knobel (2006) see new literacies as constructs which juxtapose several of the practices mentioned above. What's more, they point not just to new "technology stuff" but also new "ethos stuff" that remixes, reconfigures, and redistributes how knowledge is produced and disseminated.

As educators, shift in the literacy practices within the realm of popular culture demand our critical attention, not merely as a casual curiosity to know what or students are doing in their spare time but as a means to understand the social implications of such complex identity writing and identity shaping. Hagood (2008) reminds us that even Shakespeare and Dickens were considered popular in their time, and texts from popular culture have increasingly been given scholarly attention in education over the past two decades because of the degree to which they inform identity and belonging. If literacy is viewed within a sociohistorical context, it becomes impossible to remove it from the associated hegemony or power struggles within that sociohistorical context. Rather than focusing on the technological components of what makes literacy in this new media age, new literacy practices involve "an understanding of how digital culture locates adolescents in new ways" (Alvermann, 2002, pp. vii-ix). In fact, Kist (2005) notes that in a "massive" social turn, literacy becomes "deeply enmeshed in the culture, history, and everyday discourses of people's lives....To look at literacy out of these contexts is to miss most (if not all) of what is happening" (p. 6).

Using a multiple literacies notion based on the frame provided by Lankshear and Knobel (2003), and Torres and Mercado (2007) provide a convincing argument for critical media literacy that embraces new forms of literacy based on new technologies, and new literacies as a new way to look at the notion of literacy. For them, new literacies provide a chance to address how students engage with and through new technologies, even though they are often absent from current curriculum. Pointing to Freire's (1970) seminal work on literacy, they suggest that a critical media literacy approach offers more opportunity than the psychological and technological paradigms of the past. Put more strongly, a Freirean pedagogy to "read the word and the world" would welcome multimodal texts and the multiple perspectives from marginalized locations. With this framework in mind, I look to Kelly (1997) who reminds us of the push and pull of traditional pedagogy that at once ignores popular texts as it attempts to view reading through a progressive lens. Such tension ultimately serves to limit the pedagogy by regarding it as no more than "response." As a result of ignoring, marginalizing, or even shunning texts from popular culture, this pedagogy "fails to understand fully, the complex political relationship of culture and identity" (p. 67).

Avatars as autobiography

At the time of writing, no research literature on visual autobiographies could be located in educational databases on this particular topic. The only near mention came from Perfect (1984) in the form of a description of an elementary art activity to create an *autobiobox* (visual autobiography in a container). In this activity young children were encouraged to fill a container with items that were of personal significance as a means to tell a self-story. I will, therefore, rely on scholarship from autobiography in its traditional print form, and, as Kress and van Leeuwen (2006) did with their examination of elements of visual design, I will appropriate notions from a traditionally print-dominated genre. Where possible, and as much as is possible, I will apply these notions to a visual form. Doing this requires that I restate my understanding of how a visual creation might be situated within the realm of "writing."

For Graham (1991), autobiography in education is aligned with neopragmatist and constructivist epistemologies as it allows for an examination of the relationship between the social and the self. As do the aforementioned scholars from new literacies, Graham sees transformative opportunities present in this mode of writing as it gives students an opportunity to claim their own voice. He critiques Willinsky's claim that such new literacies can be grounded in the Romantic legacy. These legacies intended to liberate the author to write subjectively in what Wordsworth refers to as the "spontaneous overflow of powerful feelings." Despite Willinsky's (1987) contention that the roots of New Literacy might be traced back to the Romantics (specifically to the nineteenth century and the Romantic poetry project espoused by Wordsworth and Coleridge in their *Preface to the Lyrical Ballads*), Graham explains that the links between autobiography and several neo-Romantic projects "take the nature of student's self-understanding as their primary concern" (p. 144). He explains that the Romantic interest in developing the self in broader struggles of social or institutional constraint represents a multidisciplinary preoccupation. And while he acknowledges that Willinsky makes a solid case for New Literacy education being rooted in the Romantic Movement, Graham also acknowledges a contradiction in a pedagogy manifest in new literacy classrooms. The pedagogy that allows children to, "lay claim to a kind of unconscious genius which requires only a writerly opportunity" (p. 275).

Graham (1991) suggests that the role of autobiography in education is far more than "an idiosyncratic mixture of history and fiction, or as a writerly project from reclaiming lost sources of intentionality" (p. 141); rather it is both of these and perhaps more. For him, the activity of using autobiography in education appears to work in two diametrically opposed but concurrent ways. First, the act of reading and writing the self works from the inside out to express a self as something already and always constituted, and also from the outside in as a way to "work on the self through the production and consumption of a *text*" (p. 145). He argues that within constructivist models of education across all disciplines, Dewey's influence continues to resonate in the desire to give privilege to students' experience and knowledge.

Graham points to literary theorist Michael Sprinker (1980) to illuminate the importance of the poststructuralist project of autobiography. Each text acts as an expression of the relation that exists between texts; "every subject, every author, every self is the articulation of an intersubjectivity structured within and around the discourses available at any moment in time" (p. 325). Graham also looks to Bruner (1987), whose move toward self-narrative sheds light on the connection between how educators view margins and centers. He explains that autobiographical writing often yields an inevitable feeling of alienation. It also holds the challenge inherent in asking students to write personally and engage in personal disclosure. However, these challenges also hold opportunity for further exploration as they represent an opening for broader discussions around social and cultural issues. On one level, Graham explains that autobiography is

> an ancillary method in educational settings for marginalized groups like women and people of color as an example of what Freire (1970) calls *conscientization,* of seeing how subjectivity is constructed along different relations of power, and hence of being placed in a position to effect meaningful change. (p. 144)

Within education, autobiography is part of the dialectical interplay between the construction of subjectivity as a project undertaken both collectively and socially. It explores and gives voice to these sedimented layers of individual consciousness that may have been buried or silenced under pressure from dominant discourses and modes of representation in a culture.

Along with the poststructuralists, Graham (1991) argues that "the antihumanism of poststructuralism may serve to move us toward a view of autobiography in education as intertextual and intersubjective project, a project that presses hard against the positions of those who prefer to characterize autobiography as primarily the expression of a unique individual consciousness" (p. 147). The question of the origins of thought, as Graham explains, presents a real obstacle for poststructuralist theory. The ultimate source of meaning, he explains, rests with the individual. This question of origins, that is, locating the decisive source of meaning as it relates to the will of the individual, is "the single preoccupation of philosophers from Barthes, Derrida and Foucault as they attempt to 'decenter the subject.' Ultimately, Graham sees autobiography within a broader project of education as constituting "a mode of discourse whose very function is to make problematic the meaning of subjectivity within a culture" (p. 149).

Kelly's (1997) self-reflexive practice of autobiographical writing within this context serves as an example of how students can discursively produce meaning within the apparent contradiction that is implied by such poststructural pedagogy. Described as a form of highly personal and subjective writing, autobiography can offer a "discursive production of memory, history, representation, desire and knowledge while addressing head–on the implications of such insights not only for how notions of subjectivity and collectivity are understood, but, also, for how pedagogies are mobilized" (p. 48). If such meaning–making is possible through autobiographical writing, I wonder what might be possible if autobiography is produced (or re-produced) in a visual form. Graham points to literary theorist, Michael Sprinker (1980), to illuminate the importance of the poststructuralist project of autobiography.

> Every text is an articulation of the relations between texts, a product of intertextuality, a weaving together of what has already been produced elsewhere in discontinuous form; every subject, every author, every self is the articulation of an intersubjectivity structured within and around the discourses available at any moment in time. (p. 325)

After all, each of us *is* a multiplicity of subjects (Clandinin, 1985).

While acknowledging the importance of autobiographical writing in the English classroom as it represents beliefs about writing and the individual, Berlin (1992) explains that autobiography might bring together notions of the self, identity, narrative and self-expression. However, from a poststructuralist perspective, autobiography might also be regarded as an "impersonal symbolic offering" where the self is erased, and where the narrative form is more akin to a straightjacket which "positions and defines the self in a limiting kind of way" (p. 139). Following Berlin's suggestion to juxtapose autobiography with other writing forms, such as a grocery list or graffiti, highlights the culturally restrictive conventions expected from it. A deconstruction (in the Derridian sense), which examines the "differences and identities" of the form, allows us to consider the social context of writing—what Berlin refers to as the "sociolinguistics of writing" (p. 139). This is more than a mere recognition of differences in form and function among these various genres of writing—that much is easy. However, differentiating between autobiography as a fragment (imagine a visual self representation in the form of an avatar as an autobiographical expression), as opposed to *an* autobiography, implies that autobiography must take on an established form. However, while questioning the objective truth claims implied in autobiographical writing, Berlin wonders if autobiography might be "doomed to be nothing more than a series of autobiographical fragments" (p. 140). To me, however, autobiography hardly seems doomed if it is understood to be limited and partial. It makes sense that it should be understood as fragmented —even incomplete. This theory is apparent in my study. One of the teenagers who took part had a firm grasp on this concept as she commented that pictures (or avatars for that matter) are "only a moment of your life represented." Graham suggests that one way forward is to view the writer and his or her work as being a "subject-in-progress" (p. 118). In this study, the older girls seem to have a firm grasp on the notion that they are "in progress." Perhaps the problem is not that autobiography is partial and incomplete but rather that we expect it to be otherwise.

If, as educators, we are going to acknowledge individual writers and readers who are situated in and constituted by complex and often conflicting social and cultural discursive practices as they relate to race, gender, and ability, then we must also seek to understand their writing (in whatever form it takes) within "the specificity of the literate acts that those individual writers engage in" (Yagelski, 2000). It would be irresponsible for educators to accept that writing and reading are embedded within specific social contexts and then deny the influence that these contexts have on the individual. As we attend to the inherently social and cultural nature of the individual, we must not forget "the inherently individual nature of writing and reading" (p. 60). Yegelski reminds us that educators must ask the questions about what readers and writers do as they engage in these discursive practices. It is important to acknowledge the "inevitable feeling of alienation" that can be felt when writing autobiography, while attending to the resistance that students may express when they are asked to write in a deeply personal way. On "an important level autobiography is working as an ancillary method in educational settings for marginalized groups" (p. 144). It is for this reason that any form of autobiographical writing—visual or otherwise—must be undertaken with a note of caution. If we understand the writer is not autonomous and has been written by social, political, and historical discourses then the challenge becomes how do we understand the writer, either collectively or individually?

How to Write the Self with an Avatar

With an assignment to create a purposeful autobiographical avatar, the participants of this study set out to create representations of self with as much accuracy as possible. For each of the girls, the practice of representing who they are (or who they think they are) was tied to notions of appearance, personality, things they love, activities and interests, future dreams, and favourite things. What emerged almost from the beginning was a sense that these avatars were able to do something in social spaces that profile pictures could not; that is, the avatars could portend to the future and speak to dreams and wishes in a way that was not possible with traditional profile pictures. In a later chapter, I will return to explore the similarities and differences between avatars and digital pictures as they are used and as they might be used as one's profile picture on social networking sites. For now, I will come back to the *process* by which the girls created their avatars and wrote their autobiographical fragments using a visual semiotic frame. Many girls made considered and deliberate choices to represent themselves physically and to include articles that could indicate activities they were involved with. They often used favorite colours, locations, articles of clothing, or accessories to highlight parts of what they felt were "unique" identity markers. They expressed a belief that these signature expressions of identity were things that others would easily associate with them. Within the WeeWorld.com site, however, certain limitations meant that the girls were often faced with choices, and often left with little choice in terms of being able to represent themselves the way the initially wanted to.

After WeeMees had been registered, and once a user chose to update or alter her WeeMee, it would appear that she could pick one of 377 tops for her avatar. The reality was, however, that 227 (more than sixty-seven percent) of these tops required an accumulation of points. Similarly, of the 168 possible hairstyles, 36 (twenty-one percent) of these required points. Unless the girls were willing to pay for the privilege of accumulating points, they did not have access to all of the options. Ultimately, this is read as another manifestation of kinderculture's corporate consumption of childhood (Kenway and Bullen, 2001; Linn, 2000; Steinberg and Kincheloe, 1998). Clever marketers have "pried open other parent-free environments" specifically in sites like the Internet, where they know they have almost direct access to an unsupervised youth market. "Indeed, marketers are connecting with children in an increasingly close embrace that parents find difficulty to penetrate and is even affecting how kids and parents get along" (Schor, 2004, p. 17).

In all cases, the girls in this study attempted to accurately represent themselves physically beginning with skin tone, and hair color and style. With only six different skin tones to choose from, the level of accuracy was certainly not a detail that could be attended to with any level of realistic expectations; however, only one girl commented on her inability to find the right skin tone. Would they have felt the same ambivalence toward skin tone if they were African American, Asian, or Latino? While the skin tone options included shades of beige, brown and yellow, there is no expectation that one will be able to accurately find one's exact skin tone. Is this a problem? Yes, and no. When the skin tone options are presented, they are presented by having six avatars lined up from left to right presenting the various shades. The presentation of skin colour does not go from lightest to darkest or from darkest to lightest. It has in front (and to the left in a location that indicates: "start reading here") a warm pinkish beige colour; one that most Caucasians might choose. Next, and standing behind the first avatar is a pale beige, nearly white skin tone. From there and standing progressively further behind the first avatar are then deepening shades of brown. It is my belief that there is a willing acceptance for the stylized representation at this level of representation in the same way as there would be if we asked children to colour a self portrait. We would not expect a box of crayons to include all the possible skin tones, but we would still be able to read race based on a stereotyped understanding of color.

At this point, we can begin to tease out some of the theoretical considerations around this element of representation. Is race, as it is here represented (or not represented) a matter of social, historical, and cultural discourse? (I would suggest that it cannot exist in any other way). Or do the limited semiotics of this program position race within, as Berlin suggests above, the straitjacket of autobiography? Yagelski (2000) invites us to attend to the inherent complexities of discourses by asking our students what it is that they do at the point when they are asked to decide the skin color for their avatar? Does it concern them if they are not able to find their proper skin tone? What does it mean to pick the darkest brown, what does it mean to pick the lightest beige? What are the cultural codes that have been written on them that make them read these skin colors the way they do? Also, what other considerations come to mind when they read the brown skin tone? Do they then expect to see other forms of representations with the avatar?

Returning for a moment to follow up with the one girl in my study who commented on the inability to find the right skin tone; a later response from her indicated that she was more concerned when she could not find the right kind of glasses without having to pay for them. I will return to an analysis of this participant and the considerations behind how she created her avatars in the next chapter. At this time, I turn to the participants in my study to explore the notions of how their avatars can be viewed by them and by others as autobiographical fragments. The girls help to shed light on what happened when they were free to represent themselves in a seemingly limitless fashion only to learn later that their options are limited by the semiotic language and rules of the program being used and by their willingness to pay for more options.

On a number of occasions the girls expressed that they felt that accuracy was important in terms of the way their avatars might send messages about who they are to others. This was a significant concern for the girls who noted someone they did not know might view their profile pictures. The importance of accuracy was intimately tied to the notion that first impressions are important, therefore, the details that combine to make up their avatars needed to be carefully considered. Notions of accuracy were closely tied to elements of limitations, possibilities, and first impressions. As the girls created their avatars, they attempted to accurately represent themselves physically and in terms of the things that they did. Many girls included favorite colours, locations, and specific articles of clothes or accessories to highlight what they felt would be signature pieces that others would easily identify with them. Within the WeeWorld site, however, certain limitations meant that the girls often were faced with choices. This in turn meant that they were not always able to represent themselves with the degree of accuracy that they had initially intended. What participants soon learned was that the limits of the options available to them, and the limits within the program itself (i.e. that they could choose lipstick, *or* freckles, or eye liner, *or* a mole, but not any combination of these) meant that accuracy became something they were all eager to write about. Eventually this led to a lively discussion regarding the benefits and drawbacks of using avatars versus real profile pictures to make an accurate representation of self. The debate over avatars versus photographs will be further discussed shortly. In the meantime, for many, limitations in the program led them to make choices that they were not completely happy with, and in one case, a participant nearly gave up because of her frustration over not being able to create her avatar in a satisfactory manner.

A Brief Look at the Research Project

A decision to first locate and recruit participants for this study on the social networking site Facebook was my deliberate attempt to find individuals who were already engaged in online social interaction with their peers. During the initial sampling for this project, I "invited" participants to join my *Avatar Creation Group,* which was posted on Facebook. Facebook requires that groups be listed according to category and type. This particular group was classified under "Internet / Technology" and "Cyberculture." The group was set up as an "open group" where anyone could join, and all members could invite others to join. In order to gather the largest possible initial sample, there was no limitation placed on age or gender. The sample was deliberately limited to those who use Facebook and who were, by extension, connected to my initial network of "friends" (a term used on Facebook to designate contacts within one's online social network).

My justification for using this particular online site for my initial recruitment and sampling was that it provided a population of potential participants who were already immersed in the mode of social online communication that this research intended to examine. I was not looking for online gamers; I was looking for individuals who were using the Internet as a social tool. As such, the "invitation" to participate in the research was essentially an electronic version of a recruitment poster designed to find participants where they already are (rather than find them in an artificial context like a classroom where they may or may not engage in forms of social online communication). Participation was completely voluntary, and Facebook members joined the group if it was of interest to them and could leave it if they didn't want to stay. The first "friend" I invited was my sixteen-year-old daughter, not only for her interest in the study but also for her connections to a youth peer group, many of whom had expressed interest in participating in this research. The target population was teenaged girls between the ages of thirteen to seventeen, even though participation in the initial phase of this study did not limit age or gender. The initial collection of a convenience sample lasted for approximately two months until the group included 136 members. Data were collected, by means of observation field notes and thick description, and it was analyzed with a system of open coding and arranged thematically.

As the Facebook group name suggests, members of the *Avatar Creation Group* were invited to create an avatar that intentionally represented how they saw themselves. Directions were given on the group's home page, and members were encouraged to choose from a list of programs to create and upload their avatars. After conducting extensive on-line searches for avatar creation programs, three programs were chosen deliberately for this group site because they were free. The following three programs were also chosen because they had no associations with a gaming culture where alter ego personas where encouraged, and because they each had transportability built into their features. That is, the avatars created here can be used in other online and digital spaces, as apposed to the avatars on the Rogers Yahoo site, which could only (at that time anyway) stay within Rogers Yahoo itself. Below is a list of the avatar creation sites that were listed on the Avatar Creation Group's Facebook page:

http://www.weeworld.com/
http://www.doppelme.com/create/wardrobe.asp
http://birgits.net/eng/eng_grafstor.shtml

Another program http://www.zwinky.com was initially added to the list; however, after exploring the site it was determined that the similarities between Zwinky and WeeWorld negated the necessity for having a choice between the two programs. The implicit autobiographical design of these programs was also a significant factor in choosing them for this study. The list of program options is and was in no way intended to be exhaustive, but the three choices were meant to give a variety of style choices to the participants. Not surprisingly, the WeeWorld site was chosen exclusively by the case study participants as the place to create their autobiographical avatars. In the original group (which had 136 members at its peak) and where forty (40) avatars were created, all but one avatar were created using the WeeWorld.com site. The options to individualize avatars through either physical features or interest options on WeeWorld represented significantly more choices than the other programs.

It should also be noted that in the months since this study began, the WeeWorld.com site has undergone a rapid and significant expansion. While the site now includes a two-dimensional version of a *Second Life* option for WeeMee characters to socialize, the option to have the WeeMees uploaded to email signatures or to Facebook profiles (among many other "traveling" options) remains a key feature of the program. While the exporting process proved too challenging for a few participants, some who needed detailed directions, and others who, at the time, needed to be walked through the process step-by-step on the phone, the process of exporting a WeeWee has recently been drastically simplified. Directions have been streamlined to allow users to export their avatars to other locations, not only allowing users to add a personalized dimension to their email signatures, for example, but also allowing the WeeWorld brand to travel and colonize public and private spaces (Klein, 2002).

Once WeeMees have been registered with WeeWorld, for example, individuals have the option to "Export them to community blogs and websites, email signatures, mobile phones, instant messaging, or to t-shirts, bags and badges." It was this feature that interested me most, since the transportable design of these avatars invites a deliberate autobiographical consideration of how they will be created depending on where they will be used. This consideration played an important part in the participant's own observations regarding what they would or would not share in terms of profile pictures or avatars and in terms of the importance of the first impressions that their avatars would have on others.

A Wee Bit About WeeWorld.com

Since all of the participants in the case study chose to create their avatars using the WeeWorld.com site, the site itself demands some attention. However, since much discussion and analysis will be given to this site and the choices available to the participants of this study in coming chapters, I will provide only an overview of what is necessary to explain the function and options available as they relate to the purposes of this study on this site at this time. In keeping with a Web 2.0 mindset and the collaborative and participatory nature of new literacy practices, I turn to Wikipedia.com for guidance:

> A WeeMee is an animated avatar for Skype (since December 2005), Windows Live Messenger, and AOL Instant Messenger. WeeMees can be customized on the WeeWorld.com site or on AIM.com. Customizations available are similar to those on other avatar sites and include facial features, clothing, and accessories. In May, 2008, WeeWorld created "world," an addition to site where WeeMees are able to walk around (actually jumping), and chat live for the first time. The site has been criticised in the past for not having this feature until now.
>
> With a WeeMee, a "WeeWorld" personal web page is created. This is similar to a MySpace account in that it comes with a blog, the capability to add friends, to have a thought, and to post comments on other people's pages.
>
> A WeeMee can be transferred from WeeWorld to AIM, Windows Live, Skype, or a mobile phone. Some methods turn the WeeMee into a static image.
>
> In AIM, the WeeMee responds with animation based on emoticons and specific language used. While mimicking the smiley emoticons, it also has a specific range of vocabulary that it picks up on and applies into movement. (Wikipedia.com)

Once on the WeeWorld.com blue home page, users are invited to click on a number of main options. Because of the commercial aspect of this site and because there are often video advertisements streaming along the top and side of the home page, it is impossible to fully represent all that can be seen when one logs onto this site by simply taking a screen shot. It would also be impossible to completely represent all that the girls in the study saw, since the site changes advertising content on a moment-to-moment basis. Described below is a snapshot of the constantly shifting nature of this site. It provides a glimpse of the kind of thing the girls might have seen when they created their avatars.

In spite of the "no-cost" avatar creation options available to participants on WeeWorld, there are also significant, direct, and thinly veiled branding components (Klein, 2002) written into the site that must be acknowledged and considered. When the participants in the study logged onto the WeeWorld.com site during the summer of 2008, the first option provided to them was to "Create Your WeeMee, Get started, it's FREE." Alternatively, users were invited to "Chat with live friends: 24 million WeeMees and counting," or they could "Get cool stuff, play games, millions of items are downloaded a week." The screen on my home page was embellished with advertisements for cruise vacations, new music videos, or the latest gaming release. However, it is very likely that the home pages of the much younger participants had advertisements targeted to a younger audience.

The bottom of the page was divided into three main sections. One section urged users to "Get Cool Stuff for your WeeMee: Earn Green Points Now." Another section invited users to get a rating meter to find out if their "Room" is "Totally hot or totally cool." The third section invited them to "Validate their email today" and "Grab 500 points now." The points that are being referenced are used to "purchase" items for their avatars. (It should also be noted that given the nature of this site, there have been significant content changes in terms of advertising over the few months that I have been investigating the site. However, the principle behind the content remains fairly constant in that there is still a commercial component that allows or invites users to partake in opportunities in order to accumulate points that can then be used to purchase items for their WeeMees.)

Making a WeeMee: Gendered Issues of Choice

When the user clicks the button "Get Started," they are taken to another page where they are asked to choose between a male or female WeeMee, then three head shapes are offered—round, square or oval. Next, users choose from six skin tones and six eye colors. It is interesting that the three head shapes and six skin colors make no attempt to accurately encompass the range of possible shapes or colors that exist. Even as the WeeMees are intended to create a version of their creator, the expectation is that the version will be highly stylized. At each stage, the option to "Go Back" is available. At this stage, the user's WeeMee is placed in its undergarments on a themed background (which can be changed later). The default backgrounds are changed frequently to reflect the current season or holiday. For example, in October a Halloween background was provided on the WeeWorld site. At this point, the user is prompted to "get dressed." Beginning with personal features, users choose from a number of hairstyles (which can be personalized by color), and emotions. Two belly sizes are offere—either round or a lean and fit "six-pack" appearance), and three "sizes" are offered. "Size" here is code for breast size. Once the body has been completed, avatars can be adorned with clothing options, with include headwear, tops, bottoms, and footwear. Many of these can be personalized with color preferences. Among the items and articles included under the category "more stuff" are food and drinks, accessories, interests, and environments (more commonly known as backgrounds). Once the WeeMee has been completed, users are asked to register it and agree to a privacy policy.

All of these categories will be looked at in greater detail below, but this brief description is sufficient to get started with a deeper analysis. At this time it is also necessary to proceed with the caveat that this site is under constant revision, and the analysis of this engaging site represents a mere glimpse of what was seen over a particular time and does not necessarily reflect what a user might see today.

Female or male?

When creating a WeeMee, the first choice is male or female. There is no androgynous option. Even so, if a female body type is picked, the later option of adding facial hair exists even though facial hair is not something typically associated with a female gender. While this might appear to create a space for gender shifting, another feature later asks users to pick a body "shape" which ultimately has the avatar sporting a set of three different-sized breasts. By adding breasts, the option to imply any gender shifting might be erased altogether. Later options to add clothes that are culturally coded as "male" imply flexibility in how users can choose to represent themselves. Many options for less feminized clothing do exist, and often without a point value attached. In fact, articles such as the pride flag exist as an accessory that can be chosen for free. Alternatively, if a male figure is chosen in the beginning, a certain degree of gender shifting might be achieved, if so desired, by choosing hair styles that might be read as feminized.

For a male WeeMee there are several options to add long hair, and the option for "updos" exist as well. However, there are no make-up options for the male avatars, just as there are no shape options as are available for the female WeeMees. (As a note, more recent versions of this site do allow for the belly shape to be added to the female WeeMee.)

Exporting and uploading

In order to upload the WeeMee to other locations such as a Facebook page, an email signature, or even to a user's own computer file, the WeeMee must be registered. This step was necessary for the girls to share their avatars with the group. What happened next as a result of this registration opened the study up to an exploration of the commercialization of childhood because, once registered, users of the WeeWorld have the "opportunity" to add additional clothes, hairstyles and accessories to their avatars. However, there is a catch. In order to add some of these items, members must first accumulate points that can be traded or used to "buy" the items which cost points.

Once a WeeMee is registered, it is placed in its own room which can be designed and changed by the user. Another option to "Change and Shop" also appears. If a user clicks that option, the set-up in the new room is strikingly similar to the set-up that they saw when the avatars were first created, except for one critical difference—in many cases, now, items will have an icon attached to them indicating the number of points a user must have in order to "buy" the item for their WeeMee. At the time the study was completes, these "prices" ranged from 75-600 points. It needs to be noted that the point values have been getting increasingly higher as time goes on. It should also be noted that over the duration of this study the number of items with points associated with them has changed, literally on a daily basis, and has increased substantially over a period of five months as has the commercial nature of the WeeWorld.com site.

During the study, the ten girls all created their avatars from the free options that were initially available to them prior to registering their WeeMee. In some cases, once the WeeMees were registered, the girls saw the opportunity for more clothing or hairstyle options (as highlighted in Figures 3.1-3.3), and they tried to make changes at that time. They quickly discovered that unless they were willing to pay for points, they were limited to their original choices. For others, this discovery was not made until they created their second, and sometimes their third avatars. When the girls did not realize that more choices were available to them, they made no comments about the limited number of hairstyles or clothing options they had; however, it was a different story when they learned that other choices were available for a price.

After this discovery, the girls expressed dissatisfaction. The one area where the girls were most dissatisfied was the limited number of choices they had in terms of the backgrounds and accessories they could choose to accurately express their interests. In one case, one of the girls wished she could have used a gymnasium as her background; others expressed a desire to display their WeeMee on a skating rink. In all of these cases, not even a purse full of money would have helped them because those options were not available to users of the program (and are still not at the time this is being written). In an upcoming chapter the limited choices that the individual girls faced will be explored in more detail as they relate specifically to themes of gender and identity. It was at this point, when the girls were determined to make their avatars accurately reflect their identity and their personality, found that they their expression stifled.

Figure 3.1 highlights the number of choices available to girls at the time of the study when they created their WeeMee avatars. It is important to note that these were the initial choices presented to them prior to registering their avatars.

Figure 3.1. Initial avatar-making choices on WeeWorld.com as of August 5, 2008

Features	Total
Hair Salon	103
Facial Hair	50

Make-up	5
Emotions	18
Belly	2
Shape	3
Clothes	
Headwear	66
Tops	113
Bottoms	88
Footwear	32
Eyewear	44
More Stuff	
Food and Drinks	40
Interests	102
Accessories	62
Environments	44

The point values or virtual fees attached to a participant's desire to "purchase" particular items for their avatars carry the culturally coded assumption that "high-priced" items must be more valued, desirable and sought after (like high-priced running shoes might be, for example). Analyzing this element of the WeeWorld site sheds some light on how youth handle marketing and branding as well as the ubiquitous and hegemonic commercial nature of such forms of personalized "writing" (Kang and Yang, 2006). Torres and Mercado (2007) remind us that when corporate media flex their powerful, mainstream, and mainly commercial muscle, it is those from marginalized and misrepresented or underrepresented communities who suffer most. Would such commercial muscle flexing have a bearing on the participants in this study as they sought to create accurate representations of self? Scholars tell us that children and youth are most vulnerable to the messages of assimilation promoted through corporate media. They also tell us that kids are also the most in need of an alternative voice to represent themselves (Kenway and Bullen, 2001; Linn, 2000; Steinberg and Kincheloe, 1997).

To that end, when I considered the commercialized branding of aspects of the avatar program and how it becomes manifest in the autobiographical representations of the participants, I decided to stand back and see what the girls would do when faced with these choices. Would they accumulate points or would they choose their options from the bank of free articles and accessories? If they chose to "pay" for the presumably more highly valued items, what would that mean? If they decided to stick with the items that were free, what would that mean?

It is also important to note that the options available for users to collect points have also changed. When this research began, users (or parents of users) could use a major credit card, or PayPal to purchase points. At that time $5.00 USD would get a user 25,000 points. More recently multiple options are available to users to "earn" points by trying out online games. For example, users might "TRY Outsparks Groundbreaking Free Online RPG!" for 83 WeeWorld Points. They might choose to purchase a "hard-to-find, head-turning color" iPhone for 300 WeeWorld points. Or they could "Discover who loves you!" by having horoscopes sent directly to their cell phone for 413 WeeWorld Points. These commercially driven incentive options add another element to the creation of these avatars. While participants in my study certainly had the option to purchase items for their avatars, they did not do so. Several times the girls commented that they would have represented themselves differently if they had been able to choose items for their avatars that did not have a point value or a cost associated with that item. What results then, are a group of girls who have created avatars intended to be autobiographical, but those self-stories have been severely limited to the availability of free articles within the program.

What makes the various options and considerations significant, and the reason I will spend time analyzing the options available to the girls, is that by profoundly limiting their semiotic choices, concerns are raised regarding issues of access and equity. This "critical orientation" (Luke, 2002) will allow me to go beyond the cultural studies models of the 1980s and 1990s where critique and deconstruction ruled the day. Instead, I can follow Luke and ask "What are the implications of the emergence of new virtual identities and communities and issues of 'authentic' or 'masquerade' identity?" (p. 134)

In order to get a better idea about the degree to which the girls would have had their choices limited, I conducted a brief survey on October 15, 2008 in order to count the number of free options versus the number of items that had a point value attached. What this short survey does is provide a glimpse at how a willingness to pay for more choices *might* afford a WeeMee creator the added freedom to express his or her identity with more accuracy. Note the percentage of options available to the girls if they were not willing to pay extra for more choices. Also note that this site is fluid and its content is constantly being changed and updated. This list is meant to give an idea of what the girls saw at the time of the study and does not accurately represent what choices are currently available on the WeeWorld.com site. The categories tops, footwear and accessories showed the largest discrepancy in options available to the girls.

Figure 3.2. WeeMee avatar-making choices after registering as of October 15, 2008

	Items requiring points/Total items	Percent with points
Features		
Hair Salon	36/168	21.4%
Facial Hair	0/51	
Make-up	0/5	
Emotions	0/18	
Belly	0/2	
Shape	0/3	
Clothes		
Headwear	48/118	41%
Tops	227/337	67%
Bottoms	64/151	42%
Footwear	46/78	59%
Eyewear	22/66	33%
More Stuff		
Food and Drinks	16/56	29%
Interests	77/184	42%
Accessories	103/169	61%
Environments	0/43	

In a similar survey taken on January 15, 2009 I found the following similarities and changes in options for creating WeeMees after registration. Note the jump in the number of items requiring points as a form of payment. Also note the option to have a full make-up makeover was available for 1000 points. Basic body shape, single make-up option, belly size, emotions, facial hair and environments remain the only categories that are unchanged in their pre- and post-registration formats. The rest of the categories see a substantial difference in the choices a person has to create an accurate individualized avatar.

Figure 3.3. WeeMee avatar-making choices after registering as of January 15, 2009

Features	Items requiring points/Total items	% requiring points
Hair Salon	55/159	35%
Facial Hair	0/50	
Make up	0/6	
NEW!! Total Makeover option 1000 points!!!!!		
Emotions	0/18	
Belly	0/2	
Shape	0/3	
Clothes		
Headwear	60/126	48%
Tops	277/391	58%
Bottoms	82/170	48%
Footwear	49/81	60%
Eyewear	33/77	
	43%	
More Stuff		
Food and Drinks	29/69	42%
Interests	96/202	48%
Accessories	138/201	69%
Environments	0/44	

While more choices appear to be available for individuals to make their avatars in January 2009 than were possible three months earlier, the number of items requiring an accumulation of points had increased in all cases, as well. Of the new and notable options was the option for a WeeMee to have a complete makeover. Instead of being limited to only one make-up choice as the girls in the study were, the makeover option allowed avatars to at once wear all of these options in matching color schemes. While this "service" was worth a whopping 1000 points in January, in the days closer to this book's printing the makeover option had increased again. More recently it was being offered for *1500 points*. What is more interesting is a consideration of what kinds of activities one would have to engage in before being able to accumulate 1000 or 1500 points. The surveys above both show items that had popular, feminine and fashionable clothes (or what the participants in the study referred to as "girlie" items) often had a point value attached; however, many of the less mainstream items that might be used to "other" a WeeMee as a member of a non-dominant, marginalized or underrepresented social or cultural group remained free. These free items included a pride flag, a menorah, a Chinese dragon mask, a turban, an Indian sari, an indigenous mask, a cross necklace, and a pink ribbon t-shirt, which implies the message "For the Cure," a North American breast cancer awareness campaign.

While initial reaction to these accessible items is heartening, consider that fairy wings, or angel halos, having green slime splashed over a WeeMee's face, or having a WeeMee emit an imaginary puff of toxic green were all options that have points assigned to them. This option is slightly ironic since WeeMees do not have noses! It is also worth noting that some options also had the ability to infer violence (for example, there was an axe that gushed blood from the avatar's head), and glamorized binge drinking (for example, there was a football hat with two beer cans and two siphons inserted into the avatar's mouth for drinking). In the food and drink category, 29/69 choices were either considered fast food, junk food or were implied alcoholic drinks like tropical pool-side drinks, or unspecified drinks with ice cubes (possibly alcoholic in nature).

Under the "interests" category several of the items with point values assigned may not have any particular commercial fad significance but may have points associated because the items have a special function. For example for 250 points a WeeMee can sport an chameleon that actually changes color in front of our eyes, or a WeeMee can be seen twirling a hula-hoop before it eventually drops to the floor for another 250 points. If someone wants his/her WeeMee to appear like the perfect host/hostess, it can be made to pour a steaming cup of tea for 200 points. Under accessories, a WeeMee can suck on a soother (and there are even different colors to pick from) for 400 points. These items were not always available, however. One thing is clear: the creators of the WeeWorld site do seem to have a handle on the kinds of things kids of all ages think are cool.

The Forum as a Site for the Case Study

Inasmuch as possible, I wanted to create a space for girls in my study to interact online in a manner not unlike the kind of social space they were used to on Facebook. The forum was an attempt to replicate, as much as possible, a natural site for the research to occur. I understood that the site could not replicate the vastness of the social network available to the girls on Facebook. For that reason, the forum was always "sold" as a kind of online classroom where the girls would run the class and where I would simply moderate. I understood, however, that my very presence on the forum would change the dynamics between the girls and thereby make the environment more like a classroom where a teacher is present than the social networking site inhabited only by friends. By agreeing to participate, the girls joined a discussion forum within a password protected online site. This site (referred to as "the Forum" by the participants, and henceforth here) was set up through the Virtual Teacher's Centre at the Newfoundland and Labrador Teacher's Association.

Once on the Forum, the girls were instructed to set up their profile using a pseudonym and to upload their avatar. Once this was completed participants were able to begin reading and responding to the posted questions by clicking on the question links. When they responded to the question threads, their avatar would appear beside their responses.

The closed online Forum lasted for a period of approximately four to five weeks. Because of the asynchronous nature of the Forum, some participants took longer to post their responses than others. The nature of the Forum was intended to allow them to post as often as they wanted at a time that was convenient for them to do so, thus allowing for the same kind of asynchronous social engagement that they would have in their other online networks, such as Facebook. Keeping in mind the social nature of Facebook and given the everyday nature of the new literacy practice I intended to examine within this discursive space, I made deliberate efforts to create an informal and casual relationship with the girls. The girls all addressed me by my first name, and eight (8) of the ten (10) invited me to join their "friends" network on Facebook. Being open with the participants about what I was attempting to accomplish with this research and being openly nonjudgmental about their responses were important to gaining their trust. I was careful on several occasions to tell them that I was going to be on the Forum mainly to observe them, but that I would ask them to elaborate on their responses sometimes and direct the line of questioning based on their responses and their interests. In short, I let the girls know that while I might be running the study, they were setting the agenda. I deliberately gave the girls positive feedback any time they responded to a question, and I often asked them to tell me more about what they thought.

A Quick Introduction to the Girls

Before I begin, note that names of the participants have been hidden behind pseudonyms in order to protect their identities. For nine of the ten girls I am using the pseudonym that they picked as their username during the study. In many cases these pseudonyms have been shortened and numbers have been removed from them for ease of writing. While I was tempted to change the names again, I am satisfied that their anonymity is sufficiently preserved, and further changing the names removes an opportunity to address gendered assumptions as they relate specifically to their chosen names later on. In the case of the tenth girl, I have made a change to her username in order to protect her identity. In what follows, I will briefly introduce the girls and save the detailed descriptions of their avatars for chapter four.

Roxy is a fourteen-year-old from a small rural community of less than 2500 in Eastern Canada. She has well over 300 friends on the Facebook network. On her home page, she has describes her interests as figure skating, being with friends, being on the phone and her computer. When asked during the case study what five single words describe her best, Roxy lists "caring, friendly, funny, considerate, and kind?!" She suspects her friends would describe her as being "friendly and funny." She comes from one of her province's more economically challenged areas her family is working class and she is involved with a number of extracurricular and sporting activities in and out of school. More specifically, she is a figure skater who not only skates a couple of times a week in her local community during the winter, but also attends off-season figure skating schools in a nearby city (which means a substantial financial and time commitment by her family).

Star also lives in a small rural community of fewer than 2,500 people in Eastern Canada. She is thirteen years old and describes herself as "nice, intelligent, smart, friendly, and forgiving." When asked if she thought her friends would use the same words to describe her, she answered: "I think all of my friends would say the same things because all of my friends say those words to me every day." As the youngest of two girls, Star comes from a working class family who make their children their their clear priority. Her mother works several jobs in order to provide opportunities for her children. Star was an eager and active recruiter for participants in this study offering to email friends and bring her friends on board to participate in the study. She encounted a number of challenges throughout the research from the initial stages when she was attempting to create her avatar, however.

Star began having trouble with the home computer. She explained, "Well my computer is always down." Her older sister moved away to university taking the computer in her, and with it went the Internet access Star needed to participate with the study. Once the rest of the girls had completed their entries and reflections, Star was reconnected with a new laptop and chose to complete a few more questions on the Forum. At this point she answered followup questions directly with me through the message function on Facebook.

Figureskatingchic is another thirteen-year-old participant from a small rural community in Eastern Canada whose identity was clearly tied up in figure skating, as evidenced not only by her avatar's dress and skates, but also through her chosen user name. Through her contributions to the forum, Figureskatingchic made it abundantly clear that for her, figure skating is a competitive sport, and she only has one goal—that is, to win. The gender connotations of the last part of her user name (chic) will be explored later.

Of the participants in this study, **Shorty** was the oldest at seventeen. She also came from the location with the smallest population. Her rural community in Eastern Canada has about 1000 residents. She describes herself as "outgoing, extremely honest, short, random, and competitive." She believes her friends would use describe her the same way "because they have added notes on Facebook and have used very similar words." Shorty has nearly 500 friends on Facebook and told me that she used the social network approximately four times a week. As one of the participants who contributed only a handful of times, Shorty made her observations substantive, thoughtful and reflective. Though not entirely sold on the idea of making an avatar, she did admit that her cartoon identity could do things that a photograph cold not. She was emphatic about the importance of being able to create an accurate image of her.

At age thirteen, **Questionmark** also hails from a small rural community in Eastern Canada. She describes herself as "independent, loving, intelligent, involved, and unique." She told me that her friends would use similar words to describe her because, "these words show who I am, and I know it, so do others around me." She might have also included "self assured" and "confident" to her list, as these were qualities that were noted throughout her responses. She was one of the first people to join the Avatar Creation Group on Facebook (the site that was used to initially announce the study and to collect potential participants. I will provide a more detailed description of this group later in this chapter). Questionmark was also the first to post an avatar to the group site. She was the second most prolific contributer to the Forum, and Questionmark even initiaited a thread of questioning around the topic of color on the Forum. She demonstrated a relative comfort with the technical challenges in the creation of her avatar, and she navigated the case study Forum with a great deal of ease, often posting comments in different font sizes and colors to complement her reflections or comments. For example, when she made comments about her favorite colors (purple and green) she did so in purple and green text.

Princess contributed to the Forum far fewer times than the other girls in terms of the number of posts she made, however, during these posts, the degree and level of engagement and reflection were quite detailed. Princess is sixteen years old and also comes from a small rural community in Eastern Canada. During the course of the study there was a period when she was not contributing at all. During that time I attempted to contact her through her Facebook page, but her page had been taken down, so I contacted her through an email address that she had given me. As it turns out, she had been grounded and had lost her computer privileges. She did not want to talk about it any more than that. Despite this interruption, Princess did offer significant observations regarding how she created her avatar and about the inportance of being able to accurately portray who she is to others in this way. For her, avatars were far more than a physical representation, they held the opportunity to project her ambitions and dreams as well.

Cherrytree is a sixteen-year-old from a small island community off the East Coast of Canada. She describes herself as being: "caring, talkative, very cautious, friendly and funny," and she feels that her friends would agree. From her first Forum comments, she explains that her avatar is autobiographical because it "expresses who I am." For her, making the association with what she does is initially her first consideration. She wants to show that she is a singer, and that she is unique. She describes herself as blonde and proud and writes that her avatar shows that she likes to perform in front of lots of people.

Her observations about the limits of how identity and personality can be represented in an image opened many points of conversation in the Forum. She also initiated discussion around how physical appearance (either in real life or in pictures or avatars) often makes girls targets for others. Her observation that "knowing you may be judged by what you wear definitely influences the things you wear" forms the basis for further analysis as it relates to one of the study's central research questions (who do you want others to think you are?). Upon reflection during some follow-up questions, Cherrytree told me that the process of creating her avatar "really made me think twice about how I want to be viewed."

As one of the most socially interactive participants in the study, **Cutie-Pi** is a sixteen-year-old from one of the largest cities in Atlantic Canada with a population of over 100,000. Cutie-Pi describes herself as "creative, kind, intelligent, animal-loving and positive." She also notes that her friends have told her that she has these qualities. During the case study, Cutie-Pi not only responded to the questions posed to her directly on the Forum but also attempted to engage in conversations with the other participants, by commenting on their posts and by welcoming participants as they joined the study. Through the course of the study, Cutie-Pi was part of a group of participants who engaged in comments regarding the importance of accuracy as it relates to appearance in both profile pictures and in avatars. This also led to a discussion among participants regarding how pictures are sometimes edited.

As a sixteen-year-old French immersion student from one of the largest cities in Atlantic Canada, **Butterflye** describes herself as "friendly, pensive, funny, smart, musical, and kind." She adds that her friends might also call her "crazy" (implying that they might think she can be unpredictable and fun). Butterflye was the last participant to join the study, having heard about it though word of mouth from her social circle at school. When she contacted me to express her interest in the study, she had not yet joined the Facebook Avatar Creation Group. As a result, when she made her avatar she had a more thoughtful and deliberate approach than many of the other participants may have had with their first avatars. For Butterflye, there is an enormous responsibility assumed by those who represent themselves in online spaces such as Facebook, whether that representation is in the form of an avatar or a profile picture.

Livie is a fifteen-year-old who lives in a large Northern city in Western Canada. When asked to describe herself, she writes that she is "unique, artistic, honest, considerate, and friendly" and adds that she has been called all of these things. Livie admits through her comments on the Forum and in follow-up questions that she is not a fan of the popular culture scene. More specifically she writes "i don't really subscribe to a label." She admits that in the past she has been called a number of things like a "Modern Hippy" or an "Indie Kid," and that she has dressed in a number of guises over the years as she sought to find her place with the teen crowd. She claims not to be a big fan of pop culture, but she now prefers to be known as herself, and she is quite comfortable with that.

During the course of the study, Livie was by far the most prolific contributer to the Forum. After some initial challenges in getting her avatar posted to the Avatar Creation Group site, Livie engaged on a social level, often commenting on posts made by other girls, and actively inviting others to probe further. In the process of the study, Livie revealed that she has a rare medcial condition called Tuberous Sclerosis Complex (TSC), and she not only willingly and openly educated the rest of us on what living with that condition means, but in so doing, she opened the discussion to the limitations inherent in these kinds of avatar sites as they relate to the accuracy with which girls might be able to represent themselves. This inherent inability to represent herself accurately will consititute a large section of analysis in the chapters to come. As we get to know Livie a little better in the next chapter, we will find a complex teenager who is socially engaged, who refuses to buy into popular trends in fashion, music, or entertainment, and who is eager to visually tell her story. In places, this story is easy to narrate, but in other important ways, her story gets shut down before it even begins.

At this time, I will return to each girl in turn for further insight into how her WeeMee was constructed. These introductions are intended to familiarize the readers with the girls and the stories they told through their avatars. A more detailed analysis of the participants, their avatars, and their comments will be conducted thematically in later chapters.

Chapter Four

The Girls and Their Avatars: Who Do They Think They Are?

In this chapter the girls from this study reveal how they believe their avatars tell (or do not tell) accurate stories about who they are. Before any critical analysis about the process of their avatar construction can be done, further description of the girls as well as their avatars is necessary as their stories provide valuable insight into the choices they made and how these choices affected how they created their avatars. Stack and Kelly (2006) remind us to consider that it is "what do girls do, wear, believe, value and know" that allows them to see themselves as belonging to a specific social and cultural group (p. 131). In this light, their constructed representations are, at once, an effort to carve out their vital political space (Dolby, 2003) and their potential cultural significance (Morley, 1993). Considering the limitations of the avatar creation program, these girls demonstrate that they are active participants and collaborators in their own identity representation even though their avatars represent a highly staged and often limited representation of who they think they are.

What these introductions to the girls and their avatars allow is a questioning of how their desires propelled them to construct their avatars to look the way they do. What stories do they tell? What do they leave untold? As we look at the avatars and hear briefly from the girls about them, I will hint at the pedagogical opportunities that present themselves when appropriate. These opportunities will be discussed in further details in chapter eight. Finally, avatar construction as a form of identity representation is viewed for the pedagogical opportunities it holds and for its ability to create agency or to shut it down.

In the descriptions of the participants below I have, in every case possible, used their words in an effort to give their voices authenticity throughout the study. However, I have, in places, corrected some spelling mistakes from their original transcriptions. The intent of their wording has not been compromised. Their avatars appear here with full permission.

The Girls

Roxy

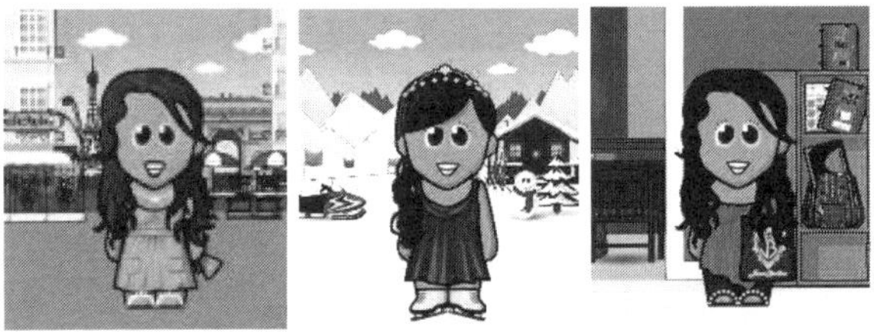

Figure 4.1. Roxy's three WeeMee avatars

When asked to explain how her first avatar was like her, Roxy told me that it reflected "me and my personality." Her response suggested that she sees "me" and her "personality" as two mutually exclusive entities. She explains that the avatar has brown hair and brown eyes, like she does, and that it is dressed in a blue dress because blue is her favorite color. In fact, a look at the three different avatars that she created reveals that each of them is wearing a different shade of blue. The facial expressions are the same in each avatar with the only difference being that the first avatar has lipstick and the other two have eyelashes. Like others in the study, Roxy indicates that she chose the Paris background of her first avatar because it is a place she would like to visit someday.

Roxy felt limited, but resigned, to the choices afforded by the WeeMee program in that it did not have her accurate color skin. Recalling that only six choices for skin tone exist for WeeMees, she wrote, "I couldn't get the right skin tone, but they are basically all the same anyways." In fact, they are not really the same—they range from pale white, to deep brown, with shades of beige, yellow and red in between. Embedded in the six available choices is an assumption about race representation that could become a pedagogical moment. What makes a person choose one shade over another when there are so few choices? What does it mean, culturally and socially, to choose a shade of beige rather than a darker shade of brown, for example? Along with not finding her exact skin tone, she also felt limited when she was not able to include glasses that suited her on her avatar. "One thing that I never added to my avatar was glasses, I could have done it but there were none that were similarly like mine, or ones that I liked." In spite of these inaccuracies, Roxy told me that she was pleased with the autobiographical nature of her avatar.

Her comments about the inaccurate skin tone and her lack of glasses will be explored more fully later.

With her second avatar, Roxy shows herself as a figure skater, though the dress might not be typical of what a figure skating dress might look like with a skirt that appears to fall from the neckline. In her description of the skating dress, Roxy describes it as purple (which she says is also her favorite color); however, it appears, at least on my screen as though it is a deep royal blue. Roxy is one of a handful of girls who said she would have preferred to have a rink for a background so that she could place her skating avatar in an appropriate environment.

She liked the color of her avatar's hair and thought the reddish color reflected her "fun outgoing" personality. This comment also opens the door for a potential teachable moment about the social and cultural assumptions of what it means to be "fun and outgoing," especially as it relates to how a person may or may not look. When asked how she is different in real life from her avatar, Roxy responds in a way that demonstrates her fun nature. She says, "my avatar has longer hair than me, and she is also a lot shorter ha ha. :]" For Roxy, the tone of her responses was light and playful. She frequently included a ☺ to her posts and often wrote in colored text to highlight any discussion that might relate to color.

Star

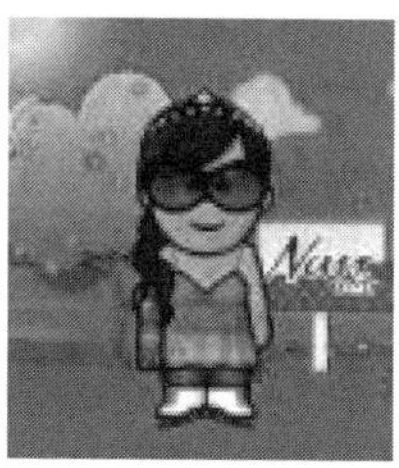

Figure 4.2. Star's only WeeMee avatar

As I alluded in Star's brief introduction previous chapter, in spite of her eagerness to participate in this study Star encountered a number of challenges that at the time prevented her from participating fully. However, these challenges turned out to be instructive and her observations, though sometimes brief, are both revealing and important. At first, Star created a WeeMee avatar that required a large number of points. However, before she could save it, she was required to pay for the privilege of the "priced" items that she had picked. These items included clothing and accessories for her avatar. Because she did not have those points accumulated, and because she had not paid for the points (and did not want to pay for the points), the site would not allow her to save her avatar as she had created it. Star was stumped, so she wrote a Facebook message to me wondering what to do. She wrote, "umm I'm done but it says to save it you have to buy points or remove the things that's in your shopping cart???" The questionmarkks indicated to me that she was unsure what she should do next.

Star seemed frustrated by the component of the WeeWorld that required a "purchase" of items with points that had to be earned or bought directly. In another Facebook message she noted, "when i tried too put sun glasses on my avatar it kept saying something about points. It got really distracting!" Eventually, she changed her avatar so that it didn't have the "pricy" items included. However, she wasn't completely satisfied with the final creation. She wrote, "i think that i could of made my avatar better beacuse i would of liked to change my backround and more things but i didn't really know how." What Star's frustration demonstrates is a breakdown in the intended autobiographical nature of this exercise, but this breakdown is also instructive. When Star was prevented from representing herself accurately because of the commercial limits of the site, the rendering of power through the visual language elements in this site begins to make itself visible. Creating a WeeMee avatar is a social practice, particularly because it was designed to be used in a social space to say: *this is who I am*. Her desire to represent herself in a particular way was shut down because she could not — and would not—pay for the privilege of including the clothes and accessories she had chosen. The consequences of such silencing will be picked up and discussed further in chapter six.

Star's problems were not limited to the construction of her WeeMee avatar. She also encountered a number of problems posting her avatar to the initial group site, and in spite of several attempts to send her written directions, I finally had to talk to her on the phone and walk her through the steps in order to help her upload her avatar and make it her profile picture. Since the time of the study, the directions for uploading, or "exporting" a WeeMee to another site such as a social networking site or an email account have been streamlined and simplified, so it is likely that these challenges were not unique to Star.

Star's one and only avatar is wearing figure skates which makes it clear that she too identifies with figure skating. Early in the study, Star was troubled by the apparent disconnect of having her avatar wear skates on a summer background. This background, incidentally, happened to be the default background at the time. She asked the group for help, "I had trouble finding different background's because I have skates on in the summer and I would really like to change my background to winter. Anyone have any answers?"

When asked to reflect on the connection between herself and her avatar, Star did not initially see a connection at all; however, as her reflections became more detailed she began to draw some comparisons. "Avatars don't say bit about your personally because it's really not a real you. it's just an online cartoon of you, but I think that the features that do tell you about who you are is your hair color, eye color, and your clothes." For Star, the accuracy of the avatar's representation was initially limited to its physical traits, not activities or personality traits. Yet in a later posting, Star comments that her avatar reveals aspects of her personality and her interests. She writes, "somethings that my avatar says about me is that I'm a really out-going person and i love fashion, and i love figure skating. but I think that some of the things that my profile picture [avatar] does not say about me is that i have lots of other cool things I love to do like play volleyball, but you can't really see that in my profile picture because I love lots of other sports too!☺"

Figureskatingchic

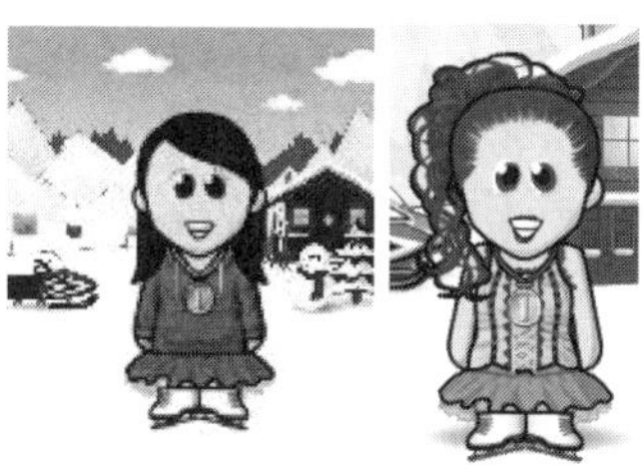

Figure 4.3. Figureskatingchic's two WeeMee avatars.

As her name implies, Figureskatingchic's identity in this exercise is tied intimately to the sport of figure skating. Of the two WeeMee avatars she created, the change in avatars represented something of an evolution of a skater from the warmup or practice session, to the skater ready to compete.

In this evolution, the background remained a winter scene; however, the hair got pulled up and the "popover sweater" was removed to reveal a competition dress. In both cases the avatar wore a gold medal to indicate not what she had done (though she has won several medals in the past), but a kind of engagement with a fantasy representation and a portent of the future. "I put the medal around my neck because I am hoping I will place this year like last year, and my skirt is the same colour as my this years dress, so I kind of revolved my person [avatar] around this years me."

In spite of this revealing fantasy, Figureskatingchic did not feel that her avatar was a completely accurate representation of her personality. She writes, "my avatar represents who I am in real life but not my whole personality." She is more specific later as she writes, "the avatars don't tell other people what my personality is, or they don't tell who we hang around with and I hang around with a lot of different people, and it don't tell people what stuff we are good at or who we are related to." In fact this notion of non-unitary subjectivity is something that other participants came to terms with as well, and it is a notion that will be taken up in further detail in chapter seven.

Figureskatingchic also picked up on an emerging theme and initiated a thread in the Forum by asking others: "Does your avatar show who you are in real life or who you would like to be?" In places where questions were asked about color, she was one of the more playful participants who responded with colored text to highlight her responses.

Even with the apparent consistency of her two avatars, Figureskatingchic expressed a frustration with the WeeWorld site, because according to her, it had too much choice. "My avatar was so hard to make. I made like three then i could not choose what one most represented me in real life." She continues by expressing a dislike for the pink laces on the figure skates—a point that became a matter of much discussion among the girls who self-identified as figure skaters, and even non-figure skaters in the group. "I was not liking that the laces were pink, they could have been white or black."

Analyzing the two avatars that Figureskatingchic created allows us to focus on detail and how she created a second avatar, not from scratch, but instead to show another side of herself. At the beginning of the study, Figureskatingchic indicated that she had created three different avatars and could not decide which to use. In the end, she presents nearly identical versions, with only the hair pulled back and the sweater removed to reveal a dress in the second version. When the two avatars are seen side by side, it is implied that this competition dress was hidden under the sweater, waiting to be revealed. She also takes the time to blow up and zoom in on her avatar making it, not the background, the complete focus of the frame. In doing this she provides an opportunity for the gaze to be focused entirely on the avatar.

Figureskatingchic revealed that her avatar was purposely a representation of the "real life me." When asked what she thinks this avatar says about her, she immediately turns to the dress which is green and apparently like the one she will compete in this year. She also refers to the medal around her neck, which serves the triple purpose of indicating her competitive nature, signifying her past success, and projecting her future results in competition. Later she refers again to the medal and explains that it is there to show everyone what she works hard for.

What was even more interesting to me was that she calls her avatar: "this years me," as if to solidify a sense of identity definition in a way that was vastly different from how others in the study viewed their avatars. While most of the other girls wrote and reflected about the impossibility for their avatar to convey all the things that they would like to say, Figureskatingchic seemed to manage to say everything she wanted to, then she repeated herself a second time, just in case her message was not clear the first time! Figureskatingchic later admits that, as they are, her avatars are unable to show her interest in other sports like volleyball and cheerleading. Even so, she keeps coming back to her figure skating identity and mentions that she "lives at the rink," and she skates "24/7." I was interested in some of the observations made by Figureskatingchic when she discussed her life as a figure skater. "My style of my avatar does reflect my style in real life because I like, live at the rink and I've always got something on like that." In fact, Figureskatingchic skates only two times a week.

Shorty

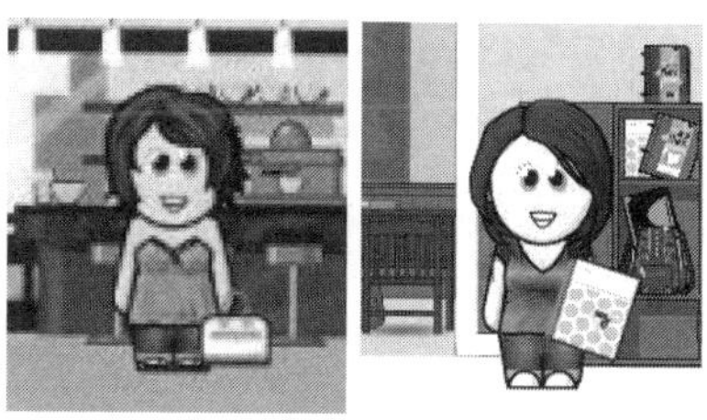

Figure 4.4. Shorty's two WeeMee avatars

On the Forum site, Shorty mentioned that if she could have, her avatar would have been animated so it could go through a typical day in her life. In spite of this inadequacy, Shorty believed that her WeeMee avatar was a good representation of her in terms of its physical traits but felt that it was not an accurate representation of her personality and interests. She describes the clothes that she typically wears as comfortable and cute, and while I might personally question the practical comfort of a strapless top (as seen in her first avatar), I do recognize the style of her avatar's tops as being current and trendy. In the popular discourse of teen fashion, therefore, it would make sense that she would label the clothes "cute." Shorty wrote that she wanted to show that she loved "to get out and be busy" which might explain the inclusion of her handbag (which implies being "out" since girls do not normally carry their handbags around their homes), but even that was not enough to enable her to include her other interests such as sports, academics and socializing with her friends. The social aspect of her personality and what might be described as her expressed fondness for family and friends was a recurring theme in her posts. Shorty felt that her avatar (or any representation of her for that matter) would be made more complete with the addition of other people. When asked to elaborate, she explained that friends and family "are a big part of my life and who I am." Shorty also made some important observations about being able to have friends in her real profile pictures in order to show what she had done or where she has been. For her, not being able to include friends in a representation like an avatar is something that limits how it can represent you as a form of autobiography.

One of my favorite participant observations from the entire study came from Shorty when she compared the limits of Facebook profile pictures to what could be done with avatars. She began, "Pictures are just a second of your life represented." She then went on to say that as a statement of how she is, avatars could represent her more *generally*. In a follow-up question, when I asked her to imagine a place where this kind of representation (the general avatar kind) might be beneficial or even necessary, she wrote: "I think a place to use the general avatar would be anything official to do with work or school. This would allow you to represent yourself truthfully but they would not be incriminating. Certain places in the backgrounds and people with you in your profile picture are too personal and not appropriate for professional relationships."

When given an opportunity to create a second avatar, Shorty was among the participants who used a school theme for her background and made a point of saying that this was appropriate at this time because school had begun and it represented a "regular school day and the kind of clothes i might wear."

Even with her expressed dissatisfaction over the limits of her avatar, she admits that if she were going to use her avatar as her profile picture on Facebook she probably would not change it. That admission helped me to believe that she had represented herself in a way that was not merely designed to satisfy me and whatever she thought I might be looking for in the study, but that the visual representation of who she thinks she is was accurate enough for her to share with her online social network as well. What might not be obvious from a black and white replication of these two avatars is that the eye color in the two avatars is not the same. In her first avatar, Shorty has blue eyes, and in the second avatar they are green.

Questionmark

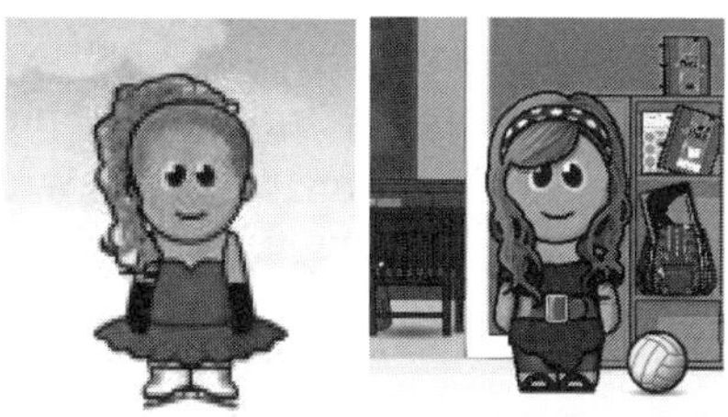

Figure 4.5. Questionmark's two WeeMee avatars

For Questionmark, the struggle to construct WeeMee avatars that could be autobiographical highlighted a number of questions around accuracy, power, and possibility for these visual representations. While Questionmark found representing herself with a WeeMee avatar fairly easy, her revelations about her limited choices indicate serious issues around notions of accuracy, particularly as they relate to ability and even gender assumptions. On a simple physical level, her avatars both have blonde hair and brown eyes and both have the same skin tone and facial expression. However, when it came to finding the right clothing and backgrounds her challenges begin.

As a figure skater (though one who participates at a purely recreational level), Questionmark used her first WeeMee avatar to represent her skating persona. She initiated a discussion about a frustration over skates with pink laces. Not only did she personally dislike the color pink, she had even larger concerns over what the pink laces implied. On the Forum, Questionmark asked, "What do you girls think when you see pink laces on my avatar??" At this point it is sufficient to allude to her dissatisfaction and promise to return to a closer examination of the gendered issue of pink laces later when the combined contributions of other girls can help to round out this discussion more completely. Suffice it to say—Questionmark was not happy about the pink laces, but her dissatisfaction with what she was able to "say" with her avatar certainly did not stop here.

In the beginning, Questionmark had trouble finding a skating dress for her avatar so she used a regular dress instead. Her observations around this reveal her sense of style and personality. "If I could have made a custom skating dress for my avatar it would have some sparkle and maybe a little less poofy. If I could have any background I wanted I would be in a skating arena, at center ice." She goes on later to explain that she does not own a proper skating dress, so finding one and making it into something that looks like a skating dress was close to what happens in her real life anyway.

A more interesting revelation came when Questionmark indicated that during the course of the study she had a broken foot, but that when she made her second WeeMee avatar, she was unable to show this. "I tried to find crutches or a cast…..but they had none." (As a side note, during the analysis of the Forum transcriptions and the writing of this book, the content of WeeWorld was analyzed on several occasions, and it is significant to note that four months after the girls created their avatars, crutches became available as an accessory.)

Questionmark also wrote about and identified quite strongly with the sport of volleyball. While the school setting and the addition of a volleyball in her second avatar helped her to depict herself in a way that represented these interests, she was not completely satisfied. She told me that she would have created her avatar in a gymnasium wearing a red and black sport jersey if that had been possible, and that it would have been more accurate this way.

However, in her quest to construct autobiographical images, Questionmark revealed that she did not get to share her interest in acting, writing, or other sports. The partiality of this form of semiotic representation reminds us of the poststructuralist caution that telling one story silences others. Examining what made the stories she *did* tell, and examining what issues undercut her telling (be they socially and culturally influenced, or found in the limits of the semiotic structures of the WeeMee options available to her), the process of "writing" who we are using an avatar site is in no way a straightforward process.

If Questionmark hadn't been the first participant in the study (and member of the original Avatar Creation Group on Facebook) I might be prone to speculate that she might have initially chosen to narrate herself as a figure skater because a community of figure skaters emerged on the Forum site. There is a sense of belonging in such affinity groups, after all. But just as Questionmark was the first to join the Avatar Creation Group, she was also the first to create a WeeMee avatar and narrate her autobiographical fragment. She was apparently acting on her own volition.

In spite of the challenges to the accuracy of her avatar, Questionmark thought it was important for her avatar to "represent who you are," and "who you want to be." She believed that accuracy was important in light of the fact that others (in the study, or wherever else the avatar appears) would be seeing it and making assumptions about her based on how the avatar looked. At one point during the study she indicated that she doesn't wear make-up in real life and that she doesn't even like make-up. True to her real-life experience, neither avatar presented here includes any of the make-up options.

Princess

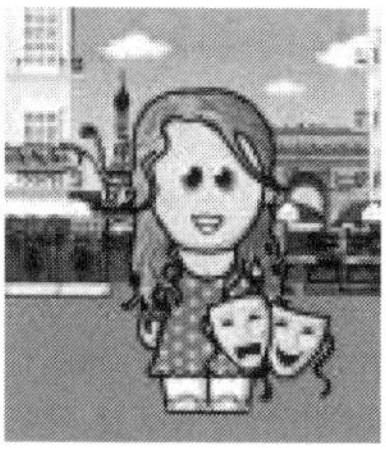

Figure 4.6. Princess's only WeeMee avatar

Princess was one of the older participants in the study. She created only one avatar which for her combined a statement of her appearance with the activities that she enjoys. For her, the first consideration in making her avatar autobiographical was also at the level of physical description. Her visual narration lists blue eyes and long blonde hair that she believes accurately represents what she looks like (although she does add, jokingly that she wouldn't mind if the WeeMee was a little taller). She muses that in real life the shade of her eyes tends to reflect the clothing that she is wearing so they are sometimes more green or hazel. She includes a comment that her avatar indicates that she likes blue (because of the color of her dress) and that blue was *one* of her favorite colors but not her very favorite. Like others in the study, she wrote about choosing colors that she liked to represent who she is. Of the dress, she explains that “it’s very me, if I had it I would wear it.” What this indicates is that Princess does not believe that her avatar’s clothing needs to be identical to something she owns in order for the avatar to provide an accurate representation of who she is. Put another way, the stylistic intent of the avatar’s clothing is more important than providing a replica article of clothing.

Princess believes that an avatar should reveal more about a person than how he or she looks, and given the opportunity to do so, she shares details about her life with us. The theater masks with her WeeMee avatar reveal an interest in drama. She later confirms this in a post and indicates that drama is a passion of hers that she intends to pursue as a career. The Paris background, she explains, offers insight to her identity at a level that might not be possible with a simple picture. Princess tells us that she has never been to Paris, and that she has included it as her background because she hopes to get there in the future. “It also shows the Eiffel tower, and I would LOVE to go there some day. I wouldn’t want to go right yet though, I would want to go when I’m old enough to pay for it myself.”

Her professed love for a future travel opportunity opens the door to another pedagogical opportunity for critical work to take place. By asking her to explain why she has chosen a background that clearly is not part of her present living arrangement, I am able to pry open a dialogue not only about her hopes and dreams for the future, but more importantly (in a pedagogical sense anyway) initiate a discussion about the cultural codes implied by the Paris background. While it is of interest that she wants to travel to Paris, it is more interesting to see (in light of the fact that she has never been there) how her knowledge of and expectations about this foreign destination have been shaped. By finding out what she knows about Paris provides an opportunity to see how family, friends and/or popular culture have shaped her knowledge about it. Has her professed interest in Paris been shaped by movies, literature, or television? If so, how? What promises does the city hold for her in her imagination? Why is it so appealing?

Princess spends more time describing her avatar and the significance of the masks: “She has the comedy and tragedy masks in her hands. I love acting and performing and I would love to pursue it as a career one day. I am in various other extra curricular activities but when I saw the masks I knew I had to use them :)!"

Princess also engaged in a discussion with other girls regarding the importance of creating an accurate representation. Like others, she also believed that girls get judged based on appearances, and that those judgments include images that represent who we are. "I think it is important to represent yourself in a way that tells more about you than just how you look because sometimes, and it's a shame, people judge you by the way you look." This discussion eventually opened up a significant line of questions and comments about the profile pictures used on Facebook and how they are similar to and different from avatars in form and function.

Cherrytree

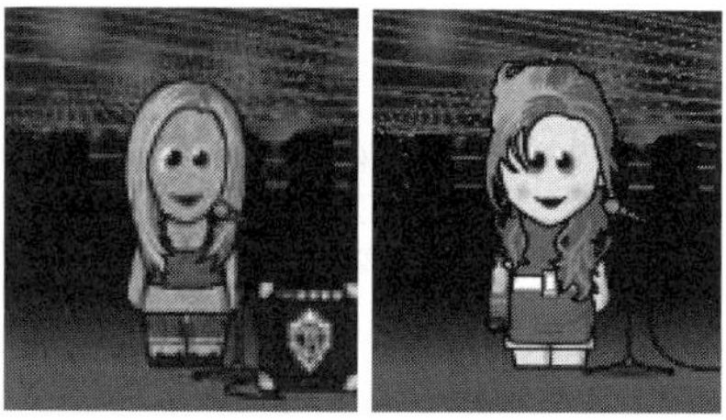

Figure 4.7. Cherrytree's two WeeMee avatars

While the backdrop of Cherrytree's two WeeMee avatars remains the same, the physical transition between the two singing avatars reveals a complex set of negotiations as Cherrytree demonstrates how attention to fine details can made a significant difference in how these avatars appear. Recalling that Cherrytree is a singer, each of her two avatars are posed on a stage with microphone in the scene, as her avatar seems poised to sing into the microphone. Initially, Cherrytree presented an avatar that shows her as confident about herself and her abilities. However, almost immediately, Cherrytree began defending the way her avatar is dressed. She writes, "My avatar may come across as "skanky" because of the belly top, but that is not what my avatar is saying about me." Given our music industry and considering the scant and revealing outfits that female singers often wear when they perform, especially in music videos, Cherrytree's first avatar hardly seems inappropriate for her location on stage. I will examine the struggle that Cherrytree had over how she feared others would assume she was “skanky” based on her avatar’s belly top in more detail in another chapter. I raise the issue here only to introduce it as a significant pedagogical opportunity that bears close consideration. Instead. I will focus on the changes that she made with her second avatar and the opportunity for critical dialogue that this transformation presented.

Cherrytree dressed her second avatar in a simple green dress and accessorized it with a white belt. She indicated in her description that she enjoys dressing up when she performs, which draws attention to the clothing choices in each of the two avatars. In the first avatar she chooses jeans, a belly top, and black shoes. The hair is neat and smooth, and she is standing with an amplifier and microphone indicating a need (or an opportunity) for a loudly projected singing voice. Looking more closely, the body of the first avatar is more shapely and buxom than is the second avatar. In the first avatar cleavage is revealed and the hips are curvaceous. In the second avatar the body represented is leaner and the clothing is less revealing. The amplifier had been removed and replaced by what appears to be a bottle of water implying, perhaps, a less raucous venue for singing. The hair is partly pulled up indicating a fancier look, and instead of having lipstick as her make-up option as she does with her first avatar, her avatar has make-up on her cheeks making it look as though she is blushing a little. Looking closer still, the second avatar has no feet. Since the option for bare feet does not exist, the failure to choose footwear results in a footless avatar.

Cherrytree’s original avatar portrayed a singer in clothing that she became uncomfortable with to the point that she initiated the option of making a second avatar in order to re-represent her autobiographical story in another way. Her apparent discomfort with her first avatar came in spite of the fact that no negative comments about her first avatar were ever made, at least not on the Forum. In fact, besides positive comments from me assuring her that I did not get any negative connotation about her based on the first avatar, no other participants made any comments or judgments about her first avatar. However, even in the absence of any negative comments, Cherrytree was quick to defend herself in an almost preventative way. She did not post often, but like the other older participants, Princess, Butterflye, and Shorty, when she did post comments they were often long and poignant, making up in quality for what might have been lacking in quantity.

Cutie-Pi

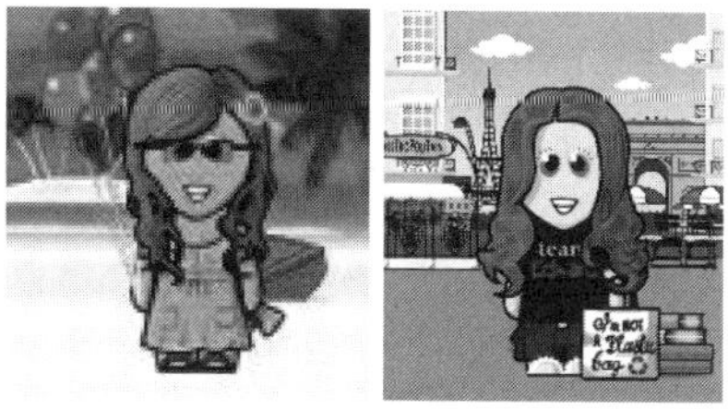

Figure 4.8. Cutie-Pi's two WeeMee avatars

With her first avatar, Cutie-Pi was less worried about finding characteristics and items that would create an accurate representation of who she is as she was with her second one. Starting off, Cutie-Pi opted to go with a more generalized self-representation that could speak to her moods and interests. She writes that her hair really is not the color of the first avatar, and that she really does not have tinted glasses. More to the point of accuracy, and unlike the other participants who placed their avatars on backgrounds that they felt said something about their current interests or their future aspirations, Cutie-Pi deliberately chose a background that was in opposition to the circumstances in her real life. For her first WeeMee avatar she chose a "beachy-summer theme" which was not at all reflective of the cold and wet weather her city had been having. Clearly, the palm trees in her background are nowhere to be found in her Atlantic Canadian home. In spite of that, she does think her avatar shows her physical features well. She indicates that she was trying to show that she is a happy person (as indicated by her avatar's smile) and reinforced that idea again with the brightly colored balloons.

When I asked her about her second avatar, Cutie-Pi told me that she spent more time making it than she had on the first one. She said that her focus this time was to present a more realistic avatar rather than to create the kind of general representation, such as she had done the first time. With the second avatar, she used lighter skin tone (which I interpreted to mean it was not tanned from being at the beach like the first one was). The second time around, she also included items that make a statement about what her interests are. The black t-shirt with the words "Team Edward" refer to an insider movement with the fans of Stephanie Meyer's enormously successful vampire novel *Twilight.* In the book series, which, in part, pits a family of vampires against a pack of werewolves, two characters challenge for the protagonist's heart. The main character, Bella, must choose between the physically and emotionally perfect Edward, and the free spirited, rebellious Jacob. On the WeeWorld site, both Team Edward and Team Jacob t-shirts were available at no cost. The "Team Edward" shirt and other options like it on WeeWorld will be discussed later for their connection to a commercial component inherent in WeeWorld and what that means in terms of identity negotiation for these girls.

Returning to Cuti-Pi's second avatar reveals another telling item. Her avatar is sporting a shopping bag that says, "I'm not a plastic bag" which signifies a commitment to environmental causes. She indicates that the Paris background, for her, is a nod to her French immersion education and for her passion for the French language. Again, what these explanations provide is a space to interrogate deeper-held meanings and assumptions about place and culture.

In her follow-up questions, Cutie-Pi revealed that as a result of the Forum discussions, she no longer edits her profile pictures. She writes, "actually I no longer use Picnik [to edit her pictures] and that makes me more comfortable with who I am :)". This resultant behavior change was neither anticipated nor called for at the outset of the study but nevertheless led to some significant analysis and reflection from the participants. These will be explored more fully in chapter seven.

Butterflye

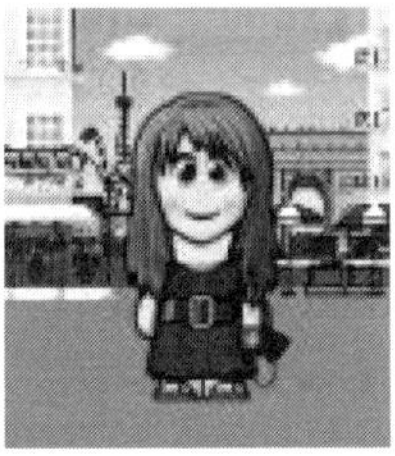

Figure 4.9: Butterflye's only WeeMee avatar

Recalling that Butterflye was late to join the case study and as a result began by deliberately trying to make her avatar autobiographical meant that she did not feel a desire to try again in order to make a more accurate WeeMee avatar (like other participants did). As a result, and as a matter of personal choice, Butterflye constructed only one avatar during her time in the study. She wrote about this process: "it is fair to say that I carefully considered what I wanted it to look like." During the follow-up questions she noted, "I spent about half an hour on my avatar, trying to find the right hairstyle and clothes to reflect both my appearance and my personality." When the time came that many of the other participants made another avatar, Butterflye chose not to. "I felt that it [the first avatar] still represented me in both appearance and personality and so I saw no need to change it to fit any new looks or characteristics."

Her avatar was designed to be a blend of who she is and also who she wants to be. She "definitely" considers her avatar's hair (blondish-brown) and eye color (blue) to be accurate representations of who she is. She acknowledges that one of her favorite colors is blue, which is why she has chosen a blue dress for her avatar. Even though she doesn't have a dress like this in her wardrobe, she tells me that she would wear something like it if she owned it. Although it may be difficult to see on a small copy of this avatar, Butterflye's WeeMee is holding an iPod. Even though the item does not have a clear brand label, Butterflye is the only girl to refer to an iPod accessory with her avatar and call it by its brand name. Even though the item bears no label, per se, the signature circle-shaped control below the screen makes it clear that the listening devise is intended to be an iPod. She tells us that the iPod indicates that she loves music, though she does not mention what type or genre she loves. She has also chosen a background of Paris because she *has* been there to visit (hence for her it is a marker of her world adventures) and she would also like to live there in the future. This ability to refer to her future aspirations reveals her belief that there are things an avatar can do better than a picture can. She suggests that avatars can show a person's aspirations, and they can allow for creative expression through choices in clothing, hair, and background. Butterflye also cautions that those choices might also be limited by the options available within the site one is using to create the avatar. As we also saw earlier with Questionmark, Roxy, and Star, the manner by which the options are limited may affect how an avatar gets constructed, and as a result significantly affects how autobiographical stories get told (or silenced).

Butterflye reveals that this avatar not only reflects her personality (by presumably showing her interests in travel and music), later she indicates that her avatar is a good representation of her because it also shows that she likes to try different styles of clothes. By including a comment about mixing and matching clothes and trying different styles, Butterflye provides a detail about her desire to experiment with different styles that would not be possible to read by simply observing her avatar alone. Without knowing her personally and seeing her "style" in person, one would have no way of knowing if the clothing she had chosen for her avatar copies, reflects, or drastically differs from what she would normally wear. All we can possibly know is limited to what we are able to see, and that is determined by what Butterflye is willing to tell us. Nothing on the avatar indicates a passion for mixing and matching clothes; in fact, her avatar is dressed in a solid blue dress from head to foot. The only break in color is provided with a red belt—this disclosure reveals again that poststructuralist notion that one story told silences another. It also highlights one of the fundamental limits of any form of autobiography in that the limited image is akin to the way language, in a written form, is always incomplete and unable to capture the vast complexities of a moment.

Butterflye reveals that her WeeMee avatar tells us that she likes eyeliner (as it is this make-up option she chooses from the six different choices available). However, later she tells us that her avatar is wearing much more eyeliner than she ever would in real life, leaving me to wonder just how much eyeliner is too much for Butterflye? The fact that she selected eyeliner over lipstick or a mole leads me to believe that the eyeliner gives her avatar the look that most represents hers.

Butterflye made a connection between how she thought her avatar represented not only what she looked like but also what she wanted to be in the future. "My avatar's kind of a blend. It shows what I look like and also what I want to be." This observation opens not only an analysis about how these visual representations are potentially autobiographical but also to an element of autobiography that might portend to the relationship between fantasy and reality. For her, individuality and accuracy were integral parts of this type of visual representation.

Even though Butterflye made fewer observations and comments in terms of the number of times she posted to the Forum (she posted six times), her postings were thoughtful, detailed, and reflective. In a detailed entry about the differences between avatars and pictures Butterflye wrote, "I think you can accurately represent yourself with both photographs and avatars, if you know what you are doing." For Butterflye, making the right kind of first impression with our pictures or our avatars was not only a matter of personal concern: it was also potentially a safety issue. "First impressions are everything, and if someone gets the wrong impression of who you are, because of your avatar or profile picture, it can be everything from embarrassing to downright dangerous." The conversation about the importance of first impressions was picked up by a few of the older participants who reiterated Butterflye's comments around safe behavior on the Internet.

This theme of Internet safety appeared again later in one of her substantial responses to follow-up questions. After being asked if this kind of work around identity and representation in social contexts should be something that schools venture into, she responded quite emphatically that it was. "I think that schools do have some business in the student's social lives, as it is the teacher's responsibility, for 8 hours a day, 5 days a week, to keep their students safe. It's only natural that they would want to discuss Internet safety, especially considering how popular websites like Facebook and MySpace are now."

Livie

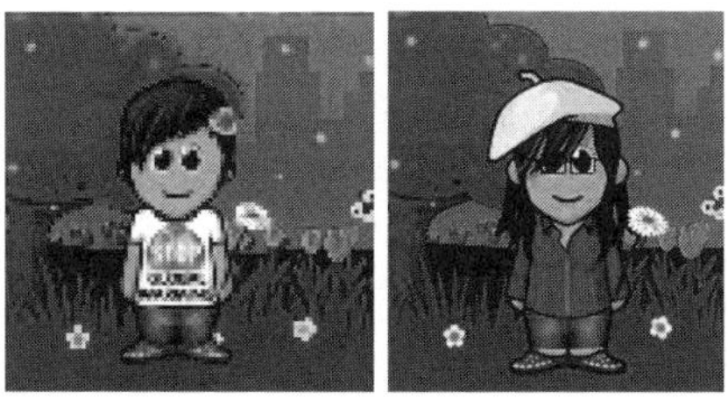

Figure 4.10. Livie's two WeeMee avatars

Livie began describing her first avatar as one that showcased her "unique style and personality." On a physical level, Livie expressed being pleased with the details of her avatar. She admits the hairstyle in the first avatar is not exactly right, but it doesn't concern her much. While the other girls included items that displayed an emphasized femininity, Livie opted for a more casual less feminized look. The background on both avatars appears to be in a city park during the summer. Live wrote that she loved nature and her surroundings and wanted to express that with her avatar. She was clear to represent herself as someone with a social conscience. Her choice of clothing in the first case makes the combined political and environmental statement: "Stop Global Warming." When I asked her about the shirt, she wrote that she didn't have one like it, but that the cause was one she believed in and she would wear the shirt if she had it. Still referring to the t-shirt and her belief in the cause it supports, she writes: “haha call me a hippy” then she tells us that she does have a shirt at home that says “Think, Care, Act, Save Darfur” which reveals a concrete example of her willingness to literally wear her political convictions to the point that she embodies them.

Livie reveals that in one of her trial versions of the first avatar, she had included an iPod as something she thought was important because she has hers with her constantly as a kind of security blanket. She described how she created skins for her iPod and kept them protected underneath a clear cover, which made her own iPod unique. The discussion led to the kinds of music she listened to, and Livie was anxious to share names of her favorite bands, most of which belong to alternative and indie pop rock genres. She revealed that she was not like the people in her city and she did not feel the need to follow the trends. In one of her posts, Livie revealed that she had noticed some t-shirts on the WeeWorld site with the name of some bands on them, but she admitted that she is not into the pop scene and was not interested in those items. She also took note of the *Twilight* t-shirts such as the Team Edward shirt that Cuti-Pi’s second avatar wore, but Livie would not be swayed by the lure of the best-selling vampire.

I left Livie for last intentionally because she had such profound observations to make. In discussions that occurred after the girls had left the Forum, I had asked her to elaborate more on how she sees herself in terms of pop culture and her connection to it. I also asked her to tell me more about her understanding of identity. Her words and sentiments are profound. This is what she wrote:

> Ah, yes pop culture:) its not that I don’t enjoy it, I mean I know more than I’d like! I just try to stay out of it, and I’m not too sure [why] I don’t really subscribe to a label, there are too many out there. I’ve been called a few things like Modern Hippy, Indie Kid, but I perfer [my own name]. I feel like teens are being clumped into different categories by other teens, like the kids that wear lots of black makeup and wear tutus and fairy wings are trying to stand out and be unique so they’re labeled Emo kids, and I don’t think that’s right because I went through a phase where I dressed like that and I was teased, before that I was another type of teen - the total opposite, a "prep" … the girls that wear name brands and are really popular... when you look at it every one struggles, everyone has good friends everyone has bad friends, we all make bad choices...to me, regardless of how people dress or act were all PEOPLE. thats why I am who I am, I want to be myself … they don’t know what to categorize me as ;) I mean, most people don’t know what to do with me!

While Livie reveals much more through discussions about her avatar, this much will suffice to paint a picture of her story as well as establish a brief understanding of who she is as we proceed to more thematic explorations of specific issues.

What Can Be Learned from Autobiographical Avatars?

WeeMee's personalized avatars have been designed to accurately represent personal identity—that is, they are intended to be miniature versions of their creators. Since they are intended to "travel" across a person's entire digital life, it makes sense to give the process of avatar construction (not to mention the product) some critical attention. Recalling my earlier cultural studies frame (see chapter two), creating a WeeMee avatar (or any personalized avatar, for that matter) for a Facebook profile page or to use as an email signature or text messaging signature is a social and political statement of who we are, who we think we are, and/or who we want others to think we are. These are all separate and distinct considerations, especially when we consider that the way these avatars get created, or authored, is not always entirely up to the creator. Because of technical challenges or limited choice, or even financial restrictions, an accurate personal identity is not always possible. When we look at the way the WeeMee avatars are created and how they are used, this same cultural studies frame invites us to look at how this site, and other commercial sites like it, works to shape how youth learn to understand themselves in and through these spaces. Questions of power and hegemony and of who controls the images that may be chosen to represent us need to be asked.

Considered by itself, the act of creating avatars for use on a social networking page or as a digital email signature might be dismissed as a trivial bit of digital play. It might also be regarded for some as low culture and even unimportant. It is, after all, an act that anyone with Internet access and a few free minutes can do, and it requires no specialized technical knowledge. It is associated most closely with a form of play on one level, and it can be seen as nothing more than a virtual game of dress-up. Yet, it is intended to be a semi-public statement of personal identity. From this perspective, the very practice that shapes how we can or cannot represent ourselves, not to mention shapes how we read the representations of others, deserves some attention. When viewed through a cultural studies lens, it is seen as a commercially and politically shaped (and shaping) discursive practice. To that end, Alvermann et al. (1999) agree that texts are always and necessarily political, because of the multiplicity of ways in which they can be read, and they agree that reading is a "social and cultural practice" (p. 2).

From a socio linguistics position, online social networking sites are what Gee (2003) might call "affinity spaces" where youth can claim agency, or define membership and group identity. Peer groups who communicate by texting or through blog postings might also be described as congregating in these affinity spaces. In these spaces, the very acts of claiming tastes and preferences and connecting with others of like tastes and preferences are all part of a young person's attempt to become located within the larger social order (Pomerantz, 2006). When these claims are connected to statements of personal identity, they become even more salient because of the constitutive effects of culture in general (and popular culture in particular). Put another way, these sites provide an agency-making space—a place where individuals can say: *this is who I am, this is what I believe,* and *this is where I belong.* When an individual is not easily able to create agency and/or establish a coherent self-identity in such a space, the resultant consequences can be profound (Dolby, 2003; Currie and Kelly, 2006). Within an avatar construction site that claims to let users make images of themselves, just as they are, what happens when the options available cannot live up to that promise? What happens when the creation of personal identity can only be done at a price? How do power and hegemony get negotiated in and through these socially discursive texts?

By returning to the girls and their avatars, I turn to Bloustien (2003), who is helpful in reminding us that any form of media production allows for a kind of "self-making," or a kind of "self-representation" and even "identity-in-progress." When we think about avatar construction sites in particular, it would seem that this is even more evident. With the WeeMee site that the girls used to make their personalized avatars, identity construction was an explicit intention not only of this study but of the site as well. It makes sense to remember that these constructed personalized identities are also designed to be fluid forms of identity construction. WeeMees never presume to be a one-time creation or a definitive representation of identity. Rather, the intention is that they can be ever-changing reflections of the personality, styles, or interests of the user.

A perspective from media studies

It is also important to remember that from a media studies perspective (Alvermann, 2002; Dolby, 2003; Luke, 2002), forms of media production also exist as serious play and when examined critically, they can help us gain insight into youth culture. Rather than treating popular and media texts as something to be avoided, or even feared for their potential to harm young minds, Buckingham (2003) shows us that protectionist missions of the past are no longer appropriate. Thankfully, younger teachers who grew up in a world mediated by electronic media are not likely to advocate against its cultural, moral, or political evils; therefore, "more playful forms of pedagogy that engage directly with young people's emotional investments in the media and with their sense of agency" (p. 314) are more likely to show up in classrooms. Yet, despite this hopeful look forward, Buckingham admits that in many places, media education "remains fundamentally modernist," and educators find that they are often suspicious of "creative play" evoked in media production in spite of acknowledging its educational potential. For teachers who did not grow up in this media-saturated world, a vast chasm of experiences separates them from their students. Notions of *identity politics* are challenged within the diverse media culture that defines the world that youth inhabit as it informs media education.

By working with the project of constructing a personalized visual identity, youth have an opportunity to see how media construction works. Buckingham (2003) regards such media production as a means and opportunity for students to reflect upon their own fluid perceptions about and within a media culture. Creating autobiographical avatars would quite comfortably, I argue, be accepted as a form of textual production, which Buckingham argues also encourages a "space for play, in which unspeakable desires can be spoken and totalizing discourses transgressed and undermined" (p. 325). In this sense, when students are encouraged to reflect upon their productions, an opportunity arises to see that both play and rationality are not necessarily opposed to one another. He adds that by accepting the existence of such texts in the classroom "desires and experiences that are often left unspoken in schools" are given a legitimate space in the classroom and where they "often policed out of existence" (p. 325). At the risk of cleansing texts of popular culture by including them in the classroom, however, teachers are encouraged to remember the inner conflict that can emerge in students when they are asked to conduct a critical reading on a text that brings them pleasure.

The Larger Context

As WeeWorld continues to partner with online and mobile service providers, it has set its sights on becoming a standard in the way identities are constructed and represented in online and mobile realities. With more than 10 million WeeMees in over 39 countries, WeeWorld literally has a global reach on a form of textual identity representation that cannot be denied. The significance of the opportunity to visually represent the self constantly within one's online and mobile discursive practices takes on a sense of urgency when it is considered beside what we know about the consumptive activities of today's youth. For example, Schor (2004) warns that "Children's social worlds are increasingly constructed around consuming, as brands and not products have come to determine who is 'in' or 'out,' who is hot or not, who deserves to have friends, or social status" (p. 11). In the chapters to come, Cherrytree, Princess, Livie, Butterflye and Cutie-Pi all demonstrate how this is manifested in their real worlds.

Any examination of visual self-writing not only as a way of knowing, discovering and analyzing the self but also as a way to acknowledge the inherent instability in meanings implied within that knowledge gives educators and students alike the chance to go beyond the skills-oriented pedagogies of the past. By acknowledging the multiple and often conflicting ways that sources struggle in a tangled nexus of power, pleasure, desire, and identity (Currie and Kelly, 2006), I am suggesting that an exploration into the power dynamics that inform these discursive practices gives voice to those most affected by society's power dynamics.

The degree to which the girls were willing to reveal or disclose their identity is significant given the rapid take-up of non-gaming avatars and the increasingly lucrative market trends associated with avatar creation and embellishment. If the degree to which avatars are being used in Korea (for more, see chapter one) is an indicator of how avatars might become popular as a kind of personal signature within digital mobile technologies, then Korea might also provide a glimpse of what is to come in North America. Similarly, if WeeWorld is to achieve what it seeks in terms of a market that caters to personalized online and mobile identity and representation, the future of avatar programming, marketing, and possession as an emerging popular discursive practice will be enormous.

Analyzing these avatars presents an opportunity to demonstrate how each of the girls became an active participant in her identity construction and representation. Like the girls in Bloustien's (2003) study who were asked to capture their life experiences using a video camera, the participants in my study also understood the act of identity construction to be an element of play that yielded a representation of self that was always in progress.

In nearly every case early in the study, the girls described being pleased with their avatars in that they were able to reflect, in some manner, uniqueness reflective of their personality. They often described their avatars in terms of having a "look" that is "very me." What that meant differed for each of the girls, though nine of the girls exhibited a style consistent with hetero-normative image of femininity (Driscoll, 2002). For the younger girls in the study, the autobiographical nature of their avatars was tied to the physical similarities between their real world identities (Gee, 2003) and their visual representations. They considered their avatars to be accurate representations if the hair and eyes were the correct color, and if clothing "styles" were close to something that they either had at home or would wear if they did have. As the study progressed, seven of the girls created second (or third) avatars in an effort to provide a more accurate representation of themselves, to attend more carefully to the details of their representations, or to better reflect their changing life circumstances. This desire to update their avatars presented an opportunity to tease out notions of the poststructuralist notion of the de-centered subject (Peters and Burbules, 2004).

Allowing the girls to create a second avatar allowed them to see their own identity as multiple and constantly shifting as they realized that they could not possibly capture everything they wanted to say about themselves with one (or more) avatar(s). Having pairs of avatars to examine in juxtaposition to one another provided an opportunity to see more than one visual telling. It was then that all of the girls began articulating an inability to represent all the things that they considered important. When they realized that their avatars were constructed using highly selective semiotic choices, some became frustrated. However, when they were presented with the opportunity to have more choices, none was willing to pay for that privilege. That refusal opened the study to an examination of alternative stories. At times, the second avatar provided a more nuanced version of the first, as was the case with Figureskatingchic's competition-ready figure skating avatar, or Cherrytree's dressed-up singer. More often the girls used the opportunity to create a second avatar to show another side of their identity. Several times this change meant incorporating a new background in order to situate or frame the avatar. Moving from beach, a soda shop, a snow-covered cabin, or an imaginary colorful cloud, four of the new avatars found a home in school that reflected a move away from summer vacation back to the books.

For the girls in this study, the avatars they created were more than physical cartoon replicas of the self. For some, they contained statements of political or ecological activism, as with Livie's "Stop Global Warming" t-shirt and Cutie-Pi's fabric shopping bag. For others, their avatars projected dreams for the future, as did Figureskatingchic's hope to win her figure skating competition again this year. For others, future dreams were embodied not in the avatar itself but instead in the background as with Princess who hoped one day to visit Paris, or with Cutie-Pi who dreamed of a warm day on the beach as an escape from the cold, wet weather she was experiencing.

A Complex Writing

What the girls' comments revealed was that autobiography, especially in its visual manifestation, provided a means to understand the constructed nature of self and identity. Their avatars were not merely autobiographical constructs, as they may have initially been intended. Instead, they became nuanced and complex, gendered, social communicative constructs, co-constituted from within the confines of the semiotic code that the WeeWorld program afforded. Through their discussions with me and with each other on the online Forum, the girls discussed the ability of avatars to be accurate representations of self. As a form of identity representation, most agreed that avatars possess the potential to represent the self "generally" because they can reflect interests and project their dreams for the future in a manner not possible in a photograph. Even with that ability, however, all of the girls ultimately preferred to use real photographs as their profile pictures on social networking sites like Facebook.

Just as Bloustien (2003) understands the participants of her study to be active participants and collaborators in their own identity representation rather than victims of the camcorder's voyeuristic gaze, I also regard my participants as active in their own project of visual identity construction. Thomas (2007) found that "identity is shaped by desire and that desire is expressed through both language and image" (p. 182). In many ways, this reflects the findings of my own study in that it took the written explanation of a visual representation to more completely clarify, justify or elaborate the intention behind the manufactured considerations behind the avatars. The difference between the studies conducted by Bloustien, Thomas, and me, however, is that with Bloustien, participants were able to capture their versions of their realities using camcorders they could limit what they revealed through the lens as well as what they kept hidden and private. In the case of Thomas' avatars, on the other hand, participants were limited to a restricted number of forms available. In my study, not only were participants limited by what they would reveal, they were limited by what they could reveal by the options and choices within the program.

Identity Collaboration

In this sense, the girls in my study are merely collaborators in their identity representation because girls using these avatar programs do not posses full control of their options. As the girls attempt to construct an autobiographical avatar, they are being hegemonically shaped to choose from among a limited number of identity representations available to them as chosen and created by the anonymous other. Given the notion of such co-production, the question then becomes, how accurate are these avatars as representations of identity? And how comfortable are the girls with these avatars as accurate visual representations? Perhaps the answer is as close as a mirror. Who among us has not been at least co-constructed by the culture that informs us? Thomas (2007) elucidates the same point:

> Our reality is where we exist semiotically at any point in time. At the same time, I am involved in a dialectic process of being—my identity is both shaped through the semiotic resources I am engaged in: text, image and sound. I am authoring myself through the multimodal texts I produce, within the various contexts and groups and worlds I am a member. (p. 8)

Thomas (2007) notes that in the online world, the confines of identity are not bound like they are in real life. "Online interaction strips away many of the usual semiotics of identity, which can be limiting, yet can also be liberating and offer the opportunity to tinker and play with elements of self" (p. 17). However, I suggest that within sites of avatar production, the usual semiotics of identity become merely re-inscribed in different terms. Turkle (1995, 2005) understands virtual space is a laboratory for identity construction (as was the make-up bag, shopping mall, and hair salon for some girls in the 60s and 70s, for example). The difference (notwithstanding the cost of the technology to hold this discursive practice in the first place) is that in the online space identity reconstruction can be afforded more economically, more rapidly, and more publicly. In fact, the online space allows for constant (or nearly constant) reinvention, re-authoring, re-writing and re-presentation.

Nixon (2002) tells us "many of these evolving literacy practices are not yet generally made central to school-based English language arts curriculum" (p. 122). The kind of visual self-representation described here certainly has not found a home in any English classrooms I have seen, but I will argue in chapter eight that perhaps it is time that it should. In the following chapter I will explore what the girls had to say about the pressure to look cool and how that affected the way they constructed their avatars. Through the process of writing their visual autobiographies, each girl at one time or another expressed that it was important for them to distinguish themselves from the crowd. They did this with and in varying degrees of detail by demonstrating subtle qualities or identity markers that were unique to them. They read the options in the avatar creation program initially as an opportunity to express their individual uniqueness. I will now turn to more in-depth analysis of the practice of fluid and active identity shaping and (re)shaping as I look at specific examples of the role that these avatars take within the limits of identity construction.

Chapter Five

That's Not Who I Am Today: Making and Remaking Identity

Much of what dominant psychology and education consider free will and expressions of innate intelligence are simply manifestations of the effects of particular social, cultural, political and economic forces. While we can make decisions on how we operate as human beings, they are never completely independent of these structuring forces.

Joe Kincheloe

When the girls in my study set out to define themselves by creating a personalized avatar, they were not long in learning that culture's hegemonic forces were at work helping to define what they could do. This chapter explores what happened when the girls created their avatars. Even with the vast range of choices the WeeMee site offers to individualize these identity constructions, it was still sometimes difficult to create the autobiographical stories that they wanted to tell. Besides their stories being limited by what they choose to tell and what they choose to keep hidden, sometimes the autobiographical intent of this exercise is shut down for another reason altogether. Share (2004) reminds us that in writing about identity, language is a non-transparent political artifact. Put another way, language is never neutral. In its traditional print form, self-writing offers a "safe place where students can take apart the culture and come to know themselves" (p. 82). I contend that even in this kind of visual manifestation self-writing can work "to expose power relations and disrupt the apparent seamlessness of autobiographical narratives (p. 82). When we look at the stories these specific girls are trying to tell and how they get told as well as the stories they cannot tell and what they do instead, we begin to confront the expressive limitations of such an exercise. But even from examples where some girls are not able to tell the stories they first try to tell, all is not lost. These girls provide a glimpse into what happens when they must go to plan

B, or even plan C. Examining how identity is visually written in this social space, then, allows us to look at how knowledge about identity and representation is created within the experiences of girl culture (Bloustien, 2003; Harris, 2004, 2003; Luke, 2002). However, before turning to the voices of the girls in the study I will briefly revisit the commercial side of WeeWorld as a site of identity construction in order to situate these examinations.

This Is Who You Ought to Be

Kenway and Bullen (2001) tell us that marketing machines have been working to colonize brand loyalties with young children from the time they were in the cradle. By the time they reach the age of twelve, corporations and marketing firms have ceased to see kids as children at all. During the preteen and early teen years, sexual identity is emerging as an issue that will continue to preoccupy the thoughts and actions of young girls for their next several years. Not only are young girls being positioned by dominant messages in mass media culture to become interested in the opposite sex, this is happening at the time that they are trying to make sense of their own sexual identity. The beauty industry finances the myth that without make-up to augment their appearance girls are simply not good enough or attractive enough this myth then fosters a life-long dependence on cosmetics and beauty products. Tweens have known for years that brand possession has the potential to act as currency in the market of peer acceptance therefore iconic associations are integral to identity (deliberately constructed or otherwise). Being ‘cool’ is also marketed as an object of desire that promises keys to the gateway of peer acceptance and belonging.

The price of accurate representation

As we saw earlier, when the girls created their avatars on the WeeWorld site they could initially choose from a number of options in terms of the clothes, hairstyles, accessories, and interests. All of these selections were free. However, once the WeeMees were registered, a virtual world colonized with advertisements opened up. The original purpose of the study was interested in seeing what the girls would do when confronted with the option to buy points or to accumulate points. I want to be clear, this is not intended to be a criticism of WeeWorld—I understand that hosting an avatar construction site of this size cannot possibly be done without support from advertisers. (For more on the issues raised in this research and the operational perspective of WeeWorld.com from its creator, Mike Kinsella, please see chapter seven.) I also want to be clear that I understand that the WeeWorld site is constantly changing and what is described here represents a snapshot in time. When I began the study, I offered participants other options for sites to use to create their avatars however none had the vast array of options available to create a personalized identity that WeeWorld did.

I wondered, would the kind of brand collateral that existed in my own youth show up in the everyday lives of these girls as they represented themselves in an online site with these avatars? Would they feel compelled to pay for more options in order to construct a more accurate representation of who they are, or would they be satisfied to write themselves within a limited semiotic frame once they were aware that other options existed? Messages on the site imply that in order to be happy avatars must have the latest clothes and accessories. In the teen market, "cool" changes quickly, and advertisers know that (Klein, 2002). On WeeWorld, flash-enabled articles (like twirling hula hoops or a pie in the face) are deliberately hard to resist in the teen market of cool. On more recent versions of WeeMee, avatars can even have a complete makeover (for a price, of course).

However, to my surprise the girls in my study were not tempted enough by the items with points attached to actually pay extra for them—that does not mean, though, that they were happy about all of their choices. In some cases, the girls were emphatic that the priced items would have let them construct a more accurate self-representation. The key to this dilemma seemed to be that they were not willing to pay for that option. Instead, they seemed willing to go with plan B and tell the next most salient story about themselves. For some girls the issues around identity and representations were certainly tied to the commercial nature of some of the items, but for others the identity-shaping elements of the process occurred on a much less superficial level. At these times, the inability to accurately represent themselves invited specific questions about appearance, ability/disability, and gender.

Something Missing

Livie's courage

In terms of accurate representations, Livie became the poster girl for being silenced (Kumashiro, 2001) when she sought to reveal a key physical trait—one that she is deeply connected to. After she had invested a significant amount of time introducing herself and her avatar to me and to the other girls on the Forum site, Livie came forward with an admission about having a medical condition that could not be expressed using the language of the program, and she was frustrated with her options. She had wanted to add freckles to her avatar, not as it turned out because she had freckles, but instead because they were the closest things she could find to represent a condition that she has. Livie writes:

> I also want to add freckles but not because I have freckles but because they would be the closest thing to looking like the angiofibromas on my face from having Tuberous Sclerosis Complex or (TSC).

When she revealed her condition to the group it felt as though she had dropped a bomb, not only because she had TSC, but because there was no way for her to show it. Livie had been diligent in helping me to understand the kind of clothes she would typically wear and the kind of music she would listen to on her iPod, and she had answered every question asked of her. However, her revelation caught me completely off guard. She had made a few subtle references to her social life and indicated that she would prefer to have a handful of true friends than a swarm of "people who secretly don't like me" pretending to belong to her tight social circle, and I had wondered about what would cause her comment about people who she believed secretly did not like her. After revealing her condition to the group, without any prompting, she posted an explanation of TSC right away.
She wrote:

> Tuberous Sclerosis is a multi-system genetic disorder that can cause tumors to form in all organs of the body; Brain, Heart, Kidneys, Lungs, Eyes and Skin. In some cases Tuberous Sclerosis can cause neurological damage causing individuals to have severe seizures, some form of disability as well as can cause kidney failure. Tuberous Sclerosis Complex (TSC) is a congenital genetic disease characterized by certain skin abnormalities and birthmarks, tuber-like growths in the eyes, the brain,

and other internal organs, and varying in 6000/10,000 persons in the population. It is often difficult to recognize as it manifests itself differently from person to person.

As well, she referred the other group members to a Facebook site created to bring awareness to this condition.

After telling us that she did not suffer from any of the severe symptoms of the condition, she did note that the condition does affect all of her organs. What came next provides valuable insight into the hegemonic pressures that Livie felt within the tangled nexus of negotiating the willingness to reveal something fundamental to her identity and the semiotic shut down she encountered when she could not do so. From Livie's perspective, including freckles on her avatar might have provided an opportunity to represent her medical condition; however, they weren't quite right so in the end she opted to have eyelashes instead. Remember that the way the program is constructed, there are five beauty options and one can be selected as a facial feature (freckles, eyeliner, eyelashes, lipstick or a mole). By choosing one option the participants are then precluded from using another. It is likely that if she had chosen the freckles we all would have just assumed it meant that she had freckles in real life. Deciding that she would reveal her TSC to the group was obviously a choice that Livie made after some consideration and one that I felt was courageous. When I told her so, she responded by telling me:

I don't feel courageous it's just my life! But people say that a lot.

What this response revealed to me was that her courage is something that others outside this study and present in her real life obviously see as well. It sheds light on the prominence of this condition in her life and on her willingness to educate others about it.

When I asked her about her decision to include the eyelashes rather than the freckles, I was curious about what thoughts would have grounded her decision to leave off an identity marker that she felt so strongly about. As it turned out, her desire to share the existence of her medical condition with others was trumped by her desire to look like a girl, or more accurately, "so my avatar didn't look like a boy." When I asked her to elaborate, she wrote:

I was happy about the choice I made with the eyelashes at the time I felt it would be the best thing to go with cause I hadn't decided if I would even have a reason to talk about my TSC but I decided to share with you!

Her ability to find agency in her condition and make its advocacy as a platform for her life is significant. Livie did not know the other girls in this study except within this online space, and perhaps she felt as though she had nothing to lose, but she had no reason to have to reveal anything about her condition to a bunch of strangers who she might never see in real life, either. She could easily have hidden behind the flawless cartoon image that the avatar provided and none of us would have known any difference. By admitting that she hadn't decided if she was going to share her condition with us she indicated an acknowledgment of the anonymity that online sites provide. After subsequent discussions, Livie revealed that she had felt safe and comfortable in this site, and that factored into her choice to share her TSC with others.

What that admission reveals speaks to the sense of trust and security that might be necessary in order to expect girls (or all youth for that matter) to open up and be as honest as possible when writing about the self.

Seeing Roxy

Roxy was unable to find a pair of glasses on WeeWorld that would accurately copy the ones she wore in real life. At first blush, that might not sound like a big deal. However, rather than having her avatar wear a pair of glasses that weren't the same style, she opted to have her avatar not wear glasses at all. In real life, Roxy explains that she always wears her glasses, so this omission represented a significant decision. She could have put any number of glasses on her avatar. But she was emphatic. Leaving the glasses off her avatars represents a fairly significant problem with how her avatar could be an accurate physical representation. Glasses are not fashion accessories for Roxy; she needs them to function. However, for her, the omission was more palatable than misrepresentation. When considered against the assignment to represent the self as accurately as possible, it became clear that the answer to the question "who do you think you are?" did not include glasses. When we think about it, however, in her private space, Roxy would see herself without glasses (perhaps she would appear as a blurred vision!) where others may not expect to see her without her glasses. Considered that way, the omission might provide a more telling look into who she thinks she is.

Roxy also noted that her avatar's skin tone was not quite accurate either. Of the six options available, it is difficult to do any more than classify an avatar within a stylized and generalized racial group. Loosely defined, they might fit the following categories (in order of color appearance from left to right on the WeeMee options page): Caucasian, Asian, Latino, Indian, Arab and African. More subtle or multi-racial representations are simply not possible. In other locations within the WeeWorld site, a sliding scale allows users to opt from a range of colors as they choose hairstyles and articles of clothing for their WeeMees. However, no such option exists at this point in the program for skin tone. While there are political, social, and cultural implications for race being so generally and stereotypically represented, I believe that the issue did not become a problem for the girls, even for Roxy, because there was an expectation that these avatars would not be real—that they are representations and stylized ones at that. The fact that the language of the program was not neutral here might be a factor for others, but it was not important to her. When commenting on her limited choices, Roxy was almost dismissive when she noted, "they are basically all the same anyway."

Questionmark's Leg Up

While identity is often closely tied to notions of race, gender and class, using a critical media lens allows us to tie appearance to belonging and belonging to consumption (Kenway and Bullen, 2001). With her first avatar, Questionmark expressed a desire to represent what she did as a way to accurately represent who she is. However, she found that she was limited by her clothing choices on WeeWorld, and as a result, she was unable to accurately represent who she is. Put another way, she was not able to tell the story about who she is the first way she wanted to, and as a result, she had to tell another story about herself. Her dilemma revolved around her desire to show that she was involved in a number of sports. The problem, however, was that she couldn't dress her avatar in clothes to show that. She writes:

> I wanted something that represented me and what I do. I love sports and there was no sports jersey there so I thought about a figure skating dress. I found a ballerina dress that looked a lot like a skating dress, so I added gloves and used that. I also found a pair of skates that made it more obvious that I was wearing a skating dress.

What this statement demonstrates is the poststructuralist caveat that telling one story silences another one (Kelly, 1997). Throughout the study, Questionmark identifies strongly with the sport of volleyball and with her school team of which she is a member. Her first preference would have been to dress her avatar in clothes that would have depicted her as a volleyball player. Even though that option was not available to her, Questionmark was clear about what she would have chosen if it had been possible. Referring to the sports jersey that would have been her first choice, she writes:

> I would have made it black and red for my school volleyball colors, I would probably have had black shorts on with running shoes.sp

When it became clear to her that a sports jersey was not available, Questionmark went looking for a second choice that might be able to depict her in another of the sports she plays. However she had no more luck finding a skating dress. The analysis of this limitation reveals not only the gendered assumptions and limiting possibilities available (or not available) through this program, but it also provides an example of how a discursive space born of this exercise opens up to interrogate dominant society's hegemonic ideology. The semiotic language of the program as it relates to choice is, in fact, not neutral—it is as gendered as a McDonald's Happy Meal,where dolls and ponies are packaged as girl toys and cars and superhero figurines get to be the boy toys.

The inability to find a sports jersey also speaks to the gendered assumptions within WeeWorld. While plenty of frilly, "girlie," or "poofy" (read: puffy) options were available, a sports jersey was not (at least nothing that she thought looked like a sports jersey). While her sport could arguably have been represented with a volleyball as an accessory (as it was in her second avatar), it is impossible for the program to make every piece of sporting equipment available to users. Instead, individuals would have to be satisfied with partial forms of representation. For example, if a male wanted to construct a hockey player for his WeeMee, then he would have to be satisfied with just hockey skates to do the trick. The option to suit up the avatar in full hockey gear, with hockey skates and a hockey stick does not (or at least did not) exist.

Returning to Questionmark and the challenges she faced when attempting to find a clothing option for her avatar brings me to her third clothing dilemma. Since Questionmark could not find a skating dress among her choices, she decided to improvise and use what she interpreted to be a "ballerina dress." While this might have appeared to be settling for another inaccurate representation, it actually mirrored her past, real-life experience. As a recreational figure skater, she does not own a real skating dress, and has, in the past, "altered" fancy dresses by hiking them up and pinning them so that they appear to be like a skating dress for events such as interclub competitions. While the ballerina dress might not appear to be a figure skating dress on her avatar, the addition of figure skates leaves little doubt to those who view/read this avatar, that the person who created it is a figure skater. Even so, Questionmark is not completely satisfied with the incomplete representation of herself. She writes:

> If I could have made a custom skating dress for my avatar it would have some sparkle and maybe a little less poofy. If I could have any background I wanted I would be in a skating arena, at center ice.

The mention of center ice highlights yet another layer of semiotic consideration these girls navigated. Being able to choose backgrounds enabled a number of the girls to literally locate or position their WeeMee in a place of personal significance. I will attend to the considerations behind some of these backgrounds shortly.

When Questionmark created a second WeeMee later in the study, she created an avatar standing at a school locker with a volleyball at its feet. The avatar's hair is pulled back with a band and it is dressed neatly for school. However, this personalized and intentionally autobiographical avatar marked a vast departure from the image that Questionmark had set out to construct. She announced:

> I broke my leg : (I tried to find crutches or a cast for my weemee but they had none :S

Because of her broken leg, she would not be playing volleyball or figure skating. Including a sad face (☹) and a confused face (:S) reveals an emotional connection to the explanatory message in the text above. It indicates that she is not happy about her broken leg or the restrictions to her activities that have come as a result of it. And she is confused about how to represent her present situation with her avatar. She was clearly saddened that she would not be playing volleyball or figure skating because of her broken leg, and she was bewildered, confused, and perplexed about how to show that. The manner by which she chose to represent herself in both of these sporting forms may initially seem like a bit of a deception, especially when the assignment of this study was to create an autobiographical avatar. After all, how can it be truthful to depict oneself as a skater when one cannot at the moment actually skate? Clearly her cast was not going to fit into her skates. But if she wanted to convey a message that she was a figure skater as a kind of general statement, then her only option was to include the figure skates (pink laces and all). Looking a little more closely, the telling of one story (her connection to figure skating) meant that she was silencing another (her connection to the school's volleyball team). Within autobiographical discourses, there is nothing surprising about that, nor should we be surprised to learn that Questionmark had to consider whether she would first represent herself as a figure skater or a volleyball player (or in another form, for that matter). Identity is multiple and often conflicted, so the act of telling or writing (even in its visual form) is limited, quite simply because language is limited.

What is perhaps even more telling is that Questionmark reveals both of these identities (the skater and the student volleyball player) instead of constructing her avatar either time with a broken leg. However, this was not her decision to make. This time, her autobiographical representation had been shaped by the choices available to her. Questionmark's dilemma is significant at the level of how ability/disability could be represented with her avatar. Not only were crutches not available for her WeeMee to indicate a broken leg, it was not possible to designate a cast on the leg of her avatar either. As I dug more closely into the options available to the girls at the time of the study, I discovered that it was not possible to represent an avatar with any form of physical disability. That has since changed.

While this issue of accurate representation also raises the notion of co-construction, I will only mention it briefly here as something I will return to in more depth in chapter six. The fact that the girls are able (or unable) to personalize their avatars with any degree of accuracy depends entirely on the options available to them as they navigate WeeWorld to construct their avatars. The personalization options are clearly created by those at WeeWorld and made available to users through their site. In short, what this means is that the girls are actually co-authors of their avatars because the site itself manages and regulates what they can or cannot choose in the process. This is neither a criticism nor is it an endorsement of WeeWorld; it is merely an observation that demands further consideration.

Returning to the matter of ability/disability, WeeMees were, and are, depicted in a standing position. The culturally coded message is that they are fully functioning and able bodied. What's more, footwear is always displayed in pairs and thus further assumes a discourse of ability. It is important to note that since the time of my study, recent addition to the WeeWorld options now include wheelchairs; however, no crutches existed at the time that this manuscript was being prepared.

Gendered choices

Returning to the avatars constructed for this study, a lively discussion evolved on the Forum based on the gendered issue of skates that have pink laces. The issue generated discussion on the Forum among figure skaters and non-figure skaters alike. The girls were faced with a conflicting choice as to whether they should use the skates on their avatars and have themselves identified as figure skaters or if they should resist the pink laces because they represented an element of "emphasized femininity" (Kelly, Pomerantz and Currie, 2005).

Figureskatingchic's identity (as one can infer from the username she chose for this study) was tied closely to everything figure skating. Both of her avatars were dressed in what would be read as skating dresses. Her entries on the Forum often referred to her time at the rink and her hopes for the upcoming competitive season. However, when it came time to weigh in on the pink laces, she was not afraid to express her feelings telling everyone on the Forum that she did not like that the laces were pink. However, in the conflicting struggle her expressed dislike of the color pink was outweighed by her desire to represent herself with the distinctly gender-coded figure skates. In the end, it was more palatable to have pink laces than it was to have no skates at all.

The importance of being able to represent herself accurately was also something that Roxy expressed, not merely because it was part of the assignment the girls agreed to by participating in the study, but because the avatar would provide a source for others to make judgments about her. This notion of being able to create an accurate first impression is interesting when we remember that Roxy did not opt to have just any old pair of glasses on her avatar. When she was unable to find glasses that were like hers, she simply left them off her avatar. When she chose to include figure skates, she did so even though she was unhappy with the color of the laces. Rather than choosing to leave the skates off her avatar altogether, this inaccurate form of representation was something she was willing to live with. This represented a significant moment in how Roxy chose to write herself because it demonstrated that figure skating was tied closely to her sense of identity, and it was not something she was willing to give up on, even if the skates she would be using were inaccurate. She wrote (in pink text this time):

> I was okay with the pink laces, but wished there were a few more colors to choose from.

On the Forum, I asked the girls to speculate about why the skates might be represented as pink, and what that might mean. Roxy was the first to consider why the skate laces might have been pink in the first place. She wrote:

> I think it is because they are figure skates, I have also noticed a few actual skaters who have pink laces. It may want to show the other users that the pink laces are showing the more feminine side of figure skating.

As a personal observation regarding the issue of the pink skate laces, I can say that at the recreational level it is possible, but still quite rare, to see a skater with pink skate laces. However, in over thirty years of being involved with figure skating I have never seen a serious skater wearing pink laces in her skates. From my perspective, pink laces on a pair of figure skates can *only* be read as a form of gender stereotyping. It should also be noted that under the male options on the WeeWorld site, figure skates are not available. Alternatively, it is only recently that hockey skates have been options available to female WeeMees. At the time the study was conducted the option to choose hockey skates was not available for female avatars.

Avatars as Non-unitary Subjectivity

Another theme emerged within the category of accuracy—or more specifically within the limitations to accuracy. It revolves around the poststructuralist partiality of representation. These limitations might be categorized as ones that exist as a result of not being able to find the options that the girls wanted (as in the angiofibromas, the crutches, or the arena background), and ones that were a result of having to make a choice (between freckles or eyelashes, lipstick, eyeliner or a mole). The difference between these categories of accuracy rests in the power of the participants to make the choice about what they will include and what they will omit. These choices differed according to context, time, and place.

Despite not being able to find the right skin tone, or not being able to find a pair of glasses that were like the ones she wore in real life, Roxy considered her avatar an accurate representation of her appearance and personality. For the younger girls in the study, appearance and personality were the qualities that they considered important in terms of how accurately their avatars were created as identity representations. For these girls, tying personality to things like their favorite colors was common. In fact, Roxy and Questionmark often posted their comments in the color they were writing about. In the following example, Roxy blends a descriptive comment about her appearance with a comment about her personality as though appearance is a measure of her personality. Also, her original text was blue:

> My avatar reflects my personality and me a lot because I have brown hair and brown eyes, also the blue dress is one of my favorite colors so that's why the dress is blue.

While the color of her hair and eyes might serve to represent what she looks like, the inclusion of a dress in one of her favorite colors reveals her belief that clothing can be tied to personality.

Roxy took little time creating a second avatar. With her second avatar, she depicts herself as a figure skater, and in so doing connects one of her passions to her personality. She writes:

> I think it is a very good representation of me because it represents a skater which I am. We both have a similar hair color and it also has figure skating clothes on, and she has a purple dress, my favorite color.

Again, she connects the notion of personality, at least in part, to clothing—and even more so with the specific color of the clothing.

What also begins to emerge from these two posts (both created on the same day and only twenty-two minutes apart) is the inability of an avatar to address the non-unitary subjectivity of each participant. In the two posts above, Roxy reveals that blue is one of her favorite colors, and purple is her favorite color, but she cannot use both at the same time. Again, the either/or structure within the program asks her to choose. By choosing one color she cannot pick the other. When she wants to allow another element of her story to come forward, her only option becomes reconstructing her present avatar.

Livie was aware of the partial nature of this form of visual writing. Part of the limited nature of this representation could certainly be tied to the restrictions of the WeeWorld site. If someone wanted to show an interest in animals by including a dog with her avatar, then she could not also indicate an interest in reading by including a pile of books. However, even if an unlimited number of options were made available, Livie felt as though her avatar could not possibly include all the things that represented her. For example, she expressed not being able to show her love for music, art, God, and family. Part of that inability is tied to the number of options a WeeMee avatar can include.

For Questionmark, understanding that her avatar could not narrate an accurate representation of her identity was a revelation. Even though she was not pleased about having to outfit her avatar in an improvised figure skating dress that was too "poofy" for her liking, and even though she did not like the pink laces that were part of the only choice of skates she could find, Questionmark was resigned to her initial avatar's improvised version of a skating dress, and she was clear to point out that her skating style and her overall style were not to be confused as one and the same. Of the skating attire, she writes:

> I don't think my clothing represents my all over style, but it represents my skating style.

By separating her overall style from her skating style, Questionmark reveals again an understanding of the partial nature of her avatar, and that it is impossible for it to represent all of who she is and all of what she does. Even though she is one of the youngest members in this study, her understanding of the limits of representation are profound and mature. She was clear in other postings that even though she figure skates, and even though her first avatar showed her as a figure skater, she did not identify with figure skating "24/7" as others did. Figure skating was one of the *many* things she does, but that was not to be confused with who she is. She even used bold type for emphasis. She writes: **My avatar shows a part of my life.**

In another similar post, she also uses boldface again in order to be perfectly clear that her avatar should not be read as her complete and inclusive likeness. She writes:

> My avatar shows a part of me but not all of me. My avatar does show that I skate but it doesn't show that I play other sports such as volleyball. It doesn't show my love of acting, or writing. My avatar has longer hair than me, and the hair color is a little more blond than mine, but weeworld didn't have my right shade.

Figureskatingchic also had a similar understanding that her avatar could not possibly represent her completely and accurately. She wrote:

> My avatar represents who I am in real life, but not my whole personality.

For a few of the older girls in the study, the interrogation into the manner by which avatars could only possibly offer a partial form of representation led them to some keen observations. For example, Livie observed that avatars or pictures both might serve the purpose of creating a representation of what we look like physically, and each might have the ability to capture a fragment of who we are; however, an image of a person, created deliberately or captured by the lens of another can only show one thing with any degree of accuracy. She writes:

> We're only judging appearances, a picture can't show you what a person is really like.

This observation ignited a debate regarding the merits of using a real picture or an avatar as a representative self-image. Which could be more accurate? What could be told with an avatar that might not be possible with a picture? What were the advantages of using a picture rather than a cartoon version of the self?

For two of the younger participants in the study, the notion that their avatars could not capture all they wanted was also a theme they considered. Despite creating two avatars that were clearly figure skaters, and after posting responses on the Forum that spoke of her commitment to the sport, Figureskatingchic wrote about what her avatar could not do:

> First the avatars don't tell other people what my personality is, or they don't tell who we hang around with and I hang around with a lot of different people, and they don't tell people what stuff we are good at or who we are related to.

Star was even more blunt in her assessment of the autobiographical limits of what avatars could do:

> Avatars don't say a bit about your personally because it's really just not the real you it's just an online cartoon of you, but I think that the features that do tell you about who you are your hair color, eye color, and your clothes. I think people just judge people on what they look like, but people got to stop judging a book by its cover.

Her final comment about being judged based on appearances was another idea that generated a lot of discussion among the girls on the Forum, and I will return to it in more detail shortly. Although Star's youthful voice is evident in the grammar of the entry above, her response also serves to provide a transition between the perceived limits of a visual autobiography and a fuller understanding of its non-unitary nature. Besides being able to represent the self physically, Star believes that her avatar can do little to connect her physical self with her personality. In other words, her avatar might be able to construct a representative body for an online space; however, it is not able to hold the missing elements of personality that would make the telling of her autobiographical fragment complete.

What is interesting about her observation, however, is not so much that she sees the avatar as incomplete, because a poststructuralist theorizing tells us that identity is always incomplete. Rather, her observation that connects appearance and social acceptance provides another ideal pedagogical opportunity to interrogate the cultural assumptions behind this statement. Why are people judged based on appearances? What are some of the media messages that youth receive that tell them people ought to be judged based on their appearance? What does appearance tell us? Even though it is easy enough for many of the girls in the study to understand that it is impossible to represent who they are within a limited visual writing of self, why then do others continue to judge based on appearance? And if the girls know they are being judged based on their appearance, how does that affect the considerations around how they construct their visual representations? How have youth been constructed to focus attention on and give emotional currency to discursive practices that focus on appearance? Methods from critical media studies (Alvermann and Hagood, 2000; Buckingham, 2003; Dolby, 2003) that focus on audience and purpose can provide guidance through these questions as teachers and students explore the messages they get from the beauty and entertainment industries. With attention to these questions and others like them, educators might find a transformational moment is made possible.

Identity Shaping, and Reshaping and Reshaping

The understanding and acceptance of multiple and shifting identity marks a vast difference from early in the last century when it was not uncommon to talk about identity as something "forged" (Turkle, 1995). The metaphor of an "iron-like solidarity captured the central value of a core identity" (p. 179). To assume multiple identities was akin to putting yourself in the company of con-artists, bigamists, Jekyll and Hyde, and split personalities. However, times have changed, and we seem to have a better idea that identity is not stable, fixed, and forged. Rather it is fluid, situated and partial. During my study, within this new technologically guided set of discursive practices, the girls seemed to have a clear understanding that identity is *not* something fixed or static, but rather it is (and should be) something constantly shifting and momentarily situated within particular social contexts, not to mention dependent upon the particular audience.

Upon culture's shifting ground, teenaged girls are presented with multiple ways of representing themselves. The literacy practices of the past have given way to new literacies, and identity is now also negotiated in virtual spaces and cyberspace. Writing about the world of instant messaging (but I believe equally relevant to my point), Stern (2007) reminds us, "Online identity construction and manipulation appear to be an enormous consideration in this communication process among adolescents" (p. 8). Arguing also from a poststructuralist perspective and drawing from Foucault where no fixed notion of identity can exist in cultural discourse, Stern understands that individuals are influenced by not only their historical locations but also by their social circumstances and discursive influences.

We are, as Clandinin (1985) tells us, all a multiplicity of subjects. As a teenager, I would have found it nearly impossible to create an avatar and represent myself as anything other than a figure skater, though I also would have struggled at having to include skates that had pink laces as some of the girls did here. Taking on the same project years later, I would have abandoned the skates in favor of a pile of books, or perhaps a diaper bag. As if to mirror the vast and varied forms of representation my imaginary avatar might have taken over the years, the girls in my study demonstrated a more immediate need to re-represent themselves in order to keep up with their always shifting, always evolving, and never constant representation of identity.

As the study progressed, seven of the girls decided that they would like to have another opportunity to create a better, more accurate autobiographical avatar, either because they felt that they had not attended to the details well enough the first time, or because their life circumstances had changed and they wanted to reflect those with a new and updated avatar. For all of them, accuracy was considered important in terms of the way their avatars might send messages about who they are to others, especially to those who might not know them. They understood the purposeful autobiographical nature of their assignment, and they set out to create deliberate self-representations.

The girls also noted that first impressions are important, and to that end the details of the avatars would have to be carefully considered. However, for many the limited options available to them on the WeeWorld site meant that they were not always able to represent themselves with the degree of accuracy that they had initially intended. Eventually this led to a lively discussion regarding the benefits and drawbacks of using avatars versus real profile pictures to make an accurate representation of self. This concept will be discussed more fully in chapter six. Suffice it to say, in one case a participant nearly gave up on the study as a result of her frustration over trying to navigate the WeeWorld site. She ended up creating an avatar that she was not happy with. For another, the evolution from her first to her second avatar represented a refining and fine-tuning of the personalized options that would create her visual autobiography.

Cherrytree's lament

Cherrytree initially seemed pleased with the autobiographical nature of her first avatar. When asked to describe her avatar, Cherrytree's response seemed full of a confident and youthful exuberance. However, one line provided a hint that her representation was not entirely perfect. With this first of two avatars, there had been an effort to represent her appearance, her interests, her talents and her personality. She wrote:

> It says that I am a singer; it says that I am unique; it says that I am blonde and proud. My avatar shows everyone who I am, I love to sing in front of people and I guess you could say rock out sometimes. The only thing difference between my avatar and me is that I don't always wear that little of clothes, hehe.

Claiming that her avatar showed that she is unique was a message echoed by several of the other girls. Cherrytree's first avatar showed a blonde singer in front of a microphone and stand. This initial expression of confidence did not last long, however, making me wonder if the "hehe' in her response might more accurately be read as a nervous laugh. As a piece of autobiographical writing the avatar was intended to show what she looked like (blonde hair and blue eyes), what she did (sing), and what she loved to do (be in front of people). It also spoke to a more difficult aspect of her personality to pin down—her confidence (I'm blonde and proud). Her initial avatar is wearing a short top that shows the avatar's midriff. It is important to note that including this top was this was not a deliberate act of resistance, nor was it an expression of social conformity. It is both and more. By alluding to this in her initial post, Cherrytree sets the stage for self-doubt and for a reconsideration of how she has represented herself. Even though no one else commented on how her avatar is dressed, her subsequent posts on the Forum site become increasingly defensive until she finally asked if she could make a new avatar.

What this development offered the research was more than an opportunity for other participants to fine tune their avatars or update their looks. Cherrytree asking to rewrite herself with another version of her avatar in an effort to undo the assumptions she thought others might have made about her opened the study to another layer of analysis. Thinking back to Ulmer's frame of "mystory" writing, this form of reflective exploration allowed Cherrytree to see beyond the actual textual production of her avatar, beyond the visual semiotic cues of color and style that comprise the avatar's construction, and allowed her to read the cultural codes and hegemonic assumptions that had been implied by her avatar. What message did the belly top actually send? How can others misread a statement of confidence and assurance as something entirely different? How do these misfires in communication occur in the first place?

A clue might be found in the combined fields of cultural studies and media studies. Audiences encode or interpret the messages in multiple ways leaving no guarantee that the dominant or hegemonic message gets taken up in the way it was intended (Stack and Kelly, 2006; Hall, 1999). Media messages are not monolithic. However, because media are such a ubiquitous force in our society, this ensures that media messages become embedded to the point that they are naturalized. We exist like fish swimming in a sea owned and directed by the media and their commercial interests. It is so present in our lives that it is like the air we breathe.

Hall has taught us that messages may be read or decoded in three distinct ways. They may operate within the dominant ideology, which is also the *preferred reading,* where what is being represented is not questioned. Depending on the social situation, other readers/viewers/listeners may apply what is known as a *negotiated code*—or an alternate position that reflects an individual's position and understanding. Messages may also promote an *oppositional code* in which the dominant code is criticized and rejected. Examining the limited/limiting discursive practices of manufactured constructions, or re-representations of reality within interpretative communities such as the social utility sites and the chat sites—an example being the research Forum—is key to understanding knowledge creation and the experiences of youth culture.

For Cherrytree, the breakdown seems to occur when she creates the first avatar using a kind of negotiated code—where the belly top is a statement of confidence. However, whether it is after a period of second thought, or whether she is influenced by another reason that she does not disclose, Cherrytree seems to understand that the belly top might present something else—a kind of dominant reading that she had not intended.

At first Cherrytree clearly says that she thinks her first avatar is a good representation of who she is. She is confident about her appearance; she even claims to be blonde and proud. She understands and rejects the cultural assumption that being blonde is not something that she should be proud of (she refers later to blonde jokes that make fun of girls with light hair). Her resistance here is at once political *and* personal. She makes the statement of pride almost defensively, as if to fend off any unsavory comments that might be coming her way (though none ever did). She made other references to the stereotypical assumptions others in her peer group (outside the study) have about blondes and about girls who might wear midriff-baring clothes. She vigorously defended her avatar's clothing against any assumption that it (and as a result she) might be misread. Her need to clarify that she is much more than the person who might be represented by these cultural and political markers reveals a pedagogical moment; an opportunity to interrogate the complex nexus between desire and belonging, agency-making, and agency-crushing opportunities that compete for voice.

A subsequent posting reveals some light on the conflicted position she finds herself in. Cherrytree commented at length on how her avatar may be dressed in a manner that may look revealing or that suggest a message that might be misread by others. She recognizes the code for such clothing might infer a certain type of behavior or personality, but she blatantly resists that dominant reading. It is worth quoting Cherrtree at length here because her words speak volumes:

> My avatar may come across as "skanky" because of the belly top,
> but that is not what my avatar is saying about me.
> It says that I can wear clothes like that and still have respect for myself and my body,
> Sometimes people judge others because of things like that.
> Although the avatar is supposed to represent me, there are still aspects of me that you have to look outside the box to see. My avatar doesn't show that there are other

> things I love besides music and clothes, such as, family and friends and theatre and movies and more.
>
> It doesn't show that I enjoy school, and that I'm an honor student.
> It doesn't show that I am very softhearted, and would do anything for my family.
> It doesn't say that I am stubborn at times, or that I worry a lot.
> It doesn't show that I'm a people person, and very good with kids.
> There are many things that the avatar doesn't show, but it's just like me.
> If you look at me, you probably wouldn't be able to see these things either.

Acknowledging the limits of her avatar against the complexity of her own personal identity, Cherrytree creates a list that allows her to claim agency in this avatar, despite the reading she assumes others might make with it. She is eager to explain that the belly top was not intended to reflect an act of resistance, and that she is not a girl who should be categorized as such. Instead she turns the tables on a hegemonic reading and in an act of conformity by claiming a "good girl" status from within her "bad girl" image.

Not long after defending her choices of clothing, Cherrytree created another avatar. She explained that she wanted to show what she would be like as a performer. While she explained that she sings classical music in several languages, as well as musical theater, pop and rock and country, it would be easy to argue that each of those musical genres would demand a more subtle rendering of visual expression than simply a performer standing behind a microphone, Cherrytree did not seem to mind the overgeneralization one bit. In fact, she seemed more focused on her avatar's clothing and hairstyle.

> I did want it to dress more like I dress, especially when I'm performing.
> I always like to get done up and wear my hair up.
> I love to wear belts and I thought this outfit best suited me.

In the end, what Cherrytree provided with her explanations highlights not only the partial nature of these avatars but also the poststructuralist notion that identity is constantly shifting. Constructing an image of an identity that is fluid represented a huge challenge, especially when we consider that the options used to do so were at once limitless, limited and limiting.

Identity and the Limitless, Limited and Limiting Avatar

At times during the study, the girls noted that the challenge for them to accurately create a representation of self was tied to the notion of excessive choice. How is it that within what initially appears to be infinite options, the girls were able to decide how they wanted to create their avatars? What would propel their will to truth? What stories would they want to tell about themselves? What stories would they keep to themselves?

For Figureskatingchic, the challenge initially was choosing which version of herself she wanted to share with others. It appeared as though she had several options.

> My avatar was so hard to make I made like three then i could not choose, what one most represented me in real life.

It was clear from the beginning that she took the assignment seriously. However, her challenge was choosing an avatar that *most* represented her. Implied in her comment is that each of the avatars she created represented her, and it was a matter of the one with the greatest degree of accuracy that was the issue. There were also other occasions during the study that other girls expressed being limited, again not by their inability to choose something they wanted like crutches or glasses but rather by the vastness of choices available within the program. Amid the process of trying to figure out how they would construct their avatars, they were negotiating larger questions that asked which story would be told and which others would be silenced as a result of their choices? By going beyond an analysis of what the girl's avatars looked like and asking the next layer of questions, a level of interrogation into the non-unitary nature of self-representation provided a valuable pedagogical space and an opportunity for the girls to slow down and tease out the nature of their choices in a way they had not done before.

I can't find a thing to wear!

Questionmark provides an example of how the girls often confronted both the limitless *and* the limiting possibilities within the avatar creation site. Before registering her WeeMee and finding out that there would be many more personalization options available to her (if she were willing to pay for them), Questionmark commented on the challenges she faced when she constructed her first avatar:

> Making my avatar was difficult because I didn't know what I wanted at first. There was so much to choose from! I chose most of it easily but the clothes and the background were harder. I wanted something that represented me and what I do. I love sports and there was no sports jersey there so I thought about a figure skating dress. I found a ballerina dress that looked a lot like a skating dress, so I added gloves and used that :) I couldn't find the right background so I just chose something plain with colors that contrasted with my clothes. I also found a pair of skates that made it more obvious that I was wearing a skating dress.

Questionmark also indicated that when she initially constructed her first avatar, she did not know that there were many more items and options available. She did not feel "limited" even though she had struggled to find a figure skating dress, a background in an arena, a sports jersey and figure skates with plain old white laces. However once she did registered her WeeMee, and especially when she went to update her avatar, many other options were presented and they were tantalizing. Once she discovered that she did have a choice between priced items and free ones, she was discouraged. Questionmark used boldface to highlight her frustration:

> I had trouble choosing the shirt because I had saw a plain shirt with a white blazer over it, **but is cost 500 points, which I didn't have!** When I chose a different shirt that was free, I had trouble choosing a color. It took me a long time to choose shoes, because **the checkered flats that I wanted also cost points, and I didn't really like any of the other shoes.**

So after creating an avatar as a figure skater, even though she had a broken leg and couldn't write that into her avatar, and after not being able to find a skating dress, or an arena background, Questionmark finds that she has to settle again for clothes that are not really her first choice. Rather than being able to include a white blazer and checkered flat shoes, she must find something else to wear. What are the forces behind Questionmark wanting the white blazer and checkered flats? How is it that when she did not know her choices were limited, she was satisfied to represent herself in a manner that was less than accurate, but when she had other options appear even though she could not (or would not) access them, she was no longer happy? What might that say, metaphorically, about our desire to have things we cannot afford? Although I have already stated that I do not believe in grand narratives and I am in no way suggesting that Questionmark's dilemma speaks for all teenaged girls, I cannot help but wonder if it might not provide a clue to the overwhelming cultural phenomena that creates need from desire.

Are we better off being satisfied with what we have than being frustrated by what we do not have? I will leave that question for now, and return to it in the last chapter.

Backgrounds Front Stage and Center

Earlier, in chapter two, I explored how the girls in this study had the option of choosing between forty different backgrounds for their WeeMees. Even though options included scenes from every season, iconic locations (like Paris or Stonehenge), and everyday places (such as a school, a dance hall, or a park), a skating rink was not one of the available options. While the study took place during the end of summer and into early autumn, Roxy and Figureskatingchic each chose to represent their figure skating avatars on the winter background. Even though the winter background bore no relation to a rink (it depicts a snow-covered cabin, and a snowmobile), they felt it would be too complicated to have the avatar appear against a summer backdrop. When I asked them to elaborate on their decisions, Figureskatingchic explained:

> My background is a snowy day because when I skate there is usually snow on the ground.

Roxy had a more detailed explanation that revealed that while connecting the background to her skating avatar was important, she was also fond of the other elements within the scene as well:

> I choose a wintry background with different shades of blues and some whites because skating is mostly a winter sport so I wanted to match the skater with a good environment, I also like the ski-doo and the snowman in the background!

In subsequent postings, Roxy noted that she enjoyed winter “somewhat” mainly because it included Christmas and because she enjoys getting out in the snow when the weather is fine. For her, then, it might appear that the background held multiple meanings and did more than serve the sole purpose of providing a plausible backdrop for a figure skater. Roxy also indicated that having the ability to change her backdrop helped to establish a liberating practice because it could enable her to keep her avatar current as she created different avatars to narrate her story more accurately. She wrote:

> One thing that an avatar can give more freedom in is the background of it, for example you can easily change from Paris to any other place with a click.

In reality, one click does not open up an endless supply of background options. A further analysis into the explanations Roxy and Figureskatingchic made about their avatars' backgrounds reveals that the decisions made by girls were (each in her own way) attempting to write their avatars within a realm of believability. In this way, staging them realistically was an important consideration.

On the other hand, even though Questionmark's first avatar was dressed as a figure skater, she resolved the background dilemma by placing her skating avatar on a cloud-like swirl of pastel colors. Once it was clear that she could not find an arena background, she chose this background, because it didn't make any kind of statement of place, and instead it allowed her to make the avatar the focal point. She explained:

> I liked the background with simple colors and not too much detail so that when people look at my avatar they will notice the background but most of the focus will be on the body itself.

For Star, the fourth girl to represent herself as a figure skater, finding the right background for her was not that simple. In fact, none of her navigations around the WeeWorld site was simple. Technical challenges haunted her from the beginning of the study until the end. Rather than being deliberate with her choice of background, Star ended up choosing a summer-themed backdrop with a "Nair" sign propped up as an advertisement. When I asked her to explain her choice for her background, she told me that it was not so much a matter of choice, because she tried to pick something else, but she couldn't figure out how to do it. Despite her efforts she was not able to find what she had been looking for. She explains:

> I had trouble finding different backgrounds because I have skates on in the summer and I would really like to change my background to winter.

She also wrote to me indicating that she had found it difficult to represent herself the way she wanted to because of the way her choices on WeeWorld were connected to points that she did not have. Later I asked Star if her trouble had originated because she had chosen items for her WeeMee that had points associated with them. She repied:

> Yes beacuse when I tried to put sun glasses on my avatar it kept saying something about points. It got really distracting!

I asked her if she thought she could have made her avatar by using the free options, or if it might have been easier if she had not had her choices restricted. She answered that she thought she could have done a better job using the items that had a point value attached. Her main compliant was that she wanted to change her background, but she didn't know how. I asked her how she felt about her background including an advertisement for Nair. She told me:

> It did kind of bother me that the Nair sign was in the backround I tried to change it but I couldn't cuz I didn't know how to.

So for Star, the limited nature of her ability to construct an accurate avatar was tied to her ability to successfully navigate the site. Her frustrations and what she does as a response become the focus of another section later on. In the meantime, I return to the avatars and what the girls told me they were able to do.

To dwell in possibility

While many girls in the study were eager to point out the limiting and at times even silencing nature of the choices they had on WeeWorld site as they created their avatars, Figureskatingchic recognized the potential for the avatar she created to do more than present an image of what she might look like. She writes:

> I think the avatar gives you more freedom because it lets you show people what you think [of] yourself.

She goes on to say that she likes having the ability to define her own identity. The fact that she can *show* others what she thinks of herself was significant to her because she felt the showing was more important that telling. For her, creating an avatar with skates, a competition dress, and a gold medal represented a more accurate statement of who she is than a picture could, perhaps because a picture could not portend to the future and project the image of herself as a champion figure skater in a way that her avatar could. For Figureskatingchic, the ability to use the avatar to embrace a fantasy world (or more accurately as she sees it, a future world) was key. When asked about the importance of constructing an avatar accurately, she wrote:

> I think it is very important because you got to show people who you are exactly.

In a way Figureskatingchic is saying that the creation of her avatar was an act, or even a performance (Butler, 1990), that depicts who she is more accurately and more honestly than words might (in the sense that actions speak louder than words). As the theme of accuracy emerged on the Forum (or more specifically the limitations to accuracy), so too did the ability to analyze the poststructuralist partiality of representation. These limitations could be categorized by omission of choices that were a result of not being able to find the options that the girls wanted (such as the angiofibromas, a sports jersey, crutches, glasses or the arena background), and ones that were a result of having to make a choice (between freckles or eyelashes, or a mole, for example). The difference between these categories of accuracy rests in the power of the participants to make the choice about what they will include and what they will omit. These choices differed according to context, time and place.

Among the limitless opportunities the WeeMee avatars gave their creators was the ability to project to a time in the future. For some, the avatars were able to provide insight into future dreams and wishes. In most cases, those dreams involved travel to a foreign land. The choice of backgrounds opened up this possibility for a number of the girls. As one of the choices of backgrounds, four of the girls included the visual representation of Paris as the background for one of their avatars. In an example of how an image does not hold monolithic meanings, it represented a stereotypical romantic getaway, an iconic cultural location that implies a love of French food, art, and architecture, and a dream for future possibilities. Stonehenge (another of the choices that the girls had), on the other hand might imply a combined attraction of mystery and history. Roxy was only one of the girls who chose to use a Paris backdrop for one of her avatars. For her, it provided a space to visually represent an element of fantasy—a dream of where would she like to travel. She wrote:

> I think the background is in Paris, and I'd LOVE to go there someday!

Princess also included the Eiffel Tower on her background and explained that she deliberately chose that background, even though she has never been there, and even though she wouldn't plan to go until she could pay for the trip herself. For her, it represented a dream for the future. For Butterflye, the Paris backdrop was a reminder of her school trip, her commitment to the French language (as a French immersion student), and her wish to return to live there one day.

Even though Cutie-Pi included the Paris background on her second avatar, it is the background of her first avatar that does something that none of the other girls did. Unlike others who used backgrounds to set an accurate stage for their avatars or even to take them away to a foreign land as a part of a dream or future fantasy, Cutie-Pi used the background to remove her from her present unpleasant situation. With Atlantic Canada experiencing one of its wettest and coldest summers on record, Cutie-Pi used a brightly colored beach theme to brighten her spirits. She explains her decision:

> During the time of creating my avatar, we were having a really cold spell. This is why I decided to go with the beachy-summer-happy theme.

For Cutie-Pi, writing her visual autobiography meant embracing an opportunity to be in a place that made her happy. Rather than saying *this is where I am today*, she chose to say *this is where I would like to be*. In a way, the beach is not that much different from the Paris background that Princess uses because she hopes to visit there one day. The difference is that for Cutie-Pi, the beach was a rejection of the present cold and damp weather that she had been experiencing. In the end, hers is a statement no less telling and no less accurate than any told (or constructed) by the other girls.

This chapter has provided an exploration into what happens when the girls are confronted by seemingly limitless avatar construction possibilities only to learn that they are in fact limited by what they can choose. This kind of silencing alone (either by necessity or by choice) may not be considered significant, but as Dolby (2003) reminds us, it does become a serious matter when considered together with the way identity is negotiated within larger peer groups and within the social discourses of youth culture. The next chapter delves even deeper into the issue of appearance. The pressure to look a particular way and the desire to be cool are placed within media discourses of fashion, beauty, and entertainment.

Chapter Six

I Can't Find a Thing to Wear! The Pressure to Look Cool

Dressing for Success

I wonder how many teachers have gone to a parent-teacher interview night or to curriculum night without first stopping to consider what to wear. When I asked a group of educators in a graduate course I am teaching how many of them had thought about such a choice, each one admitted they *had* given careful consideration to their clothing for such an evening. Male and female teachers alike admitted to dressing for such occasions with the intent of constructing a desired image. They admitted to pausing in front of the closet in order to decide what image they will portray and how they want to present themselves to parents and caregivers. One male teacher admitted that it was the only time in the school year that he wore a tie, while a woman claimed that it was the only time she wore high-heeled shoes to school.

Growing up, I recall a list of semiotic dress codes that were reinforced by my family, my peers and by popular culture: wear bright colors to a wedding, dark to a funeral, no white after Labor Day, and no high heels with short skirts. Somewhere along the way, I learned that at an interview one should dress for the position for which they are applying, and that it is better to be overdressed for an occasion than it is to be underdressed. Even though I do not recall the origins of these codes, I do know that the fashion industry seeks to give anyone who will listen an "advantage" by offering tips and suggestions that would enable us to "look better," "look the part," or, "be in style." The implied message inherent in this unsolicited advice is that to attend an event or social function in the wrong attire is mildly embarrassing at best and socially unacceptable at worst. Fashion magazines regularly reframe and resell the same old messages in articles about this season's "must have pieces," and we are grateful that they would point out fashion faux pas and teach us right from wrong. Even as a teenager I remember being highly suspicious of the constantly changing looks within the make-up industry—spring might focus on pastel lips, summer on subtle bronzer and fall meant you "must" wear the latest doe-eyed look. Even then, I sensed a more deeply entrenched conspiracy that was designed to keep me running frantically all over the cosmetics section of the department store in order to purchase products that claimed to bring, at last, satisfaction with how I looked and a sense that I finally presented myself the way I should.

The fashion industry continues to spread similar messages to rescue the stylistically impaired individuals from the social shame implied with not having the latest look. Besides finding such advice in magazines, we can now turn to reality television programs that conduct fashion interventions with unsuspecting reprobates who have been turned over by their family members or friends. The fashionably challenged offenders are then expertly advised regarding how to update their closets, maximize their clothing budget to suit their body type, embrace fashion "dos" and avoid fashion "don'ts." Some fashion messages have even become a regular staple of media's fashion industry. Ask any woman under the age of forty and she will have heard the advice regarding the way to achieve the illusion of a longer, slimmer silhouette (to dress in a monotone from head to foot). She will have been told through various media over the years that the little black dress is basic and essential (even if she doesn't own one), that horizontal stripes will make you look wide (and therefore should be avoided), and finally that the way to finish a look is to accessorize.

When I taught school, I will freely admit to carefully planning what I would wear on evenings when I would meet parents and caregivers. I did so, not because we had dress code expectations that espoused a "business casual" look (even though we did), but because of a more subtle, culturally coded expectation that teachers were to "present themselves" as professionals during such events. Often our manner of dress is dictated by the occasion for which we are dressing. I would not, for example, wear the same clothes to an interview as I would to take my children to the farm. But it is not this level of consideration that I am interested in. Rather, it is the interrogation of the cultural codes and expectations behind the tension that exists at the level of decision making—the examination of self-making (Bloustien, 2003) that interests me.

When asked to create avatars that purposely represented who they think they are, I found that the girls in my study readily tied the notion of identity to how they looked, and even more specifically to how their avatar was dressed. While they all paid attention to the details of getting their generalized skin tone and eye color right for their avatars, the considerations around how their avatars were dressed and how they wore their hair demonstrated the close association that identity and appearance have for them. If it is a given that the "art and importance of being cool" is relative (Bloustien, 2003, p. 25), and if it is also a given that if something is cool or ideal in one context does not necessarily mean that it will be cool or ideal in another, then I offer the following analysis of the girls in my study and what their representations say about who they think they are with a note of caution.

I acknowledge that even though the girls in my study were asked to present visual autobiographical representations of them in an online setting that was designed to be as natural as possible for them, I also understand that by placing myself in the study, their behavior and responses must have been shaped to some degree by their awareness of my presence. Just as when a teacher brings/allows popular cultural forms into the classroom the dynamic of the classroom changes (Knobel, 1999; Buckingham and Sefton Green, 1994), this research was designed to gain insight into a communicative literacy practice which is usually off limits to adults, or at least off limits to adult analysis of it. With this in mind, this research deliberately remains outside of the classroom. However, the hierarchal power dynamic between youth and adult still remains and must be addressed. There is also a risk inherent in trying to analyze/deconstruct/do critical work with texts that students use in their private lives and for the purpose of pleasure in what Trend (1997) calls a "regressive system of discursive positions" (p. 52), which places professionals in a hierarchal position of authority. Therefore, I proceed with this analysis with a careful eye that there may be an element of positioning that the girls engaged when creating these avatars. How did their expectation of what I may have wanted them to produce factor into these avatars? Some of the older girls in the study spent time on the Forum discussing the importance of being aware of the potential consequences of being online because, as they noted, you never know who is watching and you do not want to make a bad first impression. With that in mind, I proceed with the following analysis by giving voice to the girls wherever possible and leaving the final word to them wherever possible.

The Pressure to Buy-in to Belong

The sentiment that "Citizenship is at risk of being reduced to consumerism" (Stack and Kelly, 2006, p. 9) is one echoed by a number of scholars (Giroux, 1999, 1998; Kellner and Share, 2007; Kenway and Bullen, 2001; Klein, 2002; Schor, 2004; Steinberg and Kincheloe, 1997; Linn, 2000). Even at the level of belonging, children and teens get the clear message from the ubiquitous and predatory media that they must have the cool brands and the latest gadgets in order to belong. Often the debates around the media and its effects on children and youth ignore a critical piece—that is how adults, who created the media, have come to understand children and youth (Stack and Kelly, 2006).

Pedagogically, it would be impossible to consider how teenaged girls construct their personalized avatars without framing this understanding within the larger social and commercial ethos. The utopian reach and hegemonic pull of popular culture are contradictory in that it enables a number of agency-creating creative spaces and opportunities for youth, such as the ability to construct identities, and post pictures and/or status updates on social networking sites. At the same time, popular culture acts as an identity-defining social construct, which often serves to silence and disavow voices of those who choose, or are forced, to resist society's dominant discourses. Giroux (1999) reminds us that mass-produced images "fill our daily lives and condition our most intimate perceptions and desires" (p. 2). As an example of one such conditioning, Stern (2007) points an implicating finger at the media for preoccupation with appearance. "The media's world of adolescent girls is often characterized as particularly feminized—a world where physical beauty, sexual attractiveness, and product consumption (often that supplants both beauty and sexuality) supersede intelligence and creativity" (p. 2). For Butler (1996) gender identity is a constructed performance, something influenced by society's dominant discursive practices. As such, gender is learned culturally and performed socially. The beauty industry with its far-reaching tentacles squirms its way into nearly every site where girls are present. For some, a life-long dependence on cosmetics and beauty products starts at a very young age. "With the aid of advertising and new media forms, the market has increasingly separated children from adults and one another—offering then identities based along a consumption grid" (p. 61).

Within the WeeWorld avatar site, which initially appears to have millions of choices available for girls to create a cartoon version of themselves, the options become significantly and severely limited when one starts to consider the number of choices girls have in terms of things like skin color (there are only six choices). When considerations around the number of items available for use are taken into account, unless girls are willing to either pay for the items with cash, engage in what some would call the commodification of youth (Schor, 2004) by taking part in product surveys, or purchase popular items in exchange for WeeWorld points that provide access to the supposedly coveted highly priced avatar options, then the actual articles left over for a girl to choose from are significantly fewer than had been initially advertised.

Is it possible to create an accurate representation of self within such confines? Initially the girls said it was. If a girl chooses not to engage in the consumer-tracking behaviors and opts to create an avatar out of merely the items with no points attached, what happens then? What happens when we consider that even within the quest for accuracy there is a poststructuralist question about what does and does not get told, especially when we consider notions of audience and the expectation of who will be reading or viewing these avatars. Some might argue that it is not a big deal if a girl cannot find the pair of shoes she wants for her avatar—in terms of identity creation it is not, by itself, a significant factor. However, when taken in combination with other socially limiting discursive practices, it can have an effect over time as it contributes to a larger hegemonic, cultural ethos. On another level, Questionmark was unable to find crutches for her WeeMee. At the time of the research project, she had broken her leg and wanted to show that with her avatar. No crutches (or wheelchairs, for that matter) were available as options for the girls to choose; not even a bucketfull of accumulated points could have purchased that option for her.

When the study began, and after the girls had created the first of their autobiographical avatars, I asked them to describe these avatars to the group. Their initial descriptions shed light on the value the girls placed (at least initially) on the avatar's physical appearance. Further, for the purposes of my study, I have argued that the act of creating an autobiographical avatar is not necessarily an attempt to transcend one's real-world identity, nor does it fit with the literature around the disembodiment of the body in cyberspace. This is because, in this case, the construction of an autobiographical avatar is a deliberate attempt to represent and *re-embody* the real-world body in cyberspace.

What evolved might be compared to the theatrical notion of the "willing suspension of disbelief" where many of the girls referred to their avatars as though they really were pictures of themselves. While some girls referred to their avatars by calling them "it" or "she," more of the girls called the avatars "I" and "me." The girls described in great detail a preoccupation with their clothing choices, their hair styles, and sometimes the background upon which they placed their avatars as a way of staking their claim to who they are. In what might be considered a form of "staging," the creative decisions behind how these avatars were constructed allow for a degree of careful manipulation, not only in terms of what their avatars were wearing, but where *they would* appear in real life.

Taking another angle on this pressure to possess the goods that carry with them cultural capital, I turn to Fiske (1992) who argues that oppression is necessarily economically rooted. Those who are oppressed are able to take signs of prosperity which otherwise oppress them (money) and transform it into material positions for their own purposes. However, Fiske notes the contradiction in such practices—"the commodity fetish is deeply conflicted: it bears both the power bloc and the people. It produces and reproduces the economic system, yet simultaneously can serve the symbolic interest of those subordinated by it" (p. 157). From this perspective, I wondered if the pressure to accumulate points and have the ability to purchase the "cool" articles of clothing and accessories on WeeWorld might speak at once to the commodity fetish and the unspoken desire to have, at least in a virtual sense, what might not be possible to have in the real-life sense. Could the Paris backdrop that Princess used for her avatar and her expressed desire to visit there one day also be read as an opportunity for her to symbolically rise above her current and real-life economic position to represent her desire in a way not unlike the way Fiske argues plastic flowers can serve that same purpose for those who cannot afford to constantly replenish real ones? Princess is not likely to visit Paris any time soon. With a mother who diligently works two jobs to support five children, a family vacation is not high on her list of priorities. As a high school student, she does not have a job; therefore, she has no way of paying for such a trip. She does indicate in her responses that she would like to go when she is older and when she can pay for the trip herself. However, in all likelihood, that day is not likely to be any time soon.

Fashion at Play

> Fashion provides a range of already sanctioned codes for coherence and recognition to be cited by the girl in pursuit of identity. In synthesizing this unified character the beauty routine and the fashionable look are synecdohic of the process of adolescence. Fashion is not an individual aesthetic but a process of simultaneously producing, recording, and consuming the self. (Discoll, 2002, p. 245)

Driscoll tells us that while it is generally accepted that fashion is represented as a mass-produced expression, and while it may or may not be an expression of individuality, it is always an expression of identity in girl culture. She points to how girls manage to inflect even the most homogenizing fashions, such as school uniforms, with their own personal touches and, as such, provide insight into their own political and cultural positions: "Fashion is both change and continuity, and ambiguity particularly associated with …girls" (p. 246).

Stack and Kelly (2006) remind us to consider that it is "what do girls do, wear, believe, value and know" that allows them to see themselves as belonging to a specific social and cultural group (p. 131). In her ethnography of schoolgirl style, Pomerantz (2006) also found that "far from clueless, girls carefully and creatively use[d] style as a form of embodied subjectivity in order to negotiate their identities" (p. 176). She continues to explain that style provides a bridge between private and public space by acting as a fluid social text. Their constructed representations are at once an effort to carve out their vital political space (Dolby, 2003) and their potential cultural significance (Morley, 1993). Thomas (2007) also demonstrates that "identity is shaped by desire and that desire is expressed through both language and image" (p. 182). Considering the limitations of the avatar creation programs described earlier, the girls in this study demonstrate that they are active participants/collaborators in their own identity representation even though their avatars represent a highly staged representation of self.

As we saw in chapter five when teenaged girls try to define themselves by constructing a personalized avatar, they are not long in learning that culture's hegemonic forces are at work trying to define them, as well. This fact is significant when we remember that these preteen and early teen years are fraught with questions about emerging identity—those popular discourses about beauty and acceptance are ubiquitous (if not conflicting and confusing) in popular media.

By attempting to understand new literacy practices, particularly within popular culture, we might begin to notice that choices are limited and often determined by hegemonic and consumptive practices (Kincheloe, 2005). The WeeWorld site provides members ample opportunity for those constructing male and female WeeMees to choose from a wide variety of options to personalize their avatars. Recalling that the first choice a user makes when constructing a WeeMee avatar is the dichotomous one of picking a male or female. One might expect that this choice would open the options up into highly gendered categories of options, but such is not the case. For the most part, there is no disparity between the availability of options for males and females (except for a few notable differences that will be discussed shortly). Among the initial identity markers, users can choose from three body types (read: breast sizes) for females, and belly size for male WeeMees. In the months before this book was written, changes in the WeeWorld site were made to allow options for belly size for females as well; however, this was not the case when the study was conducted. The message these body shapes send is that female avatars will have breasts, and males will have bellies. After eye color and a facial expression are selected, female WeeMees are given a choice of "beauty" options: lipstick, eyelashes, eyeliner, blushed cheeks, or a mole. These options are not available to male avatars.

What is of interest to me at this point, however, are the sometimes-limited choices the girls encountered while they attempted to create their autobiographical avatars and how those choices either gave voice or attempted to silence the narratives they were attempting to tell. The implied messages on the WeeWorld site imply that in order to be happy your avatars must have the latest clothes and accessories. This invites us to ask the critical questions about what values are being promoted. Unlike Internet shopping that eventually delivers a tangible product, market consumption has clearly spilled over into digital spaces. It might seem odd for those unfamiliar with the digital world that teens would want to pay for items that they will never even touch.

As we saw earlier, as the girls created their avatars on the WeeWorld site they initially could choose from a number of options in terms of the clothes, hairstyles, accessories, and interests. All of these selections were free. Once the WeeMees were registered however, a virtual world which is colonized with advertisements opened up. The original purpose of the study was interested in seeing what the girls would do when confronted with the option to buy points in order to accumulate points. Would the kind of brand collateral that existed in my own youth show up in the everyday lives of these girls as they represented themselves in an online site with these avatars? Would they be satisfied to write themselves within a limited semiotic frame once they were aware that other options existed?

Gender Regimes

Buckingham (2003) argues that new media texts and environments have left us with a more heterogeneous world where boundaries between mass communication and interpersonal communication have become as blurred as the boundaries between producers and consumers. In the example of Cutie-Pi above, when she chooses to have her avatar wear a *Twilight* t-shirt, is she a producer or is she a consumer, or neither, or both or more? Gone are the days when educators can pass off the media industry as "inexorably imposing false ideologies or cultural values on passive audiences" (p. 310). As the post-industrial Western world becomes more fragmented and individualized (Trend, 2003), young people are growing up in an increasingly multicultural and heterogeneous society. Buckingham explains that this has had a significant impact on identity formation. Despite the illusion of choice provided by contemporary consumer culture, he argues that in many respects this new society is "more unequal and more polarized than those they appear to be replacing: identities and lifestyles cannot be freely chosen by all" (p. 311).

Buckingham goes on to explains that conservatives complain that childhood is disappearing and that kids are "getting older younger" (Schor, 2004), and as a result citizens aim to return to a time when children were seen but not heard. On the other hand, others (Giroux, 1999) see the traditional boundaries between childhood and adulthood being reinforced. Buckingham (2003) argues that while the social and cultural experiences of young people have dramatically changed over the past fifty years, the gap between schools and what happens in the outside world had widened. He argues that "the ways teaching and learning are organized, the kinds of skills and knowledge that are valued in assessment, and a good deal of actual curriculum content have changed only superficially since that time" (p. 312). He suggests the high energy that characterizes children's play is at odds with the passivity that increasingly permeates their schooling in terms of "the deadening influence of mechanical teaching and testing that currently prevails in many classrooms" (p. 313). In fact, some (Kenway and Bullen,

2001) argue that a new "educational fundamentalism" reinforces traditional boundaries between adults and children by moving away from the unpredictability of modern social change. Kenway and Bullen (2001) suggest that the "knowledge politics" within a consumer culture of childhood warrants a downright rebellion of formal schooling practices. To that end, it would seem that schools should be presenting ever-urgent cases for connecting the prevailing media and popular culture with the modernist project of education with its focus on rational thinking, critical consumers, and informed citizenship.

No longer can teachers claim to be the moral authority over media texts when young people are expert producers and consumers of these media texts. Buckingham argues that even in cases where teachers have managed to engage media culture successfully in the classroom, "they have sought to colonize students for their own purposes," and through this process they often end up "re-inscribing traditional notions of what counts as valid knowledge" (p. 314). Buckingham (2003) suggests that with the plethora of media options available today it is no longer safe to assume that students share similar experiences with each other, much less share those experiences with educators. However, Buckingham suggests that "students are likely to reject what teachers enjoy" (p. 315), therefore it makes little sense to push an agenda of media education from the top down. Drawing from Elizabeth Funge, Buckingham explains the disconnect between the feminist principles of ideological deconstruction and the perceptions of students regarding gender in contemporary media. From this perspective no amount of analyzing "stereotypes" and "oppressive" representations and objectification of the female body will help to make sense of the popularity of overtly sexual representations of the female body as those seen in *Sex in the City*, or *Buffy the Vampire Slayer*. More recent examples might include the Pussy Cat Dolls, Britney Spears (reinvented), and Beyonce. These later examples demonstrate "a heightened form of 'objectification' of the body with a powerful celebration of agency" (p. 315) and are capable of existing in multiple and often conflicting layers of representation indicative of the postmodern. Representations of gender, for example, are not only more complex – they can no longer be explained simply in terms of 'male gaze.'

Buckingham (2003) further explains that popular culture affords a site where identities can be constructed and contested through a playful engagement of electronic media. He understands that "media provides the basis for a kind of identity work where particular friendships and broader aspects of social identity, including gender, are being negotiated and defined" (p. 318).

Here spaces are allowed which blur the boundaries of play and seriousness and where the often-disavowed notions of pleasure are accepted. Earlier modernist notions of popular culture relied on finding serious or rational meaning to representations which "aim[ed] for 'truthful' representations of reality and thus educate[d] people into viewing the world in particular ways that are conducive to 'progress'" (p. 317). Buckingham (2003) explains that postmodernist theory relies more heavily on the ludic dimension of popular cultural texts as a means of "resistance to and oppressive modernist status quo" (p. 317).). However, for others (Best and Kellner, 2003), the refusal to adhere to totalizing discourses, which claim to reveal the "truth," is where postmodern theory is most complicit with contemporary consumer culture.

Dressing like a girl

Within the WeeWorld site, one could argue that the entire process of creating an idealized caricature and playing a kind of virtual dress up constitutes a highly gendered activity in and of itself. The make-up/beauty options for female avatars, which are absent as alternatives for the male avatars, establish an assumption that girls will want (and perhaps need) make-up and boys won't. While it might be a taken-for-granted understanding born of a societal and cultural expectation that girls will wear make-up (at least if the cosmetics industry has anything to say about it), this presents yet another pedagogical opportunity for educators to invite students to "engage in critical inquiry regarding values and cherished beliefs and to examine constructed self-images in relation to how one has learned to perceive others" (Boler, 1999, pp. 176-177). Questionmark is the only girl to purposely choose no makeup option for her avatars, because she tells us that she does not like make-up anyway and does not wear it in real life. Remember too that she is the one who would like to find a sports jersey to wear and wishes that her skating dress would not look "poofy." Livie, on the other hand, chooses eyelashes on her first avatar, but not so much as a beauty option; rather she chooses them because she is afraid that with short hair, her avatar might look like a boy. In her second avatar her hair is represented as longer and the eyelashes remain, but they are much harder to see behind her avatar's glasses and long bangs.

Turning to the girls for an examination of how fashion and dominant codes of representation get written into their personalized avatars requires that I first return to the issue of how gender regimes get taken up in youth styles and modes of cultural production like make-up, clothing, gestures, and hairstyles. Remembering that framing gender as a performance and something that is put on or embodied (Butler, 1990), each of these markers are entrenched and imbedded in cultural (D)discourses. As a result, we can look at the way the girls confront gender expectations within the confines of their avatar designs as aspects of negotiating gender codes. Some of the girls expressed feeling the pressure to create their avatars in a manner that will conform to peer expectations (which appear to have been shaped by more dominant discourses of beauty and style), and they claim that to do otherwise would be socially painful. For others, however, wearing popular styles or creating an avatar that embraces forms of emphasized femininity is unthinkable.

What these explorations offer is an opportunity to analyze the subtle and sometimes not so subtle socially and culturally encoded messages. Kellner and Share (2007) explain that within audience theory, there is a "contested terrain of cultural struggle where critical thinking skills offer potential for audiences to negotiate different readings and openly struggle with dominant discourses" (p. 13). Going one step further, not only does the question: *who do they think they are?* become central to this examination but also the companion question: *who do they want others to think they are?* is salient. Constructing an avatar that is intended to represent their identity is an exercise that forces the girls to consider how they want their avatars to be read by others. They must negotiate the stories they want to tell. And as they reveal so clearly on the Forum in their discussions with me and with each other—these representations often start with a physical description and a careful consideration of what they were going to have their avatars wear.

The discussion around pink skate laces from chapter five provides another opportunity to open dialogue around color and gender, attitudes towards figure skating and expectations or assumptions that are carried about athletes in various sports. What does it mean to be a female figure skater in Western society? Is it necessary for figure skates to have pink laces? Publicly, figure skating is already seen as a sport dominated by female participants at every level. If a male wanted to create a WeeMee avatar with figure skates, it would have pink laces too. What hetero-normative and culturally coded message does that imply about male figure skaters? Does it say that figure skating is a feminine activity so that, by extension, the male figure skater must also possess feminine qualities? While it might be fair to say that there are some openly gay male figure skaters, there are also openly straight male figure skaters, too. I doubt very much that many of them (gay or straight) would be too thrilled about the pink laces. The question for me is why are there no figure skates for male WeeMees to choose, only hockey skates? The message implied is that girls figure skate and boys play hockey. For that matter, what does this choice say about the culturally coded message regarding hockey? The option on WeeWorld now allows female avatars to wear hockey skates. What does it mean to be a female hockey player? The possibilities for such explorations and dialogue are vast.

Dressing the margins

Within the WeeWorld site I noted that a number of items that might be associated with marginalized or subjugated populations such as a pride flag, an Indian sari, a turban, a menorah, and a wheelchair were available without points attached. While this list is in no way exhaustive, it does point to a commitment by the creators of this site to at least make items available to those who would want to use them in a way that would not further silence their autobiographical representations. However, this list also provides another opportunity to pause and ask more critical questions regarding stereotypes. How are stereotypes of race and gender written and read through these pieces? If, as we have learned for the girls and their observations around their avatars, any representation is necessarily incomplete because identity is constantly shifting, what does it mean to code race and gender with one of these limited semiotic choices?

Going one step more, what does it mean that the above gender and racially coded articles are free, but that the *Twilight* t-shirts, Jonas Brothers articles, *High School Musical*, and Avril Lavigne pieces are also free? Perhaps this gives us some insight into what we might learn from the corporate branding machine that attempts to colonize the virtual bodies of children and youth. Getting kids to create an avatar that sports a Jonas Brothers t-Shirt here for free may represent a missed financial opportunity for those who license Jonas Brothers' merchandise, but it is much more likely that the free promotion they gain from having a virtual billboard embodying an endorsement for, and an advertisement of, the new Disney singing siblings is far greater in the end.

Color commentary

Giroux (1998) cites Jacques Derrida's explanation of "performative interpretation" to elucidate how we "understand and come to know ourselves and others." The suggestion is that this cannot be removed from "how we are represented and imagine ourselves" (p. 14). On a number of occasions during the course of the study, the girls posted descriptions of their avatars in order to explain what their avatars looked like. The purpose was not merely to get a written confirmation that what I saw was in fact what the girls had intended to represent, but it was also designed to tease out more entrenched beliefs regarding what their fashion choices might mean to them and to others. This performative interpretation might be exemplified in what Princess wrote about her avatar as she provided comments on her avatar's clothing choice in a manner that would make any junior fashion writer proud. She immerses herself in the language of fashion as she describes her avatar in the third person:

> She is wearing a blue top with white polka dots. I really liked this shade of blue and the polka dots I think represent that bit of "organized chaos" in my life. She is also wearing white pants, which I think look very sophisticated to others. She is also wearing really pretty sparkly blue shoes, which I think tie the whole outfit together.

What this entry demonstrates is a methodological description that attends to each article of clothing and accessory individually and provides a comment about how the sum of each individual piece is greater than their parts as they contribute thematically to a greater picture of "organized chaos." What makes this comment interesting is not so much the description of what her avatar is wearing, but that Princess believes the white pants will be considered a sophisticated choice. Where does this belief come from? What would make a sixteen-year-old think that the perception held by others is that white pants are sophisticated? Are white pants sophisticated? And what "others" is she thinking about? Within Western culture certain fashion "dos" and "don'ts" regularly make their way through the teen and young adult fashion magazine circuit, not to mention daytime talk shows and primetime makeover programs. Sophisticated white arguably finds mention here.

The notion that white pants are sophisticated and that sparkly blue shoes are "pretty" implies a level of emphasized femininity that is more obvious when juxtaposed to the way Livie deliberately represented herself with her avatars. Rather than commenting on how an ensemble was put together,

Livie chose to focus on the political nature of her "Stop Global Warming" t-shirt and limited the rest of her comments regarding her avatar's fashion style to a passing comment that "it's pretty casual."

On several occasions, Questionmark provided long and detailed descriptions of what her avatar was wearing. Her written explanations were often in colored text, coded to mimic the color of the article of clothing she was describing. As did Princess above, she provided an explanation of each article in turn, often making a comment about how a particular color looks on her or justifying the choice before making a summative comment about the ensemble. She writes:

> My shirt- I chose purple for my shirt because I really like the color purple and I think it is one of the colors that look the best on me.
> Headband-I chose purple and white for my headband because these 2 colors go together nicely. And I like polka-dots quite a bit :)
> Pants- I like my jeans to be blue.. Nothing else, just plain old blue!
> Belt- I chose gray for my belt because I think that it matches quite well with purple!
> Shoes- I chose to use brown shoes because I think they tie together my outfit, because brown looks very good with all of the colors in my avatar.

Throughout the description we can observe her desire to create a harmonious ensemble that will not only match, but will also look good on her. The message that clothes must not only look good, but look good on you is one that she took time to share during another post. When discussing her real-life style, Questionmark indicated that she feels a pressure to wear clothes that might be in style (she specifically referenced the trend to low-waist pants and skinny jeans), but that given a choice she would choose comfort over style any day. She told me that in real life she often wears jeans and a t-shirt. She does not like wearing clothing that has to be constantly tugged or checked to make sure she isn't showing something she shouldn't be. Even though she prefers to dress comfortably she often opts for the stylish options, revealing a pressure to belong and to conform is sometimes more important to her than comfort. What her response helps to demonstrate is that notions of style and appearance in real life or as represented on an avatar, are rarely straightforward in a young girl's world.

Even from Livie's deliberately carved out, unique, and alternative social space, she claims a label that highlights the cultural studies belief that we all have been written by social, cultural, historical discursive practices and that despite claiming agency and uniqueness, even "alternative" identity is something that is culturally coded and recognizable. Put another way, when Livie makes claims that she does not subscribe to a label or any particular fashion trend, she does so ironically by associating with a clothing chain that caters to a particular fashion style. Recalling her earlier statement about identity, Livie has been called an "indie kid," a "hipie," and "alternative pop rocker"; however, even though she wants to be seen as unique (or more accurately, not susceptible to the dominant fashion trends from popular culture), and the fact that she does not want to be labeled anymore, she finds uniqueness in a store that caters to those who want to define cool as something different than mainstream. She writes:

> I still like to look unique, so I love shopping at Urban Outfitters.

That's not who I am

What the participants in my study demonstrated was that there was a pressure to look a particular way and they were willing, in some cases, to put their own interests aside in order to represent themselves in a way that would be read or interpreted by others as socially acceptable. The girls revealed that most of this pressure comes from their immediate peer group. Cherrytree explained that some girls judge other girls based on what they wear. Not only is it an issue that she has struggled with in her real life, but remember that Cherrytree struggled with the image her first avatar was giving (see chapter five for a more detailed account). More specifically, she wrote that some people might see it as "skanky" because it was wearing a midriff-baring top. She meant for it to show her confidence and her outgoing personality. Where the impression that the avatar appeared "skanky" came from I will never know—it certainly did not happen in the Forum discussions. Nevertheless, what is important to this analysis is that she felt a real pressure that other girls would judge her. Perhaps we should not be surprised, after all reality television shows regularly judge contestants and kick off the least popular or least desirable ones, thereby creating the message that to succeed you must look or behave in a certain way. Facebook even has several applications that can be downloaded to a user's homepage to allow "friends" to rate their look. There is even a "hot" meter that can be added so that friends can rate how attractive a person looks. Given these and other practices, it should probably not be surprising that girls feel the pressure of being judged by others.

Acknowledging the limits of her avatar against the complexity of her own personal identity, Cherrytree creates a list that allows her to claim agency in this avatar, despite the reading she assumes others might make with it. Her use of the term "skanky" is consistent with a label that Pomerantz (2006) observed popular girls using to classify each other. The classification "used the label to diminish the power of the less popular girls in the school" (p. 180). It is described as a look that includes tight, revealing clothing, and an abundance of dark eye makeup and lip liner. To be "skanky" in Pomerantz's study was to look "sluty," though it did not necessarily mean that a girl slept around. Instead, skanky meant that a girl revealed too much skin in a way that was not considered sexy.

In this case, Cherrytree is clear to explain that the belly top was not intended to reflect an act of resistance and that she is not a girl who should be categorized as such. Her reflection above is consistent with Currie and Kelly's (2006) findings. It is worth quoting them at length here:

> The seeming duplicity of girls' behavior mirrors a disjuncture between a discourse of meritocracy as the pedagogical foundation of their education and the everyday reality of how gendered hierarchies operate. In other words, the school itself contributes to what have been identified as the 'problematic' behaviors of girls through the everyday exercise of labeling and classifying students. (p. 170)

By initially claiming agency in the choice of clothing she has used for her avatar, Cherrytree appears confident and even a little defiant. She will not be judged or affected by the way others judge her. However, this defiance and confidence soon gave way to a change of heart as she opted to create a new avatar, one that she believed more accurately represents who she is. Later, she writes at length about how she is profoundly impacted by the opinions of others as they relate specifically to how she looks. She echoes what Currie and Kelly (2006) reveal, which is that while girls can do almost anything, there is a double standard that thrives. This double standard ensures that girls are still judged based on their looks, and if looks fail to fit within the boundaries of hetero-normative and emphasized femininity, then a girl's reputation can be "'ruined' by sexually-demeaning labels" (p. 170). As quick as that the judgment of others can be rendered, based on what those in power deems appropriate and acceptable. It is little wonder, then, that the girls expressed a need to construct their avatars as accurately as possible, not to mention edit and touch up their photographs before posting them anywhere public.

As Kelly et al. (2005) show us, it is not merely how girls represent themselves physically that matters in terms of how they define themselves in their social discursive spaces; rather, what these girls do, what they wear, what they believe, value, and know all contribute to how they see themselves and how they struggle to possess social and cultural significance. It is difficult to say whether her initial avatar was made in haste or if much consideration was put into the level of accuracy that Cherrytree would demand with her second avatar. What was clear was that for Cherrytree, and others as well, the semiotic possibilities within this visual form of writing are limited in terms of what they can do. With her observation that by looking at her alone we would not be able to read all the other complex layers that make up who she is and the impossibility of any form of reading (or writing for that matter), Cherrytree sums up one of the basic assumptions in poststructuralist theory. By slowing down to consider the messages that her constructed visual autobiographical fragments were sending, she demonstrated that her own self-conscious awareness could not be removed from how she thought others would read this image. Her concern for what others will think about her avatar, and by extension about her, also sheds light on how important it is for these girls that they have an opportunity to accurately represent themselves when the task is to visually write who they are. The possibility for mixed messages is extreme.

What Cherrytree provided with her explanation around her avatars not only highlights the partial nature of what these avatars can represent (that is the poststructuralist notion that identity is constantly shifting), but that there is, as Stuart Hall has taught us, no guarantee that the message delivered will be the same as the message received. Within the complex adolescent world that depends so profoundly on peer acceptance, where image and appearance mean cultural capital or social banishment, accurate presentation and representation can be costly.

Pressure to Edit Who You Are

In a culture that teaches our youth to search for perfection (particularly in their physical appearance) there is enormous pressure to conform to a certain look as a means to gain sought-after social acceptance. In short, looking good means having social currency. This pressure is evident in the comments the girls made regarding their desire to edit their own profile pictures. Discussions arose around editing pictures and the deliberate construction and presentation of identity in social online spaces. The older girls in the study all wrote at length about feeling pressure to look good—not for their personal satisfaction but rather in order to fit with what was expected from them socially. They told me that they felt this pressure from their peers specifically and from media and society more generally. As a result, it was perhaps not surprising to observe no apparent crisis of conscience regarding the editing of photographs.

After seeing the struggle that Cherrytree endured and considering the pressure young people often feel to conform and to belong, a discussion developed on the Forum concerning matters of accuracy. A debate about whether avatars or real photographs could provide the most accurate self-representation led to a question regarding how profile pictures are used for social networking sites more generally. This question will be explored in more depth in chapter seven. However, for now, suffice it to say that the girls discussed how and why they believed it was important for their Facebook profile pictures to be an accurate representation of who they are given the social nature of the site.

Questionmark was one of the first girls to weigh in on the matter of editing Facebook profile pictures and the photos that she posts on her page. Her explanation sheds light on the social and cultural implications of this popular discursive practice:

> I edit photos. I add a phrase or saying. There is a photo altering option, which allows you to blur blemishes, sharpen photos, whiten teeth, remove red eye and other things that try to make your photo flawless. Although this still leaves imperfections, I often use the red eye removal, and photo sharpener. I don't like the "plastic" look of a photo when everything is made to be perfect, because you can really tell that it was done by computer. If I edit a picture and really like it, then I often use it as my profile picture on Facebook, because even though I like my profile picture to represent me, that doesn't mean that I need to always have pictures of me on it. I can represent myself through pictures of my friends, family, and interests.

With this explanation, Questionmark provides insight into the various semiotic tools available to her (and others) as they represent themselves in online networking spaces. Given what we know about how the girls think it is important to be accurately represented in these social online spaces, their desire to change what might be argued is a more realistic and accurate representation (the unaltered photograph) demands further analysis because it also provides guidance as to how the girls construct their avatars. The ability to touch up and alter a photograph provides, in effect, a form of identity reconstruction that would not have been possible for youth thirty years ago.

Back then, if a person was unlucky enough to have a bad picture taken the best that he or she could hope for was that the picture could be destroyed and the negative might get lost. The desire to touch up a photograph also speaks to the social pressure to conform to a certain ideal. Even though we know that such cosmetic alterations are regular practice in the way celebrities and fashion models are represented in the media, a more complex rendering of this notion provides justification for why educators need to allow for critical analysis of beauty expectations in their classrooms.

The girls understand that the images on television and in magazines are manipulated, and for some this understanding seems to lead to an expectation that they can (or should) be doing the same. Perhaps image manipulation has become an accepted practice—for some of the girls that certainly seemed to be the case. Programs like Photoshop make it simple to doctor digital photographs, clean up "imperfections' and even stylize images. But why would a teenaged girl feel the need to touch up a photograph? Is it because perfection is desired or even expected? The answer might seem obvious. Who among us likes to have a bad photograph taken, much less have a bad picture posted or circulated? Perhaps the bigger question rests in an exploration of what constitutes a good photograph? What is ideal? What kind of photograph are these girls willing to put up on their Facebook pages? When asked to comment on the way they edit profile pictures for Facebook, Cutie-Pi offered some insight by revealing how she chooses a photograph for her profile picture on Facebook and what she has done in the past in terms of editing those photographs.

> I have to admit, I always edit my profile pictures. I use some of the things mentioned, such as blemish cover-ups, tints, and many other special effects. It makes me more comfortable I guess when my profile picture is something that looks flawless and "pretty" even though I know it's fake. I'll think a second time when I go to edit pictures again, as to not over do it and change completely who I really am. Before writing this comment, I never really thought about what I was doing when I edited my pictures.

On the other side of the spectrum, Livie, weighed in on her feelings regarding editing profile pictures. She revealed that she never ever edits her photos aside from cropping them. However she has made significant accommodations in her profile pictures that did not require editing. She explains:

> before I had facebook, on things like msn or yahoo I would use a picture of a sunset or flowers or something. I was just really concerned with what people would think of me, I was made fun of alot and called ugly in grade school, but I've grown as a person, and now I know im not ugly I acctually really like how I look, and not because boys have started telling me it! because I'm not interested in them at this moment !!… and besides that, I'm a good person on the inside and I have friends and family who accept me and that's all that matters, I don't need to seek the validation of others.

For Livie, the way around finding that perfect photograph was to avoid posting a portrait-style photograph at all. The fact that she chose other symbolic representations to say, "this is me" on her online communication sites is significant. For her, the idea of beauty is something more illusive than something that can be captured with a photograph of a person; it comes from inside a person. She has embraced her Tuberous Sclerosis Complex (TSC) and likes who she is, in every respect. What's more, she does not seem to need the approval of others.

Princess does not feel the need to have the approval from others as she created her autobiographical avatar. However, for her it makes little sense to try to create a WeeMee that might give the wrong impression. She believes there is an expectation that her avatar should represent the same kind of image as she demonstrates in real life. She writes:

> If you are the kind of person who loves the outdoors and who is a very girly girl, then why would your avatar be inside wearing an outfit that makes a bold statement. I'm just saying that sometimes first impressions can be the worst impressions, if done wrong and inaccurate :)

Being judged

I asked the girls on the Forum if they thought that others make judgments about who they are and what they are like based on their Facebook profile pictures or based on how they represent themselves with an avatar. It was an issue that arose from their discussions about accuracy and first impressions, and it demanded further investigation. For the older girls, the responses were overwhelmingly clear.

Princess weighed in on the repercussions of creating images that may not be accurate. As Cherrytree had stated earlier, Princess reported that she feels the pressure of being judged by others based not only on how she looks in real life but based on how her avatar is constructed. It seems that even in this playful space, the representation of appearance is serious business. She explains:

> Sometimes, and it's a shame, people judge you by the way you look. Most times people don't want to get to know you before he/she decides if you are a nice or good person or not, they just look at your outfit [or in this case a picture] and if you don't look like someone who they would be friends with then they just pass you in the hallway.

For Cutie-Pi, her response was much the same:

> For sure! It is common today to be automatically judged as something just by the way you look. Some people make comments and I'm like, "you don't even know me, how could you make assumptions like that?"
> Snap judgments are made everyday, and it's hardly fair to start off a relationship badly just because of an appearance.

What Cutie-Pi reveals here is a deeper set of social practices that deny membership and belonging based on appearance. While it is important for an educator to address the cruel social dynamics of such an occasion, an opportunity also exists to address the larger social issues related to how young people can find their way through such a struggle. Certainly incidents like the one described above are not isolated; they are part of the social dynamics that make up the world of adolescence.

Butterflye provides another sad account of what her experiences have taught her about the social pressure to provide an accurate representation of identity on these public/private online spaces. Her comments are particularly relevant in terms of what they say about the choices girls make when constructing their avatars or choosing pictures to represent them on social networking sites. By referring to the attention-getting phenomenon of teens posting pictures of riotous parties and raucous behavior in order to gain social acceptance with peers, she stressed the importance of first impressions by using a bold font:

> The school society…can create some serious pressure. It's like the whole issue on MySpace, which has now moved over to Facebook, where people are posting pictures that aren't necessarily appropriate, in order to get attention. I think profile pictures should reflect who you are, not who society tells us you should be. **First impressions are everything, and if someone gets the wrong impression of who you are, because of your avatar or profile picture, it can be everything from embarrassing to downright dangerous.**

Embedded in this comment is a glimpse at the potential reach that social networking sites have on these girls. Butterflye not only tells us that first impressions matter intensely, but she suggests that they are just as important in a digital realm as they are in person. In fact, given the amount of time that youth spend in the digital realm and given the extended social reach that social networking sites provide them, one might speculate that first impressions are perhaps more important in the digital realm than they are in person.

On the Forum, Cutie-Pi connected this apparent need to create accurate representations with the pressure she felt about being judged by others based on appearances. In her experience, such judgments came swiftly in both digital and real life spaces. In her experience¸ such judgments were based on appearance.

> It is common today, to be automatically judged as something just by the way you look.

During some follow-up questions I asked her to reflect more on her observations about how some people seem to make assumptions based on how others dress. I asked her to clarify her comments about how she did not think it was fair to start off a relationship based on a snap judgment about appearance. I also asked her to comment on where she thought this pressure came from. Cutie-Pi's response is enlightening:

> We as a society should base our opinion of people more on the inside and less on the outside. What can you really tell by the way someone looks?
> It's unfair really. In the media, outward appearances are "important" more so than inward. At least, that's how I feel it's portrayed. Others may be sucked into this conceited way of thinking but I know better, or at least I try. Pressure come from peers mostly. In the big picture though, it would be the media.

Cutie-Pi's observation brings us full circle back to the media with the hegemonic messages that reach us in the cradle and follow us to the grave with increasingly cunning attempts to shape our desires, manipulate our wants and redefine our needs (Kenway and Bullen, 2001; Schor, 2004). Advertisements embedded in print, film, and on television tell us that in order to be desirable we must conform to ideals of beauty and fashion. The message is that to do otherwise is to be outcast. However, despite trying, corporate giants cannot guarantee that their messages designed to tempt us to consume their products will be read and taken up the way they have intended. Despite their efforts to make youth conform, there is no guarantee that they will. As we have just heard from Butterflye, Princess, Cherrytree and Cutie-Pi, in spite of their own strong desire to be regarded as unique individuals with their own styles, they still feel the pressure to conform one way or another. We also see this pressure manifested in the way they create their avatars.

Looking forward to chapter seven, I will examine the poststructuralist notion that identity is something always in the process of being formed but never fully formed. The girls understand that avatars can only represent a snapshot of who they are. As such snapshots, we explore the notion of using avatars as their profile pictures on Facebook. The girls then reflect back over the study and reveal what they have learned. It seems that the practice of slowing down to consider notions of identity and representation provides some of the study's most valuable findings.

Chapter Seven

"Just a second of your life represented." What Avatars Can and Cannot Do

Culture is the medium through which children fashion their individual and collective identities and learn, in part, how to narrate themselves in relation to others. Culture is also shifting ground where new and old literacies —ways of understanding the world —are produced and legitimated in the service of national identity, public life, and civic responsibility. As a site of learning and struggle, culture becomes the primary referent for understanding the multiple sites in which pedagogy works, power operates, and authority is secured or contested.

Henry Giroux

Fluid Representation and Identity (Re)negotiation

Statements of identity, or how we narrate ourselves in relation to others, cannot be removed from how we engage with culture or how culture engages with us. Butler (1996) shows us that identity can be understood as a performance—a deliberate act of conformity and/or resistance to culture's discourses. Such performances resonate in how we represent ourselves both to and in the world; these performances are limited by the economic recourses we have at our disposal, not to mention the historical and cultural location we inhabit. If we pause to examine the multiple ways in which identity is performed, we might notice that the performance is influenced as well by our audience. What we choose to reveal and what we choose to conceal often depends on whom we are revealing our identity to or whom we are concealing it from. Of course, these choices are never quite as cut and dried as this discussion might imply. How we perform our identity that is, how we dress, how we wear our hair, how we act, and what we say are also influenced, in some way, by our relationship with culture. But culture, as Giroux reminds us above, is constantly changing—it is a shifting ground. Similarly, expressions of individuality and identity, such as styles and trends are fleeting, as are our desires and intentions.

If the intention is to narrate or perform one's identity by creating a visual representation of who we are, and this representation is for use in a public/private communicative space, then a visual representation of our identity might be also considered as a form of autobiography: a visual telling of who we are. This view requires that we acknowledge the role of autobiography as a format that adds layers of meaning to our histories, one that questions the discursive practice of not only memory, but also of our constructed truths. From there, we are able to move beyond a more traditional vision of autobiography that seeks to privilege what it makes visible (Scott, 1991). From this perspective we must ask how is it that some experiences are considered more salient than others? What desire moves us to reveal or to conceal elements of our identity, and how does the fluid nature of culture and identity factor into our telling?

This chapter will explore the way autobiographical avatars were (and could be) used, and how the nature of their use in social networking spaces shaped how they were created and how others would interpret them. I begin by drawing on Thomas (2007), who looks at avatar construction as an opportunity to explore the "play between the construction and self-construction of subjectivity, or identity" (p. 21). Even with the avatars in her study, which were designed to serve a vastly different purpose, one can draw some comparisons. The autobiographical avatars in my study are also highly staged documents of identity in the making, described as constructed snapshots of the self at one moment in time. The deliberate nature of their construction means that they also reveal and conceal selectively. Complicating the accuracy of the telling, however, are the limitations placed on the girls based on the semiotics of the site they have used. Because they are limited to using the options provided on the WeeWorld site, the girls cannot be regarded as sole creators of their avatars. At best they are co-producers who share authorship with those who have created the avatar-making site itself. I will return to this notion later in this chapter.

In nearly every case early in the study the girls are described being pleased with their avatars because they were able to represent, in some manner, what they believed to be a uniqueness reflective of their personality. They often described their avatars having a "look" that is "very me." What that meant differed for each of the girls, though nine of the girls exhibited a style consistent with dominant, hetero-normative image of femininity (Driscoll, 2002). For the younger girls in the study the autobiographical nature of their avatars was limited to the physical similarities between their real world identities (Gee, 2003) and their visual representations. They considered their avatars to be accurate representations if the hair and eyes were the correct color and if clothing "styles" were close to something that they either had at home or would wear if they did have. On the other hand, the older girls constructed their avatars to reveal interests and dreams as well as their physical appearance. As well, they learned that the autobiographical nature of the exercise was nearly impossible to accomplish because any form of self-representation is always partial and always in progress.

Despite its inability to offer an unlimited number of options for free, WeeWorld did provide an opportunity for the girls to fairly accurately represent themselves. However, the temptation to create a more accurate avatar was not great enough to entice these girls to pay real money in order to gain access to "more valuable" clothing, accessories, and items for their WeeMees. As the study progressed, seven of the girls created a second (or third) avatar in an effort to provide a more accurate representation of themselves, to attend more carefully to the details of their representations, or to better reflect their changing life circumstances. By creating a second avatar the girls began to see their identity as something fluid and constantly shifting, rather than something fixed. At times the second avatar provided a more nuanced version of the first, as was the case with Figureskatingchic's competition-ready figure skating avatar or Cherrytree's slimmed-down but dressed-up singer. More often, however, the girls used the second avatar as an opportunity to show another side of their identity as they seemed to embrace the notion that this form of identity representation was indeed partial and incomplete. The girls quickly realized that they could not possibly capture everything they wanted to "say" about themselves with one (or more) avatar(s). When pairs of avatars were juxtaposed, the girls began articulating an inability to represent all the things that they considered important.

When they realized that their avatars were constructed using highly selective semiotic choices, some also became frustrated. However, when they were presented with the opportunity to have more choices, none were willing to pay for that privilege. What the girls revealed was that autobiography, especially in this visual manifestation, provided a means to understand the constructed yet fluid nature of identity and representation. Through their discussions with me and with each other on the Forum, they discussed how important it was for avatars to provide accurate representations of identity. As a form of identity representation, most agreed that avatars possess the potential to represent "generally" given their ability to reflect interests and project dreams for the future in a manner not possible in a photograph. On several occasions the act of creating a second avatar meant incorporating a new background in order to situate or frame the avatar. The girls changed the backgrounds to the beach, a soda shop, a snow-covered cabin, or an imaginary colorful cloud; interestingly, four of the new avatars were found on a backdrop that situated them in school. Despite the similar backgrounds, each girl felt that her avatar was still unique.

When I began the study, I made the assumption that the girls in this study would have some sort of epiphany when they were asked to confront the notion of identity as something partial, shifting, and situated within particular social and cultural contexts. I was wrong. While some girls did admit that they had never thought about some of the concepts around representation and identity creation before, they all seemed to rest comfortably with the notion that narrating identity this way was partial and in many cases fictional.

The Serious Business of Identity at Play

If the playful construction of an avatar can be viewed as a form of writing, and more specifically as a visual autobiography, then the semiotic considerations that underwrite its construction demand attention for their historical and political nature. Constructing an avatar designed to be a kind of digital signature is more than a virtual game of dress-up. It is a statement of who we are, or who we want others to think we are within a social online context. Even more to the point, these avatars enable us to examine how knowledge about identity gets created within the experience of girlhood culture. However, when these playful constructions are constituted in and through language (that is, the visual language of the available choices on the avatar site), then the way that identity gets represented is serious business. As a social discursive practice, larger cultural ideologies like beauty, gender, and ability/disability must be factored into the considerations of construction.

Avatars are intended to create and/or reveal an identity in cyberspace (Kang and Yang, 2006). While the form of identity that avatars may reveal ranges from deliberately autobiographical to that of an alter ego type, the notion of an avatar as a constructed form of self-disclosure is similar. The impact of being able to visually represent oneself constantly within one's online and mobile discursive practices is significant when it is considered beside what we know about the consumptive activities of today's youth. The visual language, or the semiotic codes represented in and through both forms of avatars convey messages about appearance, fashion, beauty, ability, and gender. Given the rapid take up of non-gaming avatars and the increasingly lucrative market trends associated with avatar creation and embellishment in places like Korea, this is significant (for more, see chapter one). When combined with the expressed desire for the creators of WeeWorld.com to become the standard in personalized online and mobile identity creation in North America and Europe, this kind of identity construction and representation demands attention. If WeeWorld.com and its 10 million WeeMees in over 39 different countries is to achieve what it seeks in terms of an emerging market that caters to online and mobile textual identity representation, the future of avatar creation of this kind will be enormous.

It is likely that how and where these avatars are being used shape how they are created. Given their presence in the digital spaces of social acceptance (on email, blogs, IM, and social networking profiles), details are important. There is a cultural currency to belonging, and as Schor (2004) reminds us, what you possess often determines if you belong. Even more to the point, she explains, "Children's social worlds are increasingly constructed around consuming, as brands and not products have come to determine who is 'in' or 'out,' who is hot or not, who deserves to have friends, or social status" (p. 11). The way in which power is negotiated in social environments like schools and on social networking sites suggests that the ways teenagers represent themselves in these environments are given a further consideration. All of the girls in this study felt their avatars made a statement about who they are. Yet, overwhelmingly, they felt they would be judged based on their appearance in online environments as they are in school or other social environments. The girls noted that first impressions are important, and to that end, the details of their avatars were carefully considered as they were constructed. With this in mind, it should not be surprising that the girls were willing and eager to use editing software on the photographs they used as profile pictures. It seems that image is important, even in their online spaces.

Research conducted by Kafai et al. (2007) found that avatar appearance was extremely important for those teens participating in the online *Second Life* community, Whyville, because it allowed participants to make friends and flirt with members of the opposite sex. There was cultural currency in looking good. "Looking 'good' is a way of demonstrating social status and more likely to get people to talk to you" (p. 33). While the communities in our studies might differ drastically, there is a common thread in how appearance was seen as something that affected social status. For the girls in this study, the avatars they created were more than physical cartoon replicas of the self. For some, they contained statements of political or ecological activism, as with Livie's Darfur t-shirt and Cutie-Pi's fabric shopping bag. For others their avatars projected dreams for the future, as did Figureskatingchic's hope to win her figure skating competition again this year. For others, future dreams were embodied not in the avatar itself but instead in the background as with Princess, who hoped one day to visit Paris, or with Cutie-Pi, who dreamed of a warm day on the beach as an escape from the cold, wet weather she was experiencing.

> Inside the school, overt and covert negotiations take place that are contingent upon the meanings that are created within its social world, meanings that differ from city to city, neighbourhood to neighbourhood, and school to school. This contextualized understanding of style enables a deeper understanding of girls' identities as complex and constantly on the move. (Pomerantz, 2006, p. 189)

What Pomerantz offers is an acknowledgment that youth identity is not only fluid, but at this age belonging is tied in part to fashion. Recalling Driscoll's (2002) observation that fashion is mass-produced and therefore is rarely an expression of individuality, the girls in my study nevertheless connected their avatar's fashion choices with their expression of individuality. Like the girls in Bloustien's (2003) study who were asked to capture their life experiences using a video camera, the participants in my study also understood that this act of identity construction is playful. They learned that the autobiographical nature of the exercise was nearly impossible to accomplish because any form of self-representation is always partial and always in progress. The powerful political social systems that operate within school culture suggest that a teacher might be better prepared to interrogate the nuances and subtleties of youth identity and belonging than a researcher, because of her position within the site of these local political and social discourses. The final chapter will offer suggestions for how this might happen.

Evidence at home

One does not need to turn to the scholars to confirm that belonging is an important preoccupation in an adolescent girl's life. Thinking back to my own adolescence, the questions of "do I fit in?" and "where do I belong?" were constant preoccupations. The accompanying and sometimes narcissistic questions like: "what will they think?" and "how do I look?" would have been equally predominant concern, as much as I hate to admit it. When I observe my own teenage daughter today as she attempts to find her way in the world, I see these same questions manifest themselves. I regularly hear things like: *Is my hair all right? Do these pants make me look fat? How does this shirt look? Gah!* My sixteen-year-old daughter has a well defined yet evolving sense of her own style and she has set clear parameters around what she will and will not wear. Besides banishing anything pink from her wardrobe, she has made some of her style choices based on her five-foot-nine-inch frame—like no heels, almost ever. But others, like her refusal to wear expensive brand name clothes (unless she can find them on a clearance rack) are only broken by the claim that because of her height, Abercrombie and Fitch seems to be the only brand that makes pants long enough for her legs. On the surface such style decisions may be just about clothes, but when we consider that we *are* socially, culturally, historically, and politically situated based in part on appearance we might see that there is more at stake. A large part of what we wear or choose to wear, and even what we choose not to wear, bears relevance to our identity construction. This also serves to point to the complex and often conflicted process of negotiation through which teenaged girls attempt to claim their space of potential cultural significance. It also represents a real and tangible example of how a teenaged girl might attempt to maneuver around sites of power and authority as she attempts to narrate her own identity in relation to others, especially her peers.

In my own research, I found that the girls in my study regarded appearance as something not only tied closely to how they look physically (through representations of their skin tone, eye color and hair color), but also how they (re)present themselves to the world and in the world (in terms of style and accessories). Seen this way, concerns about appearance represent a nearly constant but always fluid tie to identity negotiation and construction.

Back in the 1980s when I was a teenage girl struggling to fit in, I remember transferring to a school in North York (north of Toronto) during grade eleven so that I could continue training with my coach at a nearby figure skating club for the competitive season. Coming from the small Maritime city of Fredericton, New Brunswick, I felt the culture shock of a big city school most deeply at the level of identity and representation. Besides being overwhelmed by the newness of the school and the absence of a social network there, I wasn't wearing the right clothes. The manner by which I was narrating myself to others within the cultural capital language of appearance screamed out "I don't fit in here!" I had known enough to recognize that "deck shoes" or flat leather loafers were "in" so I had managed to snag myself a pair of those before starting school. At the same time in Toronto, Izod had taken off as the brand of the moment, and little alligators adorned everything from shirts to sox. By wearing logos on our clothes rather than on the tags inside our clothes, adults, children and even infants had become walking billboards. Klein (2002) acknowledges that the logos "served the same social function as keeping the clothing's price tag on" (p. 28). I remember making a frantic phone call to my mother back home and telling her I felt like I was going to school in a swamp. "Everyone is wearing clothing with alligators, so please send something, anything, with an alligator on it." Even if no one seemed to notice, I felt like a social reject. There was cultural currency and acceptance in those emblems of prosperity and preppiness. Looking back, I am sure I was not the only student at the school who did not have an Izod shirt, but it certainly felt that way. Stern (2007) tells us "adolescent girls are particularly prone to crisis in identity as a result of dominant cultural and media discourses" (p. 2). I was certainly one of those girls, and the "alligator incident" was certainly a "crisis in identity" for me. Such crises in identity occur just as easily today, perhaps even more easily, as the preoccupation to express one's potential cultural significance is no longer limited to how one presents oneself in real life in terms of fashion or physical appearance. It would be difficult to deny the gravity of such considerations in the lives of many teenaged girls.

What has changed, however, is the manner by which teenaged girls have opportunity to represent themselves to the world and in the world. One of the differences between the 1980s and now can be tied to the social communicative practices of the time. As teenagers in the 1980s, my friends gathered in cliques and hung out in small groups where we made plans to get together some more. We talked perhaps for hours on the phone (not on our own cell phone but on a family land line before call waiting had been invented), and we talked with only one friend at a time. If we were doing something deviant like planning to drink beer on the train tracks, we tried to stay out of sight and not get caught. We certainly had no desire (or means for that matter) of sharing what we considered madcap debauchery with the world, although there was some social status to be gained by having the cool crowd learn that we were planning to be engaged in a behavior that parents and teachers would deem unacceptable. Stories and secrets more regularly stayed within tightly guarded social groups and were spread or shared only by word of mouth. Rumors were hard to confirm or deny.

In a way, the transition to a sharing and surveillance culture enabled by both technology and social networking sites like Facebook and MySpace mirrors the social and political transition that occurred when society moved from an oral culture to one that disseminated information using a mass reproducible print text. Currently, texts and especially images, claim to hold the objectivity of proof—a move away from the possibility of boastful embellishment or a guarded and embarrassed downplay. With new technology, the pictures taken by tiny digital cameras, camera phones, or videophones provide an opportunity to possess actual cultural significance. The tools become the means to prove one's place, and the social networking sites become the new forum for spreading the word and disseminating the social news.

However identity and representation demand another layer of consideration when we acknowledge that images do not necessarily appear in their original form. Because of nearly infinite editing possibilities that guide negotiations regarding what stories we choose to tell and which ones we choose to leave behind, the images we see are not necessarily what were taken in the first place. Also note that before the turn from oral to print culture any form of embellishment or change in the original text might have been considered plagiarism. Today, while embellishing images is sometimes still considered scandalous, as when Katie Couric's photos were doctored for the promotional advertisements for her move to the evening news, on a social level and in online social spaces there is no similar expectation of authenticity. Editing photographs has become an artistic practice that is not only accepted, but in many cases it is also expected. Not only did most of the girls in my study *not* seem to be affronted by the evolution of what some might regard as an Orwellian culture, they seemed eager to embrace it and seek out new literacy practices that might allow their images to be snapped up, altered, improved, uploaded, and shared in cyberspace. There does not appear to be a significant crisis of conscience in practices that carefully manipulate identity construction.

The enormous popularity of sites like YouTube and Facebook that provide the ability to upload almost anything from almost anywhere in almost any form has revolutionized the way youth can think about notions of identity and representation. Social communicative practices include the nearly constant reinvention of self, acted out through practices of updating and posting multiple profile pictures and images along with frequent status updates to share among sometimes hundreds of friends. These practices, in essence, tell vast social networks in a serial form: *this is who I am*, and *this is where I belong*, and *this is what I'm wearing now* and, *by the way, do you like what I'm wearing?* The mythic resonance of the notion that "you are who you pretend to be" harkens to the plotline of *Pygmalion* and Eliza Dolittle's mythical transformation and to the power of fantasy, where individuals are not limited by our histories but can have the power to recreate ourselves (Turkle, 1995, p. 192). One such opportunity to create or recreate identity is with the personalized avatars designed to be used in our online social spaces. WeeMees, designed to be email or instant messaging signatures, or even social networking profile pictures, provide users with the opportunity to say—*look, this is who I am.*

Using Avatars as Profile Pictures

Speaking to the possibility of only partial identity representation and the nearly constant identity (re)negotiation and (re)presentation within the shifting cultural landscape, the girls in this study engaged in a lively discussion around the importance of their Facebook profile pictures. That led to a discussion about which form would make a better profile picture: an avatar or a photograph? I asked the girls explicitly what might be the benefits of using one form over the other. Their responses provided a range of thoughts about what they could and could not do with both forms of representation. At issue was what purpose a profile picture was intended to serve on a social networking site. All of the girls ultimately preferred to use real photographs as their profile pictures on sites like Facebook. For some, it was the importance of posting something not only accurate but could serve as a public statement of identity. In this context, an avatar had the potential to express interests, wishes, or dreams in a way not possible with an unaltered photograph. For most of the girls the primary concern was that it be current.

For them, the fluid nature of social networking sites demands a level of engagement that is committed to keeping things fresh. While digital photographs seem to promise a realistic representation of who they are, they all believed that their profile pictures represented a statement about their potential cultural significance (though they did not use those exact words), and choosing a profile picture (in whatever form) was an act not to be taken lightly.

Current events

The pressure to keep current pictures posted on their Facebook pages was something the girls noted in their Forum discussions. Their reasons were varied but ultimately seemed tied to a kind of cultural currency within online social networking practices. Undercutting many of the girls' responses was the notion of an unwritten code of conduct and an expectation that they would keep the images on their profile pictures current. Butterflye explains how, in whatever form, this is critical. She also notes the challenge inherent in keeping current if individuals use avatars for their profile pictures.

> I think it's important to update your profile picture every so often, just to show that yes, you do change. To show a new hairstyle, or to show that you've grown up a bit, or whatever. I think it's important to show your current look in your profile picture so that people with whom you communicate through Facebook, for example, a friend who's moved to another province, what you look like and what's going on in your life. With avatars, it's slightly harder to do this, as it's not your own face in the picture, it's a generated image of you, almost a caricature. However, with avatars, it's easier to show your aspirations.

Butterflye's comment that profile pictures should be kept current ignited a flurry of responses from the girls who all agreed that it was essential. I wanted to get a sense of how feasible it would be to expect these girls to use an avatar in place of a photograph as their profile picture on Facebook—if only for a short period of time. In order to do that, however, I first needed to get a sense of how they viewed their profile pictures. What purpose did they serve? When asked how often they changed their profile pictures on Facebook, Livie explained that she didn't change her pictures often, but was guided instead by a desire to show her friends if she had done something significant. She explained:

> It really depends, I like to keep the same one for a while depending on how much I like it. If I go on trips and I have a lot of pictures I want has my profile picture I may change it twice a month.

Butterflye also reported using her profile pictures to stay current with things she had done and places she had been. For her, being current with these forms of representation is "incredibly" important. Her comments are positioned within the context of her being a constant user of Facebook, as she provides a cautionary note for others. She wrote:

> I'm on Facebook at least once every day (I'm addicted), and I think it's incredibly important that your profile picture gives the right impression to people. You want to show who you are, what you look like and maybe even one or two of your interests in just one picture, but you still don't want to give too much away, just in case. I change my profile picture fairly often. If I go on a vacation or I'm at a party and I like the picture of me, I'll use it as my profile picture.

For Roxy the importance of having a current profile picture on her Facebook page (in what ever form it happened to be) was a paramount consideration, as well. However, it was tied less to current events and more to her current look. She wrote:

> I think that you should update your pictures regularly so that people can see how you have changed, etc. I change my pictures usually whenever I get new pics up.

Cutie-Pi agreed. The fact that teenage girls often change their looks makes it even more imperative to keep profile pictures current. She writes:

> We are always changing our looks so I agree that if you want to be accurate profile picture can be changed quite often!

In fact, the thought of leaving a stale profile picture up was unfathomable for most girls in the study. Not only was there an underlying assumption that an old photograph would be inaccurate, the girls felt that they will be judged based on their looks (as we saw earlier). They wrote about the pressure they felt to represent themselves in a manner that is either in keeping with dominant social discourses (i.e., to represent themselves in a way others would think is pretty), or with the counter hegemonic discourses they have embraced (as with Livie's rejection of popular styles).

While Shorty made her avatar for this study, she only put it up on her Facebook page for a few hours. Despite reporting that she was happy with the way her avatar represents who she is, she is cautious about how she represents herself on this kind of semi-public space. Her observations about avatars and photographs highlight a central component of *any* form of visual representation, which is at the heart of autobiography. These forms of representation are necessarily partial. As well, the nature of narrating a self-story (in a written or visual form) is constructed and deliberate. She explains:

> I think pictures are just a second of your life represented. With avatars you can represent who you are more generally, I prefer using pictures because they show what you are doing or where you were when you took that picture and you can have your friends in with you.

The practice of including friends in her profile pictures was something that may not have been echoed by the other girls in their comments, but it was a practice in which nearly every girl had engaged. At one time or another during the course of the study, nearly every girl had a Facebook profile picture that included someone else with her. The inclusion of others in such pictures allows for a social statement of belonging that cannot be created with the WeeMee site, at least not yet.

When Questionmark addressed the notion of using an avatar as her profile picture she explained that she would need to make some changes to her avatar before posting it on Facebook. Recalling the challenges she had creating her avatar on the WeeMee site in the first place, one wonders how many obstacles she might encounter trying to create these avatars. She explains:

> If my avatar was going to be used as my display picture on Facebook then I would consider the time of year. For example in winter I might use my current avatar and in summer I might make a new one with a new background and different clothes. I might also consider what I like to do in that season, I might put a volleyball in my spring avatar because that is when I play volleyball most, and maybe a swimming related object in my summer avatar.

What her comments reveal is an understanding of context. For her, an avatar would need to represent time (as in the proper season), and events particular to that time (as in volleyball in the spring, or swimming in the summer). She also appears to be aware of her audience, that is the friends who would see the avatar-as-profile-picture. She is aware not only of the consideration of what this avatar might say about her—but also how her network of friends might read this avatar. What might it say? And what does she want them to think it says?

Livie also revealed that if she used her avatar as her profile picture she might want to change the clothes. Again, for her, the rationale is complex. It not only gets tied to her artistic and creative expression, but it is also related to notions of accuracy, audience, and context. Beyond that she highlights an understanding that a display picture (or profile picture) need not be limited to a self-image. For her the practice of creating a profile picture with an image *other than* herself also reflects moments in her personal journey with TSC. Her words speak of the pain and isolation of not fitting in, but they also help us to understand why she may not have been as keen as the other girls to use a photograph of her as a profile picture before now.

> I love to take photographs I was a photography student. There are so many pictures I would love as my display pictures I love people to see the places I've been. I've also had this long struggle with being happy with my appearance for a number of reasons actually I would have never had a real picture of me on Facebook or MSN, Yahoo any thing like that I would always make avatars through Yahoo and put them up. Now I'm more confident in who I am and the way I look that I want to put up pictures to show people I'm happy with myself :)

Recalling Livie's earlier comments about refusing to edit or touch her photographs, her desire to now put pictures of herself up points to a self-acceptance that might not have been obvious earlier. When we remember how limited she was with her attempt to construct a WeeMee, it is probably not surprising that she is not keen to post an avatar as her profile picture. No matter how much other girls argued that avatars might make good profile pictures, she was not going to buy into the notion that this avatar was a "wee Livie." She wrote in bold face to emphasize her point:

> **It is a good representation of me but thing is, it's not me it's a cartoon.**

Even though a digital picture of her would not *be* her in Plato's sense that it's an image of her, and a sunflower (or any other inanimate object she might choose for her profile picture) is also not her, rather it's a representation of one of her interests, Livie could not be sold on the idea of making her avatar her Facebook profile picture.

On the other hand, Roxy found that the difference between having a real picture or an avatar as her profile picture highlighted the potential for creating a strong connection between identity and appearance, particularly in terms of clothing choice. Remember that earlier Roxy had drawn a connection between her appearance and her personality. For her, appearance reflected her personality.

> I think that the difference of having an avatar as a profile picture is that it can reflect your personality a lot better because you can actually add what kind of clothes you want on it, and different hairstyles, etc. I think it shows more of who you are than a photograph.

The idea that her style of clothing (even if they are in virtual form) can make a statement about the kind of person she is suggests that Roxy believes that clothes do make the person. Even more to the point, she believes that particular clothes represent a particular kind of person. This makes me wonder why Roxy felt that a photograph would not represent who she is as accurately as an avatar could? Is it because the avatar is more deliberately constructed than a photograph? A photograph (presumably unaltered) would capture what she looks like in a particular moment. For many of the other girls, this very point is why they favored pictures over avatars.

However, Roxy's comment highlights a subtle distinction in terms of how it relates to her conflicted understanding of style and how it is connected to personality. It also reflects an understanding about her avatar's constructed style as it relates to her personal style. It suggests that what she wears in real life on any given day *does not necessarily* reflect who she is as accurately as a constructed avatar might. For Roxy, it is the deliberate nature of choice that gives her avatar more accuracy in terms of representing of who she is, generally speaking. Being able to pick out clothes and hairstyles for her avatar gives her the freedom to construct a sort of idealized version of who she thinks she is or who she wants others to think she is. She believes that the freedom to choose these style details gives her more control over how her personality is represented than might be possible with a photograph. Essentially, she says that her true style cannot be represented by what she wears in real-life. This surprised me, because in real life, would she not be wearing clothes that *are* her style? If not, then this speaks to the notion that outward appearance in general, and clothing in particular, *are not* accurate indicators of who she thinks she is in real life, only in the abstract.

As we think more about Roxy's comment, perhaps the conflict makes sense when we think about the clothes in our own closet. Are there items that get worn but that do not reflect who we think we are? Perhaps there are items that we have been given but that we would have never picked for ourselves, or perhaps there are items that have long out of style but that still serve a functional purpose. Taken this way, Roxy's comment begins to make sense. Perhaps for Roxy, identity is not tied to what we wear, rather to what our clothes represent, and it is that kind of representation that can be done more easily with an avatar.

With another perspective, Cutie-Pi found that the inability of avatars to portray "flaws" was actually a drawback for this form of representation. Her observation is interesting when we remember that she often alters her photographs to get rid of any flaws. She writes:

> I used my avatar as my profile picture for a while but as Livie said, I prefer real photographs. Yes the avatar can show a close representation of who you are but it's more fake than a actual human being. I do not have a perfect complexion nor do I have the "perfect" body shape that the avatars I have seen have. For both photographs and avatars: we're only judging appearances, a picture can't show you what a person is really like.

It is also interesting to note that she regards the cartoon WeeMee as having a perfect body (even with its disproportionately large head, and no nose). She acknowledges the inability for a picture or an avatar to "really" represent what a person is like. Is it even possible for an image to show what a person is like?

Butterflye provides a clue in her lengthy post that expresses what she believed were the critical differences between having a real picture or an avatar as a profile picture on social networking sites. For her, the possibilities available within the WeeMee site posed both representational opportunities and limitations. She began by explaining what she saw as the advantage of using both forms:

> I think you can accurately represent yourself with both photographs and avatars, if you know what you're doing. With avatars, you're limited to what the site selects for hairstyles, clothes and interests, but with photos, it's harder to show what you'd like to be in the future. Both have their limitations and both have their advantages, and it's really up to the user to decide which one to use.

> Creating an avatar, in my opinion, gives you more freedom than a photograph in some ways, and less freedom in others. For instance, you can change the background of your avatar; change the clothes, the mood, the hairstyle, pretty much whatever you want to change. However, you can also do this by simply taking or uploading a different picture. Also, with a photograph it's YOUR face that's in it.

The Pedagogical Implications of Slowing Down

One of the most significant observations from this study came in the last few days with the final responses and follow-up questions. Several girls revealed that they had never been challenged to slow down and critically reflect about the constructed nature of identity. However, by doing so here they reported having a deeper understanding of themselves and of how others might see them. When the girls in this study were first asked to consider who they think they are, and in relation to the avatars they created who they wanted others to think they are, a dialogue began around the perceptions of other teens, and how the girls often felt judged based on how they looked or what they were wearing. The girls' comments reveal a desire to make a good first impression. This desire takes on added weight when considered against the claims that the girls were limited to how they could express themselves based on limited options and financial restrictions within the avatar program itself. If belonging to a group, or gaining acceptance in a group, or the *perception* that one might gain acceptance with a group is tied, even in a small way, to looking and dressing in a particular way or to representing oneself in a particular way, then the commercial pressures that attempt to control desire (Shor, 2004) is undeniable. If appearance holds social currency, and desire cannot meet reality in terms of representation, then what is at stake for teenage girls?

The pedagogical considerations evolving out of that one set of collective observations demonstrate the importance of teaching students about how meanings and identities are regulated, shaped, and negotiated through discourses in popular culture. If left unattended, they get taken up, normalized and assumed as naturally occurring states of being. Giroux (1999) is even more explicit:

> At issue for parents, educators, and others is how culture, especially media culture, has become a substantial, if not the primary educational force in regulating the meanings, values, and tastes that set out the norms that offer up and legitimate particular subject positions —what it means to claim an identity. (p. 2 - 3)

When working critically with this avatar program as a text from popular culture and as a site explicitly designed to get youth to define and represent themselves, an opportunity to consider how such programs shape youth culture is present. Exploring the constructed nature of these avatars and questioning the origins of their representations and the self-perception of identity are projects worthy of the cultural studies quest for voice. In fact, in this regard it doesn't matter that the girls are not able to narrate their identity accurately within the limits of WeeWorld. It is the exploration of what couldn't be narrated that provides the richest pedagogical opportunity. In a critical sense, it is pedagogy that draws attention to the relationship between knowledge, authority and power, and more explicitly, to how knowledge gets taken up or denied. It questions relationships of power and how knowledge is implicated in these relationships. And it examines what Giroux calls the "circuits of power" that shape identities within social and historical discourses.

The critical interrogation of the assumptions behind this form of visual writing does not fit neatly into the modes of standardized accountability that are so desired by institutions that govern and regulate pedagogy and curriculum. The literature critical of the slow take-up of such progressive literacies is also vast. And what the literature clearly calls for is just such pedagogy (Coiro et al., 2008; Gee, 2003; Hagood, 2008; Knobel, 1999; Kress, 2003; Kress and van Leeuwen, 2006; Lankshear and Knobel, 2006, 2003; Thomas, 2007, 2004).

Because youth learn so much about identity and representation through the media, then it makes sense for educators to critically attend to relevant forms of media education in order to help students become critical and sophisticated citizens rather than merely and solely sophisticated consumers (Kellner and Share, 2007). By attending to the complex conceptual landscape avatar of construction, I argue that students should be allowed to read and write themselves visually and reflect on what these representations did and did not, could or could not say. By embracing avatar design as a legitimate form of social knowledge, educators and students have an opportunity to engage with core curricular notions of aesthetic expression, citizenship, identity and representation in a way that traditional print-centered texts cannot allow.

Even though media culture implicitly assumes (or encodes) society's hegemonic ideology where messages are designed to reproduce dominant principles, these representations also present a location for ideological struggle between dominant ideology, negotiated codes, or oppositional codes (Hall, 1999). The transformational possibilities resultant from this kind of self-exploratory writing rest in the writer's ability to examine "the breaks, fissures, aporias and absences in his/her text to probe more deeply into the culturally mediated themes and implications for social justice" (Shore, 2004, p. 78). But before these explorations can happen, a safe space for exploring must be created. In school, autobiography, especially in its visual manifestation, might provide one such space as it invites students to understand the constructed nature of the sources, structures, and frames of reference that shape identity. I asked the participants of my study whether or not they had ever done any work on autobiography in school, and if they had ever been asked to represent themselves visually. They responded that they had not.

However, for all the literature supporting the pedagogical importance of exploring notions of identity and representation in culturally situated texts, and for the invitation found in curricular documents for educators to engage the same, one might expect an exercise in identity construction (an any number of forms) might find its way, even in a small way, into the classroom. I asked the girls if they had ever done similar work in school, and their responses were all the same. Their answers point not only to a lack of this kind of work in their experience, but perhaps more importantly, to a desire to have it included, and recognition of the value it might hold. They understood that WeeMees are typically used for social purposes, and that Facebook profile pictures (in both picture and avatar form) are chosen for their social intent, not their educational purposes. However, the girls were able to see a value in bringing this playful, everyday literacy into the classroom. Butterflye wrote:

> I think that schools do have some business in the student's social lives, as it is the teacher's responsibility, for 8 hours a day, 5 days a week, to keep their students safe. It's only natural that they would want to discuss Internet safety, especially considering how popular websites like Facebook and MySpace are now. I think that schools and teachers have a certain place in the social and communication practices of students, but that a person's social life is their own.

Questionmark was clear about what the process of creating and critically discussing the process of creating did for her. Her comment also reveals what appears to be a revelation regarding a divide between who we think we are and who others think we are.

> This opportunity was amazing and it helped me find out more about myself by thinking about all of the questions on the forum. It has taught me about identity because when I looked at the other girls avatars I almost made a puzzle in my head and thought that by looking at an avatar that they made, I knew who they are, but when I read their responses to some of the questions, I realized that some people see themselves differently than others see them. This isn't a bad thing in my opinion, just something that I never really thought about before.

Butterflye sees a similar divide between who we think we are and who others think we are with avatars, even more so than with pictures. In her opinion, the disconnect between how the girls chose to represent themselves and how others interpreted these representations is made more obvious within the deliberate constructed nature of the avatars. Remember that Butterflye believed avatars could depict a person *generally* because they had the ability to project to the future and to represent dreams and wishes in a way that photographs could not. This engagement with who we hope to become was a key consideration for her. This disconnect also provided a valuable learning opportunity for Butterflye. She wrote:

> During the course of this study, I came to realize that people don't always see themselves as others see them, and that their avatars, more so than display pictures, really represented this.

A Matter of Collaborative Identity

From one perspective, the practice of carefully manipulated identity construction might be regarded as deceitful. Carefully staging and constructing an avatar designed to narrate (and/or silence) a version of who we are might be regarded as a deliberate attempt to shape perception. But is this practice really any different that the kind of performed identity we engage in every day as we dress and head out the door to greet the world? I wonder, do we not engage in a similar kind of careful selection and staging of our identity, dependent on who we will see and what we will do any given day? Finding a parallel between WeeWorld and our real world, are we not also limited by the choices we can afford as we look into our closets and decide what to wear? And furthermore, are our choices not determined by some other power? Are we not enticed by media advertisements to spend our money on new fashions and trendy accessories all aimed to better define who we are? In this sense, constructing an avatar to represent our identity is really not much different than getting dressed in the morning. However, just because the practice of constructing an avatar can be likened to an everyday practice does not mean it is not worthy of critical exploration. Quite the contrary.

The act of deliberately constructing an avatar, even with the intention to create an autobiographical telling, might be likened to the notion of creating a willing suspension of disbelief. English teachers everywhere are familiar with the act of performance that created a veil of truth where cardboard trees are seen as a forest and a darkened stage represents nighttime. When the girls created their avatars, they did not demonstrate a significant crisis when they were unable to find the choices they wanted to represent who they are. In fact, creating and posting autobiographical images (in multiple formats) is part of their social reality. Not only did most of the girls in my study not seem to be affronted by the evolution of what some might regard as an Orwellian culture, they seemed eager to embrace it and seek out discursive practices that might allow their images to be snapped up, altered, improved, uploaded, and shared in cyberspace.

What makes youth (re)present their identity in a manner that is socially acceptable? How much of how they represent themselves is in response to how they want others to see them? In other words, who do the girls want others to think they are? The girls in my study told me that they feel pressure to conform, and they admit to altering or editing images of themselves as a result of this pressure. Perception matters. When we recall that their avatars represent an attempt to carve out actual cultural and political significance, then we must critically attend to the considerations behind how these constructions are negotiated. When we know that these avatars are part of what marketers would have as an emerging trend in the colonization of childhood, then we must pay attention to how constructed identities are silenced and shaped. We ignore them only at our own peril.

Just as Bloustien understands the participants of her study to be active participants and collaborators in their own identity representation rather than victims of the camcorder's voyeuristic gaze, I also regard my participants as active in their own project of visual identity construction. Thomas (2007) found that "identity is shaped by desire and that desire is expressed through both language and image" (p. 182). In many ways, this reflects what I found in that it took the written explanation of a visual representation to more completely clarify, justify, or elaborate the intention supporting the manufactured considerations behind the avatars. The difference between the studies conducted by Bloustien, Thomas, and me, however, is that with Bloustien participants were able to capture their versions of their realities using camcorders, they could limit what they revealed through the lens as well as what they kept hidden and private. In the case of Thomas' avatars, participants were limited to a select number of forms available to them in Whyville. In my study, the girls were limited to what they revealed by choosing what they would say and what they would withhold, but also they were limited to the options and choices within the program, not to mention further limited if they chose (for whatever reason) not to purchase items for their avatars.

In this sense, the girls in my study learned that they are merely collaborators in this form of identity representation. As the girls attempt to construct an autobiographical avatar, they are being guided to choose from among a limited number of identity representations available to them as chosen and created by the anonymous other. Given the notion of such co-production, the question then becomes how accurate are these avatars as a representation of identity? How comfortable are the girls with these avatars as accurate visual representations?

Thomas (2007) notes that online, the confines of identity are not bound like they are in real life. "Online interaction strips away many of the usual semiotics of identity, which can be limiting, yet can also be liberating and offer the opportunity to tinker and play with elements of self" (p. 17). However, as I have argued in this book that within sites of avatar production, the usual semiotics of identity become merely re-inscribed in different terms. Turkle (1995, 2005) understands virtual space to be a laboratory for identity construction (as was the make-up bag, shopping mall and hair salon for girls in the 60s and 70s, for example). The difference is (notwithstanding the cost of the technology to hold this discursive practice in the first place) that in the online space identity reconstruction can be afforded more economically, more rapidly, and more publicly. In fact, the online space allows for constant (or nearly constant) reinvention, re-authoring, and re-writing. The salient question becomes, is online reinvention more or less accurate?

Looking Forward: Avatars Play at School

Coiro et al., 2008 remind us that in order to build a larger conceptual picture of what might be possible within a framework of new literacy practices, we must find ways to connect smaller pieces of research literature, such as the one offered here, to larger conceptual frameworks that bring together not only specific components but also substantial dimensions as they relate to macro concerns. By working with the project of constructing visual identity, a group of teenage girls had an opportunity to see how identity construction works. In a way, their project is not unlike the work that Buckingham (2003) has done in media classes where students have an opportunity to reflect upon their own fluid perceptions about and within a media culture. I argue that creating autobiographical avatars, could quite comfortably be accepted as a form of textual production. Buckingham argues that such texts encourage a "space for play, in which unspeakable desires can be spoken and totalizing discourses transgressed and undermined" (p. 325). In this sense, when students are encouraged to reflect upon the process of construction and the decisions behind their semiotic choices, an opportunity arises to see that play and rationality are not necessarily opposed to one another. He adds that by accepting the existence of such texts in the classroom "desires and experiences that are often left unspoken in schools" are given a legitimate space in the classroom where they "often policed out of existence" (p. 325).

Kenway and Bullen (2001) suggest that the "knowledge politics" within a consumer culture of childhood warrant, a downright rebellion against formal schooling practices. To that end, it would seem that schools *should be* presenting ever-urgent cases for connecting the prevailing media culture with the modernist project of education with its focus on rational thinking, critical consumers and informed citizenship. No longer can teachers claim to be the moral authority over media texts when young people are expert producers and consumers of these media texts. Buckingham argues that even in cases where teachers have managed to engage media culture successfully in the classroom, "they have sought to colonize students for their own purposes," and through this process they often end up "re-inscribing traditional notions of what counts as valid knowledge" (p. 314). It would be imperative then that any in-class research be student guided and create what Kelly (2006) referred to as that "safe space" for student voices to emerge.

Building Pedagogical Bridges with Avatars

By looking at avatar creation within twin frames as a visual autobiography and a playful new literacy, deliberately autobiographical avatar construction can find a home in a realm that has been traditionally reserved for print text. By going beyond the skills-oriented pedagogies of the past, Street (1995) suggests that "Those who write from a critical literacy perspective call for teachers to uncover these power dynamics for kids and that all voices in our classrooms need to be allowed to be heard, regardless of preference of medium" (p. 7). By acknowledging the multiple and often conflicting ways that students struggle in a tangled nexus of power, pleasure, desire, and identity (Currie and Kelly, 2006), I am suggesting that there is a pedagogical opportunity for an exploration into the power dynamics that inform these discursive practices. Besides the critical engagement that comes from self-reflective work, such visual autobiographies might provide an opportunity to give voice to those most affected by society's hegemony by allowing students to consider how identity is shaped and even who shapes it.

As technology and programming continue to advance, avatar creation programs will undoubtedly evolve to include a broader range of possibilities. If the girls in this study had been given money and unrestricted access to choose whatever items they wanted in the avatar construction process, it would be interesting to know if they would tell their stories differently. Would the addition of commodified items, positioned as valuable, impact a desire to represent the self in a different way? Would there be a difference between how boys and girls take up the project of autobiographical avatar production? Further research could explore these questions.

Bringing autobiographical avatars and social online spaces into the classroom might also answer the call for youth to create alternative forms of media self-representations as suggested by Kelly (2006). Kelly finds that youth have difficulty getting their real stories told in mainstream venues because of the way "corporate dominated mainstream media filter out or distort their attempts to publicize alternative discourses" (p. 36). To that end, she has found that youth have reported success through such publications as "zines," or websites. I offer that creating avatars within one of these alternative discursive spaces and using it as a point of analysis in the classroom might also provide an opportunity for youth to maintain the control over their own voice through these publications.

From what we know about teenage identity, belonging and acceptance are among the most often cited concerns of youth (Bloustien, 2003; Kelly, Pomerantz and Currie, 2006; Driscoll, 2002). As the divide between the real world and school continues to widen, finding a genre to bridge the gap seems to increase in urgency. This literature also sheds light on what might be possible when students are encouraged to engage in a genre of autobiographical writing/representing in an attempt to trouble the social construction of self within a quest for different perspectives. McRobbie (1994) suggests that youth styles and preferences offer an "intense activity of cultural production" (p. 161) in central activities of cultural production and social transformation. To that end, autobiographical avatars might be viewed as instruments of agency or forms of resistance within the milieu of social and cultural belonging. The questions surrounding the construction or "writing" of these virtual selves become especially salient when we remember that "the body does not disappear in cyberspace, and that the on-line interactions of a mediated body have consequences in the mundane world of the classroom" (Kolko, 1999, p. 177).

We saw implications of bodies that refused to disappear online when Livie revealed that she could not represent her TSC, and Questionmark could not represent her broken leg. One might be tempted to blame this on the nature of co-production or co-authoring of these avatars as the semiotic choices are limited to those provided by the producers of the avatar-making programs. Indeed, these factors do contribute to the limiting manner by which avatars can be (or cannot be) written. However, in that sense, all forms of autobiography are necessarily limited. The limitations come not only in the form of the desire to tell or to choice to veil the self, but also in the command the author has over the language used in the telling. Voice, then, is limited by the capacity to tell. When the girls were not able to find the semiotic choices they needed to visually write their stories, they were denied voice. Such silencing may be akin to trying to write in a foreign language.

However, what I saw with the girls who has their first stories silenced by the inability to tell what they wanted to led to other aspects of their stories getting told—aspects we might have never seen had their first choices been written. Such pedagogical opportunities might easily slip past if we are not paying attention. When Livie could not tell the story of her TSC, she opted to choose eyelashes for her avatar, explaining that she did not want her avatar to look like a boy. In spite of connecting strongly with a fashion that appears to be opposed to an "emphasized femininity" (Kelly et al., 2006), this choice is telling. When Questionmark had an element of her story silenced, she simply turned to another. When the story of a broken-legged volleyball player could not be told, we got to see the articulate young student and schoolgirl instead. A simple shift in stories allows for a glimpse into that which may otherwise have remained silenced.

Through the analysis of the avatars created for this research, autobiography has been placed in a visual realm as a way of knowing typically reserved for the academically privileged written word. If language and discourse are not neutral in any form and are not natural modes of communication, but rather are entangled within power relations as well as social and historical phenomena, then the way we (re)present ourselves is tainted by discursive practice as well as by social and power relationships. As such, there is an inherent instability in meanings—specifically in terms like race, gender, and sex as we explore the "semiotics of identity" (Thomas, 2007). According to Hall (1999) it is impossible to separate understanding from how meaning is created. Simply put, how we make meaning in our world depends on the language we use to externalize our meaning, and this depends on what we bring to the concept being represented. The very act of representing a concept is not fixed, but instead it is constitutive and unique, tangled within power relations. In this sense, social and historical occurrences, our speech, our discursive practices, our social relations, and our power relationships are contaminated.

Looking Forward

Share (2004) asks, "how does school, a public and social space become a more hospitable place for self-writing? Where can students talk to each other about the ways in which they use writing as a support through the struggle of adolescence" (p. 82)? It is not the actual creating of these autobiographical avatars that makes them significant inclusions to an English pedagogy, it is in the analysis of how they were created, in the consideration of what was said and what was left out, in what students wanted to say but could not, and what they were forced to say instead. Echoing a theme that emerged from Kelly's (2006) work, Share (2004) finds that such "writing offers a safe place where students can take apart the culture and come to know themselves" (p. 82).

While education and pedagogy within the discipline of English still operate from the privileged place of the printed word, I do not expect visual literacy practices in the form of avatar design to take over English language arts classrooms like a wild fire. Engaging in the excavation of complex layers of sedimented knowledge is complex and time-consuming work, and it is certainly not for the faint of heart. It is among the most rewarding and meaningful work that I believe can be done in an English classroom. Not only does it allow students to experiment in a visual semiotic forms of meaning making that they are already good at, it asks them to work with a subject they are intimately familiar with and expert in (themselves). The questions that dig layers below the veneer of physical representation and outward appearance shed light on how constructed realities have been borne out in the representation of self.

Back to the Beginning

"Closing by return" was a favorite writing technique of my former high school teacher, and it also makes sense to return to the observation that provided the genesis for this research as a way to attempt to make sense of it. I return to Cooper's morning show observation that he could not find any fat avatars within the gaming culture. I recall a similar observation from Thomas (2004) that appeared to have been made almost as much in passing in her research on digital literacies of the cybergirl. And I recall the three body options available for WeeMees, none of which could possibly be considered "fat." I also recall that many "flaws" were not possible to represent on a WeeMee at the time my study was conducted. There were no options for pimples, misplaced dimples, cellulite, scars, or tumors. No crutches, no tattoos, and no body piercings other than those implied on earlobes existed then either. In this context it makes sense that "fat" avatars were not possible, perhaps because being overweight represents a pathologized social and cultural taboo. Driscoll (2002) tells us "health models are highly visible in late modern everyday life, from educational systems through changing medical standards to media dissemination of diet and weight-loss narratives and advertisements" (p. 253). The dominant message is clear: be thin, and you look great. If you are overweight, then you have some work to do. What the non-existence of fat avatars reflects then is what we might expect within a wider discourse of health and media representations.

In the end, the fact that no fat WeeMees existed really didn't matter. None of the girls in my study lamented that they could not represent themselves in a larger size. But if we stop to think about it, how many of us would? Just like the teachers picking out their outfits for parent teacher interviews or youth creating a profile picture to post on Facebook, the idea of presenting oneself in the best light possible can be read as an exercise in acceptance and social conformity. It can also be read as an exercise in social expectation. When I began this research, I had a hunch that young girls would be troubled if they could not represent who they are or who they think they are with accuracy. And there were certainly occasions when the girls were limited by the choices available to them. Since that time I have had an opportunity to correspond with Mike Kinsella, the creator of WeeWorld.com regarding some of the artistic choices that are available on the site. We discussed what I had initially seen as limited options on the WeeWorld site and the repercussions this had for finding proper skin tones and ability/disability options. This discussion resulted in an enlightening exchange. And as is often the case when one begins to ask questions, it became clear that the decisions to include or exclude certain racial features were carefully considered, and the voices of users were considered. Kinsella wrote:

> The WeeMee was the first on-line personal virtual character and we were very careful to try and be as inclusive as possible. We did quite a bit of user group research to try and define what would be viewed as representative and what could be misconstrued as racist for example. There were some real surprises, for example when we added "Oriental" eyes there was a lot of disquiet about how they should be slanted etc. A lot of negative energy if you will. The feedback was that Oriental users did not want that feature. To me it was bizarre but hey the customer is always right.
>
> You can imagine Connie how difficult it is to represent all possible permutations of life essentially, but we have tried…honest. A lot of the newer Tween sites that have essentially tried to ape WeeWorld's success, seem to miss the point by trying to over-sexualize the teen group and completely ignore the fact that they are developing human beings with interests and issues. I have seen WeeMees discuss the death of a parent and have their virtual WeeMee friends offer support and condolences. WeeMees practise going to the prom or align themselves with Green issues. It's a rite of passage that wasn't there when I was growing up. As you suggest it's another channel to try out stuff and find out who you are. For all its cartoon quality it's a real community where users are more confident in expressing their feelings from behind the WeeMee mask than they are in "real" life. Quite fascinating. (Personal email communication, June 5, 2009)

The notion of the WeeMee being a mask is a fascinating one. Like Butler's performance or masquerade, perhaps the personalized avatar is best understood as something that is put on; something worn in digital spaces, and in places of social networking. As Thomas (2007) points out, even though cyberspace may be a disembodied space, "the lived experience of participating in virtual worlds becomes an embodied phenomenological experience" (p. 155). Even in this embodied state, however, this work of exploring identity and how it is represented can never be done completely. Approaching the creation of the avatars, these texts represent a highly staged representation of self—a document of the self in the making, a self in process—or simply a snapshot of the self at one culturally located moment in time. However, these avatars, despite their intention to be so, cannot ever be complete because we are always and only ever partially able to represent whom we are. One might successfully trace the process of making and remaking these avatars rather than just examine the final finished product. However, it must first be acknowledged that identity is never finished; it always involves a process of trying on and changing; making and remaking.

In the final chapter, I will provide an argument for how the kind of avatar construction examined though this study might find a legitimate home within the form of media literacy espoused by Cope and Kalantzis (1999), Kellner and Share (2007), and Kress (2003). If autobiographical avatar design finds a home in English language arts or media classrooms, it could allow for a critique of ideology as it welcomes the kind of analysis that questions the politics of representation. For those in marginalized groups, new technologies and new literacy practices can provide a means for them to find a voice and claim agency. For those members of the dominant group, on the other hand, this form of media literacy that engages the social realities by placing them under a critical lens. The question that remains is whether educators will be brave enough to break with the traditional pedagogies and not only ask students "who do you think you are?" but critically explore the vital political space they attempt to claim in their constructed responses. Within a discourse of social justice, making visible the constructed nature of girlhood as did Kelly, Pomerantz and Currie (2006) allows for a pedagogy that considers how gendered identities get enacted or embodied online and how they reflect wider discourses offline. The online nature of chat rooms, social utility sites and instant messaging allows to deliberation and reflection within the social communicative process. "Because online communications are textual, they are 'frozen,' thus rendering them more open to girls' critical interrogation across time" (p. 23). While these researchers suggest that educators ask their students to keep a journal to reflect on social gender construction, they also propose that creating avatars might present a pedagogical opportunity for students and educators alike. Moreover, I would suggest that constructing avatars of either the autobiographical or alter ego variety might open discussions to gendered identity construction in meaningful ways. Research that examines the comparison of both visual and traditionally written autobiographies might shed light on the pedagogical potential for such exploration.

Chapter Eight

DIY: Making Avatars in English Class

Teaching and learning the culture of the book is no longer the staple of what it means to be literate. Children learn more from exposure to popular cultural forms, which provide a new cultural register of what it means to be literate. This suggests a cultural pedagogy, rooted in cultural practices, that utilizes students' knowledge and experience of popular cultural forms. Students should be taught to critically analyze the messages produced by the electronically mediated popular culture, but they must also be able to master the skills and technology to produce these forms, making their own films, videos, and music.

Henry Giroux

The Shifting Ground of English

Once the cornerstone of English curricula, literacy and what it means to be literate have shifted—significantly so. It has been widely acknowledged that the definition of literacy includes far more than the ability to decode print text. Meaning is constructed and interpreted from all forms of text, not just from print. Evolving technologies are not merely tools to disseminate old forms of representation through newer and flashier means; rather, evolving technology itself can invite new ways of making meaning, creating, and reading text (Cope and Kalantzis, 1999; Kress, 2003). At a time when policy makers continue to privilege literacy in traditional print terms and call on schools to be accountable for ensuring that all students achieve literacy proficiency, there are those who believe literacy education requires a more expansive vision specifically for those students who are systematically disadvantaged (Coiro et al., 2007): "Overcoming this disadvantage presupposes becoming even clearer about what constitutes new literacies than political constituencies currently are about what constitutes conventional literacy" (p. 9).

Making the distinction clear, however, seems like an uphill battle in some locations. In spite of what the literature and the experts in new literacies tell us, the political leadership guiding curricular initiatives in Atlantic Canada are either ignoring or missing the point of new literacy pedagogies. With this kind of political leadership there can be little wonder why educators are failing to embrace new literacy pedagogies in their classrooms. Instead of asking questions about the purpose of school, the conceptualization of how curricula is organized, what counts as literacy, and how educators approach the pedagogical act of knowledge production, the educational leadership in Atlantic Canada is leading teachers off a cliff to nowhere. In an action plan released in September 2009 by the Council of Atlantic Ministers of Education and Training entitled "Literacy—Key to Learning and Path to Prosperity: An Action Plan for Atlantic Canada, 2009-2014" there is not one mention of new literacy practices. No mention is made of visual literacy, critical literacy, media literacy or multimodal literacy. Instead, literacy here remains steeped in an outdated and narrowly conceived print-centered tradition and wrapped in a tidy package promising job prosperity.

So it is with the caution heeded to become clearer about what constitutes new literacies that I will attempt to make clear that applications to English curricula can make avatar construction a valid form of new literacy. Underlying my argument is a belief that ignoring multimodal texts with all of their embedded social and cultural significance is a grave error. When educators fail to understand what is at stake by privileging only a print-centered curriculum we become complicit in the systemic harm that dominant discourses may cause. We must learn more about identity and about how to behave through the media in all of its various forms, and we must critically attend to media education in order to help students become critical and sophisticated citizens, not just sophisticated consumers (Dolby, 2003; Giroux, 1999). "A critical cultural and media literacy, divorced from the cultural and contradictory experiences of everyday life, can readily deteriorate into another set of unimaginative print-based exercises" (Luke, 1997, p. 46). For teachers, being able to acknowledge the experiences of their students and take seriously their individual voices means not slipping into the familiar celebration of personal response narratives but bravely and boldly embracing the popular as pedagogical. And while educators may fall back on the cry that we must teach to the standardized test (that exists in the form of twelfth grade public examinations here in Newfoundland and Labrador), it is possible for a playful everyday literacy practice to find a home in the classroom. Elsewhere I have argued that avatar design might offer an opportunity to bridge the gap that exists between curriculum intent and practice in Atlantic Canada (Morrison, 2009) where even with guiding foundation documents inviting educators to include multimodal forms of representation in their English classes, the strict adherence to written examinations sends a clear message that the only form of meaning-making with value is the written word. If it can happen here, it can surely happen elsewhere.

This final chapter offers an argument for introducing avatar design to secondary English language arts curricula as a kind of bridge between curricular intent and practice. Drawing on a cultural studies framework, I suggest that the form of visual, autobiographical representation (or avatar creation) discussed throughout this book ought to be positioned as a legitimate source of social knowledge that combines the academic rigor of autobiography with a semiotic approach to multimodal forms of representation within the boundaries of the English curriculum. Finally, I will offer a number of activities and exercises that take avatar creation a step further in order to engage youth in a number of new literacy practices that will make their English classes more meaningful, collaborative, participatory, and fun.

What Is the Purpose of the English Curriculum?

In order to have a discussion of what English as a discipline might look like through a cultural studies lens, I must first situate the discipline within a brief cultural, historical and economic context. Over the past century, English as a discipline of study has represented more than a place from which to transmit information or skills. In its numerous forms, English has served as a vehicle for social stability, morality, social control or cultural emancipation, particularly in times of historic, social, and economic instability (Ball, Kenny, Gardiner, 1990; Berlin, 1993; Pirie, 1992; Willinsky, 2000, 1998). Whether clinging to an elitist and outdated literary canon or providing a progressive or radical location that empowers the working class or marginalized groups, the relationship between English, literacy, the citizen, and the state highlights the evolving struggle among competing paradigms within English language arts education. It has evolved from a vulgar, cheap, educational alternative to the Classics, to a place as a gatekeeper subject with mandated outcomes, standards, and competencies. Within its numerous incarnations, English has informed political epistemology by positioning the student differently in relation to the subject knowledge, teacher, and state. In some camps, English has been implicated in the perpetuation of social inequality and hegemony, and it is out of this location that a cultural studies version of English evolves, in part, as an attempt to provide a space for democratic relations for marginalized or disavowed groups. By exploring the deeper social, political, historic, and economic systems that affect and inform texts and discursive practices, English as cultural studies becomes a multi- or trans-disciplinary educational project, moving back and forth between specific cultural texts and their place in a larger sets of discourses (Morgan, 2000).

Historically, English as a subject evolved to develop literacy in Britain in the late 1800s as the final phase of British Imperialism's colonizing project and in response to the expanding technological ability to mass-produce print texts (Willinsky, 2000). In the nineteenth century, reading, writing, and literacy together would become what we now know as the subject of English and attempt to provide social stability. It would promote a common language, instill a national pride, and endorse a cultural heritage (Buckingham and Sefton-Green, 1994) for the masses of working class who were regarded to be in a state of moral decay (Ball et al., 1990). This belief was bolstered by 'scientific' studies, which established Anglo-Saxons as a superior 'racial' tribe (Berlin, 1993). A canon of an Anglo-Protestant literature attempted at once to replace the position occupied by Latin and Greek and also sought to revive and secure the Anglo-Saxon heritage within a ruling group now threatened by increased immigration. Within the academy, English served this purpose by creating a hierarchy of culture. A key figure in the establishment of the literary elements of high and low culture was Matthew Arnold who believed that literature provided the working class with something to indulge in and look up to. As a civilizing project its high moral purpose was to minimize, if not eradicate, the differences between classes.

During the 1930s and 1940s in Britain, Leavis and the Cambridge school suggested that social harmony could be achieved through literature in English and, in particular, through the establishment of a literary canon with a moral vision that could help the working class determine good from bad in art, literature, and cinema. As a practical and educational project, Leavisite English remained through the moral panics of both world wars, and some argue that it continues to thrive in places yet today (Morgan, 1995; Pirie, 1993). In the 1950s this movement, combined with a deskilled labor force and an employment economy as mass culture developed, rose in popularity and threatened established moral sensibilities and values (During, 1999). In response, English studies provided a refuge with ethical and political values central to the democratic educational mission, as it remained the historical center of liberal education (Berlin, 1993).

Ball et al., (1990) provide an account of the shifts in paradigms which occur with the study of English. By the 1960s Leavisite English was being critiqued for its high moral purpose and its refusal to budge from the canon while the learner and first-hand meaning and the daily life of the authentic child were becoming important as an educational project. Now more like an anthropologist than a preacher, the English teacher began collecting and mapping cultural experiences, paying particular attention to the values of subjugated groups (working class, blacks, and women, for example). In this movement, literature focused less on standard forms of expression in its accompanying form and format and embraced a pluralistic vision of values and morals. With this, there was a growing discomfort in exclusively promoting the morality of a group of white, dead, male authors (hooks, 2003). At this time, a multi-disciplinary approach to literature provided a glimpse into a future notion of English as culture studies in its broad scope of texts and sources. Teaching methods promoted a greater sense of autonomy and freedom to students as teachers acted as facilitators; mixed groups replaced streaming; oracy gained acceptance; and emphasis and there was a focus on learning rather than on teaching. Finally, this period saw a deliberate attempt to engage with student experiences in an attempt to make curriculum relevant.

At this time a distinction between the London and Cambridge schools was manifested not in two separate versions of English but rather in two separate visions of society, civilization, and citizenship (Ball et al., 1990). Within the Cambridge version, English teachers preserved the great literary heritage with a nostalgic harkening back to a better time when the social order and morality were investments of society. By contrast, the London version of English celebrated the immediacy of the student experiences by focusing on social injustices and personal experience and took seriously the lack of opportunity and alienation suffered by working class children (Buckingham and Sefton-Green, 1994). It also emphasized solidarity rather than upward mobility. As well, within the London position divisions between progressive and radical educators were highlighted by differences in pedagogical approaches. Willinsky (2000) points to the progressive educational movement as the greatest challenge to education during the past century. John Dewey stated that in order to create a democratic curriculum, the center of the curriculum should no longer be the great works of literature but the experience of the child instead. Within progressive camps, mixed ability groups, creative writing, worksheets, and themed projects experience celebrated working class culture as "vital, meaningful and valid" (Ball et al., 1990) in its culture, language, and self-expression. Meanwhile, radical educators inched ever closer to a cultural studies approach to English as they moved beyond a celebration of working class life with a critical analysis of the political, social, and economic conditions that produce social inequity. Critical literacy and culture's hegemonic effects challenged the established curriculum.

What Is English for?

Recent curriculum documents for English Language Arts teachers in Atlantic Canada and elsewhere in Canada (Burn and Nixon, 2005) draw on globalization, multiple intelligence theories, learning theories, new technologies, and evolving textual constructions. Our common English curriculum in Atlantic Canada requires students to read and write, listen and speak, view and represent. They are meant to engage with and produce their own visual texts in both still and moving form. An expanded notion of text moves beyond a print-based definition to one which includes a definition that embraces any oral, written or visual language event. The definition of literacy has evolved to include those expressions (besides print text) which extend the conceptual landscape to ground meaning making. This expanded version of literacy willingly encompasses images, sounds, and gestures, not to mention the multimodal expressions of meaning found in wireless and digital forms of expression (Kress, 2003; Thoman and Jolls, 2004). For Barrell and Hammett, the curricular documents in Atlantic Canada are not only "well defined" but also "quite radical in their breadth and vision" (p. 15). They argue, "transmission models" of teaching are replaced by "inquiry and project based learning" while "representations of student learning now include visual and other non-traditional ways of representing knowledge. Online publishing and broadcasting of student work is encouraged" (p. 15).

Burn and Nixon (2005) explain that along with Canada, parts of New Zealand and Australia have also afforded the visual image "an equal place alongside reading, writing and speaking as cornerstones of the English curriculum" (p. 2). The authors acknowledge that while the viewing component within the English curriculum has seen a more rapid take-up in places like Canada, New Zealand and Australia, the production of visual texts has been more slowly integrated as common pedagogical practice. They argue that here, representation within the English curriculum in the United Kingdom is denied a place of endorsement at the root of public accountability. Since examinations in English remain "resolutely monomodal" there and for the most part here as well, as print text remains the privileged form of meaning making and assessment. The problem is not that curriculum developers don't understand what needs to be done; the problem is that what needs to be done isn't getting done. However, before we blame educators for ignoring the intention of their curricular guides and foundational documents, we must remember that they are serving the master of accountability—the standardized tests and public examinations.

In some locations English has shifted from a canon-based curriculum to a discipline on the verge of becoming a curriculum that focuses on communication, as it has in South Africa (Kress, 2005). The shift to a semiotic version of English as opposed to one that is strictly of a linguistic frame represents a turn toward cultural studies in its acceptance of popular media texts and its willingness to hear the subjugated voices that had been silenced by traditional authoritarian and canon-based pedagogies. Besides recognizing the multimodal text as a legitimate from of meaning making within the English curriculum, Kress argues "one needs to see language as partial" (p. 97). Written language alone is incapable of capturing the richness of experience we might attempt to describe because language is limited, and by extension we are limited when we attempt to rely on language alone.

If written language alone were a sufficient medium for narrative, description, argument, or persuasion, we would still stand on the street corners handing out written pamphlets to disseminate our information. But we don't because we have access to technology that allows us to layer our written words with images, sound and movement. Our evolving technology enables not only rapid dispersal of information, but also it provides an opportunity for shared conversations and new forms of knowledge creation across space and time. It's as if the interactive advantages of the oral cultures of the past have met the advantages of a written culture. It is no longer a case of either /or; it's now both and more.

Kress (2005) states, "What English is for has been, and should continue to be, the issue of how we represent ourselves in our world and how we make sense of representations for us in our world" (p. 98). I agree. Despite my enthusiasm for avatars, I am not advocating ditching the written word in favor of creating cartoon images. In fact, in my explanation of some of the new literacy activities I suggest later in this chapter, I will ask that students draw heavily on the written word as it works in tandem with the avatars to create meaning. However, my argument for more inclusive and expansive forms of representation acknowledges that there are times when images do a better job at representing than words do.

Drawing from Barthes, Kress (2005) invites educators to ask students what forms of communication are relevant to them (as opposed to having forms of communication imposed upon them by those in power). The similar call for curriculum that is relevant to students is not something new (Davis et al., 2008). Not commonly taken up by educators, however, is a broad acceptance that the forms of communication that students use in their social practices (like instant messaging or social networking, for example) should be valued. We regularly hear discourses about the degradation of spelling, grammar and usage being blamed on texting and instant messaging. Kress (2005) asks educators to include these forms of communication without apology. He explains that English has traditionally been a curriculum of values, but he urges that instead it should become a curriculum "not of ethical systems, but of principles of making ethical judgments, that is, judgments about value" (p. 99). For Kress, the question of the purpose of English is a question about "how we represent ourselves in the world and how we make sense of representations for us in our world" (p. 98). Added to this, I ask, what is the value of including autobiographical avatars in the English language arts classroom? Can they be justified as forms of visual writing, visual autobiography, cultural artifact or new literacy? In order to consider the specifics of plopping WeeMee avatars into the English curriculum beside the likes of *Julius Caesar* and *To Kill a Mockingbird*, I look to Kress (2005) to consider broader questions like: what is the purpose of the English curriculum, what is English for, and what should English do? I would add, how do practices in visual literacy fit within the notions of what English is designed to do? These questions serve as a guide for me here.

Situating the Visual and Multimodal in English

Though we might think of the discipline of English being traditionally and overwhelmingly about our relationship with the printed word, the relationship between the discipline of English and the visual image is a long and storied one (Burn and Nixon, 2005). In fact, Burn and Nixon cite a number of historical examples that elucidate this relationship:

> The illuminated manuscripts of medieval romance; the woodcuts of 17C chapbooks and 18C broadsheet ballads; the painting and poetry of the pre-Raphaelites; Dickens illustrated by Cruikshank, Milton by Blake, Coleridge by Doré, Ted Hughes by Leonard Baskin; the art of the modern picture book; the graphic novel; the comic strip from DC and Marvel to manga, the modern audio-visual narratives of film, television and computer games. (p. 1)

Using David Holbrook's seminal textbook *English for Maturity* (1961) as an example of how a text could influence a generation of educators to steer clear of the lowbrow meaning making texts from popular culture, Burn and Nixon argue that including visual and multimodal texts in the English classroom has historically depended on three intellectual arguments. The first argument is semiotic in nature and depends on Saussure's seminal linguistic triad of the signified, the sign, and the signifier. Here *signs* were understood to have two features: they gain meaning through their relationships to each other rather than through their relationship to something outside language. The *sign* is broken into *signifier*, which often takes form as a written or spoken word, sound, or visual appearance of a word, a phrase, or an image, and the *signified,* which can be understood as a concept or representation or meaning. As Saussure understood it, if things/objects/concepts named by language already existed or pre-existed outside language, then exact translations would be possible across languages—but they don't. Since humans are creatures of difference, the relationship between signifier and signified is arbitrary. There are no givens in a language that is based on differential, though not entirely disordered, meanings. The differences found in *signifieds* were understood to exist interrelated in complex structures (hence structuralism) or relations. Using an overly simplistic example, the differential pair mother/father relates to the pair male/female,\ and even to the pair parent/child (Blake et al., 1998). To learn a language is to understand the complex structures of signifieds that exist within it. The structuralist argument follows that communication between subjects would not be possible between private language systems unless some common ground could be found. Poststructuralists took Saussure's linguistic triad another step by expressing an interest in the *origins* of the relationships to the word (particularly as they relate to power and the unconscious) by demonstrating that meanings *are* unstable and that language and discourse *are not* neutral, nor are they natural modes of communication.

The second argument for including visual texts in the English classroom is multimodal in nature. Kress (2005) argues for the social semiotics of the visual and multimodal image. By encouraging students to produce and create texts in multimodal forms, he encourages English teachers make room for genuine exploration (a notion also held by Buckingham (2003). By presenting an argument for the inclusion of multimodal texts, as apposed to the strict and rigid adherence to texts in their print form, Kress (2005) suggests that seeing texts as multimodal enables them to hold layers of meaning, each partial and incomplete, but nonetheless necessary to the contribution of the greater whole. This reconsideration of the boundaries, which hold language within the English curriculum, helps to frame avatar design within that same curriculum as a legitimate form of study. In what Kress argues is a return to practical criticism, the semiotic details of how something is represented get taken a step further to consider where elements fit historically. As educators did with the historical specificity and historical locations of words, Kress suggests that educators ask students to pay attention to the details, except this time, "the frame is set differently, much more widely" (p. 98). While he suggests details like print layout, font, style, and size be considered as layers of meaning in a text, I add that deliberately adding images, and at times self-images to writing, or even in place of it, a greater opportunity for meaning making is encouraged.

The third argument is cultural and tied to William's (1958) version of cultural studies that recognizes popular media texts as sites of "authentic culture of ordinary people" (Burn and Nixon, 2005, p. 1). According to Arthur Applebee (in Bush, 1995) English curriculum should ideally enhance and maintain the conversational feature of a culture. In that sense, curriculum should invite students into the culturally relevant conversation. In fact, this notion speaks to a return of English's earlier intents (Pirie, 1993). For many years, Giroux (1994) has argued that texts from "everyday life" (p. 112) should be allowed to enter into the classroom in order to legitimately be positioned as forms of social knowledge. Kumashiro (2001) argues that English is the discipline most often critiqued for teaching partial materials because of its reliance on a canon. Along with the stereotypes and mis-knowledges that come from families, peers and the media, Kumashiro (2001) explains that students are also influenced by the "capitalist structures and colonialist ideologies" (p. 6) that infuse English curricula and constitute their underlying story. Over a decade and a half ago Pirie pointed out that we remain in the shadow of a legacy of nineteenth century schoolmasters who saw literature as secular scriptures. Unfortunately, his words still resonate truth today.

> Our training as teachers of English may have inculcated us in a conviction that popular culture is debased and shallow and that great works of literature are somehow better for the soul; in its most malignant form this becomes a battle to preserve the citadel of high culture against the barbarians at the gate. (Pirie, 1993, p. 23)

He asks, "With that kind of mission, you're hardly likely to encourage students to scrutinize your "scriptures" as artifact" (p. 21). When I work with pre-service teachers in English methodology courses, they come full of an expectation that they will become the guardians of the canon and that they will maintain literature's location as the citadel of high culture. They come to the program, in most cases, fresh off an English degree and they are proud of what they have learned. However, as the year progresses, and as they return from their internships, they see the value of connecting to students at a place of interest and relevance. They embrace opportunities to use new and evolving technology in the classroom and they see the need to include collaborative pedagogies in their classrooms.

These three arguments—the semiotic, the multimodal, and the cultural—all play an integral role in how my version or vision of English is conceived. The question of the degree to which any of youth's new literacy practices should or should not make their way into the English curriculum remains a matter of scholarly debate. The shift to a semiotic version of English as opposed to one that is strictly of a linguistic frame represents a turn toward cultural studies in its acceptance of popular media texts and its willingness to hear the subjugated voices that had been silenced by traditional authoritarian and canon-based pedagogies. Besides recognizing the multimodal text as a legitimate form of meaning making within the English curriculum, Kress argues "one needs to see language as partial" (p. 97). By encouraging students to produce and create texts in multimodal forms, English teachers make room for genuine exploration (a notion also held by Buckingham and Sefton Green, 1997).

However, in spite of the apparent symbiotic relationship between the written word and the visual image that accompanies it—the debate between those in Leavisite and cultural studies camps still wages on as English educators continue to struggle over the sanctity, prominence, and exclusivity of the written word as the definitive form of meaning making. While I will not be caught espousing the death of the written word entirely, I do stand comfortably with those who argue that it is no longer the primary source of meaning making in the world. As a case in point, I draw attention to the way people have been collectively moved to respond to the crisis in global warming after viewing the images of the melting Antarctic ice shelf depicted in Al Gore's documentary, *An Inconvenient Truth.* Globally citizens responded to countries and communities in need after images of the 2006 Boxing Day tsunami in the South Pacific, or the levee breaches in New Orleans. Images of loss and suffering and devastation prove to be more powerfully and politically motivating forces than written words could possibly be.

For this reason, I hold with those who believe that the screen has replaced the page and that the visual image carries more power, prominence and persuasion in our culture than does the written word, particularly as it is disseminated throughout popular culture. Kress (2005) holds, "The dominant technology for dissemination at the moment is the screen, and it is influencing the book. It's important to think of the technology of writing or of the visual representation as quite distinct from the technology of dissemination. The media, the screen, the book—will continue, but their relations to modes will change" (pp. 104-105). Central to Kress's argument is that the boundaries that we use to define language need to be redefined in the shift from a linguistic to a semiotic focus. Rather than asking students to focus their attention on the features and elements of language on the page, a semiotic turn would ask them to pay attention to everything on the page: font size, spacing, illustrations, layout, the type of paper, etc. This renewed attention to detail brings students back to a time of "practical criticism," where educators and students might get "a more profound understanding of language than we had" (Kress, 2005, p. 101). This semiotic turn might also be applied to the visual image.

Rather than clinging to the once "restrictive preoccupation with interpretation and analysis [we turn] to a recognition of the creative possibilities of producing the visual as still image, video, game, comic-book;" Burn and Nixon (2005) argue that the grammar and literacy practices employed within the digital authoring technologies put the "'culture' back into ICT, a task which English teachers are well equipped to do" (p. 4). For that reason, I will argue for a movement toward a cultural studies framework in the discipline of English, away from one which clings, at times desperately, to the written word as the sole medium for communication and meaning making, and to the "entrenched elitism in dominant literacy practices" (Morgan, 2000, p. 70). Burn and Nixon (2005) point to the near-exclusivity of the written word as a form of summative evaluation as a case in point:

> While no one now would endorse the virulent objections to the visual as the enemy of the word as proposed by the disciples of Leavis, it is undeniable that the English curriculum becomes resolutely monomodal at the ultimate point of public accountability—in the exam hall, where pictures all but fade away. (p. 2)

Educators, who in many locations seem to be riding the accountability train, abandon the visual and the moving image as a means to make, create, or compose meaning. Many educators in the Leavisite camp will argue, as they have for generations, that the well-written word is the basis for good communication and organized thought, and for that reason there must be a basic level of competence that students attain before they leave high school. Students must read Shakespeare, even in what Kress (2005) calls its "skeletal" form even though it is difficult, arduous, and largely irrelevant material for many if not most students. They must learn to write essays, even though upon close examination of the professions that students will have to choose from as they make their way into the world, the skills of essay writing are not atop the list for many professions. I believe it remains so even more now as we shift further into a world dependent on digital technology and images as modes of communication and personal and public expression. If the written word is no longer the primary form of making meaning in public discourse, then we ought not spend the overwhelming majority of our time as English teachers preparing students to be the writers that they will never be, and never need to be, but rather, we might do better to engage students in forms of analysis and production of visual images, moving and still.

Do Avatars Belong in School? The Case of Media Literacy

Alvermann, Moon and Hagood (1999) provide an argument for how such opportunities for critical media literacy can provide a discursive space for students to find agency by evoking Saussure's semiotic approach to texts of popular culture. For Alvermann et al., engaging in the production of popular texts, such as the ones described here, permits an understanding of the cultural signs all around us within schools and within the realm of popular culture as it informs social, economic, and political position. They also add that critical media literacy creates communities "of active readers and writers who can be expected to exercise some degree of agency in deciding what textual positions they will assume or resist as they interact in complex social and cultural contexts" (p. 2). Whether drawing from Butler's notion of identity representation as an embodied performance or Lacan's belief that identity is intimately connected to unconscious desires and further manifested through discourses and how the body is represented, identity cannot be removed from one's engagement with the cultural. For young people, this engagement is often most closely tied to those elements of culture that are popular. Discourse itself is enacted in ways that are popular.

It is no longer good enough for students to merely become critical readers of popular culture; if educators hope to develop critical thought and foster a deeper understanding of the way media texts are entrenched with value-laden, politically driven content, then they must also be willing to teach students how the actual production of texts shapes the way messages are delivered and received. In order to understand first-hand the constructed nature of representation, students need to learn to write, represent, construct, and compose for themselves. What the introduction of avatars to English class offers is a way in which educators can engage students in a form of textual production that is at once personal and playful but that offers the discursive space to engage in ideology with seriousness and complexity. Kellner and Share (2007) show us that forms of alternative media production, such as the avatar construction proposed here, "help engage students to challenge media texts and narratives that appear natural and transparent" (p. 4).

Kelly (2006) also suggests that educational researchers can help play a role in creating spaces for youth to produce their own self-representations by engaging them as co-researchers and positioning them in their research as "youth as knowers" (p. 40). Following Fine, Weis, Weseen, and Wong (2003), she calls for "safe spaces," where educators can also foster programs and activities that allow "subaltern counter-publics" (p. 41). I suggest that allowing for the creation of autobiographical avatars within the cushion of visual literacy provided in English curricula might be seen as one such safe space. However, questions remain regarding how established pedagogical and discursive practices underwrite the construction of autobiographical avatars. Only when self-writing exercises such as these find their way into regular classroom practices and are regarded as valid and valuable pedagogical practices will educators have an opportunity to create a hospitable place for students to understand how their own identity is constructed, located, and situated within a broader cultural frame. At a time when youth are most concerned about matters of self and belonging, it makes sense to work with them as they seek to define themselves within their complex and often conflicted world. When we focus too much on methods and on standards demanded by the kinds of accountability sought through standardized testing, then we miss the opportunity to connect literacy (in its plurality) to social and cultural change on a broader level. What we need is for critical spaces to be opened up where students can engage in the critical relocating of their stories.

What Is English For?

Traditionally texts from popular culture have been ignored, marginalized, or even shunned for their association with a low culture (Dolby, 2003; Giroux, 1999; Luke, 2002; Pirie, 1993). But as traditional pedagogy ignores popular texts it also attempts to view reading through a progressive lens, which ultimately serves to limit it by regarding it as no more than "response." Kelly (1997) reveals that this view "simultaneously fails to understand fully, the complex political relationship of culture and identity" (p. 67). As an alternative, Kelly suggests the self-reflexive practice of autobiographical writing may provide a way to make sense of that complex relationship. She demonstrates that autobiography is a form of highly personal and subjective writing that can offer a "discursive production of memory, history, representation, desire and knowledge while addressing head-on the implications of such insights not only for how notions of subjectivity and collectivity are understood, but, also, for how pedagogies are mobilized" (p. 48). If such meaning-making is possible through autobiographical writing, this research seeks to explore what might be possible if autobiography is produced (or re-produced) in a visual form.

My argument is that students should be given an opportunity to learn the basic skills for writing and reading well—but that they should also learn how to write or compose multimodal texts, and expression should not be limited to written essays (as it is in exam situations). Writing well is still the domain of those in fields of communication, journalism, and academia; and there are those who believe it will remain so (Kress, 2005); however, asking students to privilege writing over all other forms of communication and meaning making (as is done in summative evaluation), is like insisting that all students take the bell ringer anatomy exam[1] in order to prepare them for a potential career in the medical field. It makes no more sense to insist that a student heading toward a career in the trades be asked to make meaning by using the exclusive format of as essay than it would be for a student heading toward a career in journalism to take the anatomy bell ringer exam—just in case. That is not to say that students do not need to acquire a set of competencies in writing and anatomy, but it also does not mean they necessarily need to become experts either.

Kress's (2005) research observed that a divide in how curriculum is delivered still ranges vastly from a traditional, authoritarian and science-like attention to the texts prescribed by a national curriculum (in the United Kingdom, for example), to a constructivist, learner-centered model that permits contemporary, popular media texts to frame how students learn to understand themselves and the world they inhabit. However, he does acknowledge that despite the differences he observed, it seemed clear that "a battle had been won—a recognition of the value of culture other than elite culture" (p. 103).

What Should English Do?

Barrell and Hammett, (2002) ask, "What are the rich literacies and educational experiences that young people need to experience in a digitized world" (p. 14)? Knobel argues that the everyday literacy practices are used to negotiate computer-mediated networks and other forms of technology within postindustrial society rapidly, easily and continuously. To that end, I also believe that it makes sense for pedagogy and curriculum to reflect such forms of multimodal expression within a postindustrial world that depends on such forms of expression every day. To remain stagnant and cling to only print-centered versions of literacy today would surely be as erroneous as clinging to strictly oral culture after the advent of the printing press. Within an ethos of ubiquitous connectivity, communication to and with one's peer group via social networks such as Facebook and MySpace, across any number of forms of electronic media from everyday life are central to negotiating notions of the subject, identity, representation, and social knowledge. By embracing the conversational features of youth culture in these contexts, many argue that educators can find a pedagogical opportunity for welcoming such new and everyday literacy practices into the classroom (Alvermann and Hagood, 2000; Buckingham, 2003; Dolby, 2003; Giroux, 1998). However, rather than willingly opening the study of English to multimodal texts, the discipline of English has remained the "study of linguistic and literary texts, to the exclusion of all else" (Burn and Nixon, 2005, p. 1).

An Argument for Avatars in English Class

In order to argue for the inclusion of such autobiographical avatars, I must first position the practice as a new literacy practice—one common with youth in their daily personal, public communicative and expressive discourses. Lankshear and Knobel (2003, 2006) embrace everyday literacy practices as those events of meaning making that move beyond print decoding to include expressions and practices that are limited only by new and evolving technologies. For them, the definition of literacy moves beyond a static decoding of print on a page to encompass multiple and evolving practices in reading, writing, composing, viewing, listening and communicating as legitimate forms of social knowledge. However, this acknowldgement of a new literacy practice as a form of social knowledge does not necessarily require it be included in the curriculum. In fact, Lankshear and Knobel argue that educators would do well to focus on the position of the new literacy practice first and to avoid ruining a personal, social practice by bringing it into the classroom, where it has the potential to be analyzed to death.

With that in mind, I will continue with my justification for introducing autobiographical avatar design into the English classroom in a way that I believe attends to the desire to remain removed from the social communicative practices of youth but that also acknowledges these practices for their important contribution to youth identity construction. If the population of this research project had been drawn from the millions of youth who had already made WeeMee avatars and who were already participating with them on the online site WeeWorld, perhaps the argument could be made that introducing such a new literacy practice into the classroom might be in the realm of what Lankshear and Knobel (2006) call imposing "outsider ways on insider sensibilities" (p. 245). However, this project deliberately introduced the new literacy practice of autobiographical avatar design to a population of teenaged girls who were actively participating on the online social networking site, Facebook, but who had never created an avatar, much less an avatar that would be deliberately autobiographical. Participants were not prior members of WeeWorld. In that sense and in this context, the introduction of a new literacy practice was deliberately artificial. The purpose of the study, therefore, was not to "displace established literacies" (p. 245), but to complement already established ones by pushing autobiography into the realm of visual expression and positioning it with a cultural studies frame as a practice that might shed insight on notions of youth identity, representation, agency and voice.

Ask the Experts

I asked the participants of my study whether or not they had ever done any work on autobiography in school, and if they had ever been asked to represent themselves visually.

> The closest thing to an autobiography I've ever done in school was last year, when we wrote speeches in my French class to describe ourselves. As for visual representations, I've done nothing of the sort, but I think it would be a great idea for an English project. Maybe I'll suggest that to my teacher... I'm not sure whether or not any of my teachers would ask me to visually represent myself in order to tell a story, but, as I said, it would be a great idea for a project. (Butterflye)

> I think it would be so cool to do something like this for an assignment in English, but I don't think many teachers would ask students to represent themselves in a visual way…it could be considered too easy. But I guess if you answered a bunch of questions and wrote an autobiography to go with it. It would be really interesting to see how everyone seen themselves and if the way their avatar looks is the way everyone else seen them as being in real life. I think it would be really cool. (Cherrytree)

> I've never had to do anything like this for a school project, even though it would make a very interesting assignment. I think that each one of the avatars do tell a story, when you think about each aspect of the avatar was chosen for a specific reason and it's kind of like a puzzle to figure out what the story behind it is. A possible English project would be for everyone to create an avatar anonymously, and the teacher could post them on the wall and have a sort of guessing game to figure out who owns each one. Looking at certain characteristics represented in the avatar I'm sure it would be a challenge to narrow it down according to the people you know. (Cutie-Pi)

> I think that when an assignment like this is first assigned you think that it is easy marks and it will be really easy, but as you get into it you find out about yourself and you want to know more. A project like this will get you to find out a lot about yourself and find out who you are. (Questionmark)

Students from both intermediate and senior high school express not only what they see as the value of such an exercise after participating in the case study but also how unlikely it is that any of their teachers would take up the project of visual representation as something legitimate within an English classroom. Whether the visual autobiography is positioned as something "too easy" as Cherrytree suggests, or if it still requires the validation of something written in the form of an autobiography in order to make it substantive and perhaps even legitimate, the message from these students is clear. If it's not in written form, visual representation doesn't count the same way that written words do. The message that students have absorbed over time is that words are more important than images, and answering content questions is more valuable than hermeneutic interpretation. Yet, if we examine their Facebook pages, a quick glance will prove that pictures and images dominate a large portion of the forum. Words punctuate the images with tags, comments and descriptors, but these pages also allow participants to show who they are by plastering them with pictures and images.

So even though scholars have made what seems to be a clear case for self-writing in the English classroom (Graham, 1991; Kalmer, 2001; Pirie, 1993), educators continue to focus on methods and on standards demanded by the kinds of accountability sought through standardized testing (Coiro et al., 2008). Such visual self-writing allows students to connect new literacy practices to social and cultural change on a broader level. What we need is for critical spaces to be opened up where students can engage in the critical relocating of their stories. Given the growth and popularity of social networking sites like Facebook as a location for identity construction and social communication, this research is valuable because it allows for a glimpse into how teenage girls engage within interpretative communities and social networking sites that are key to understanding knowledge creation and the experiences of youth culture. What makes autobiographical avatar design and analysis significant is that it provides a space to merge a new and everyday literacy practice in a manner that is not far removed from something that students might engage with in their spare time, with a rigorous analysis of self and identity that is demanded by autobiography.

DIY: How and Why to Use Avatars in English Class

We are told that, as educators, one of the best practices we can adopt in our classrooms is to get to know our students, to learn who they are, and to understand where they come from (Davis et al., 2008). When educators know what interests their students have, then they can choose material that connects curriculum to students' interest. What better way to get to know them than by asking them to show you who they are? As a break from the tired: "tell me what you like to do when you're not in school" paragraph, teachers can begin by asking students to create an avatar that represents who they think they are. For practical purposes, educators will need to have access to multiple computers with Internet access to the sites used to create these avatars. The programs offered as choices in my own study were: www.weeworld.com, www.doppleme.com and www.birgits.net. Other related programs such as www.zwinky.com also exist. Educators could also invite students to suggest another program with the only condition being that the avatars have the capacity to be autobiographical. It should be noted that sites that construct avatars for gaming purposes where identities are intentionally altered and fantasized would not serve the purpose of this exercise.

Setting up the activity could take on many forms. Teachers could allow students to each pick the avatar creation program of their choice, or they could ask all students to use the same program in order to remain consistent in the types of analysis they will conduct with the students. In a computer lab, or as a home assignment, students would be asked to produce and print an autobiographical avatar. And this would be the starting place for the kind of self-reflexive work that Kelly (1997) suggests.

If the class decides to use the program available through WeeWorld.com, discussion around the very first step—the gender selection—would become a point of entry to the either/or structuralist bifurcation of gender, which leaves no room for gender bending or gender shifting for those creating the avatar. This immediate gendering places some students in a place of discomfort; however, for the educator, this offers a pedagogical opportunity as a teachable moment for discussing society's gendered assumptions.

As educators, we can ask our students to engage in an examination of how these autobiographical avatars represent, construct or reconstruct identity. Questions of how and why do youth represent themselves the way they do within a turbulent and unpredictable culture become salient. By indicating their preferences, youth attempt to become located within the larger social order (Pomerantz, 2006). Any understanding of how youth write themselves, and their stories (even if these are fragments of their stories), must include an analysis of the expectations their creators have about how they will be read. How do youth passively receive or actively negotiate meaning? And since meaning making cannot occur in a vacuum, the theoretical assumptions around visual communication and audience will also need to be explored. These are all points that might start larger group and class discussions, or they might just as easily be conversations that occur between teacher and student in the form of a reflective journal.

When students in a classroom are given the assignment to create an autobiographical avatar and asked to represent themselves with as much accuracy as possible, issues of important first impressions and accuracy are likely to surface almost immediately. Appearances are important to teenaged students, even if they are setting out to represent themselves in cartoon form. For many, limitations in the program will lead them to make choices that they may not be completely happy with, as was Livie with her options of choosing between the freckles which might provide a hint toward her medical condition and the eyelashes which would signal to others that even with a short haircut she was indeed a girl. Some may attempted to accurately represent themselves physically while others may attempt to create their avatar to show what they do as a means to show who they are.

Here is a list of some possible guiding questions:

- Describe your avatar.
- Does your avatar show who you are in real life?
- How accurate is the physical portrayal?
- Do you think it is a good representation of you?
- How is it like you?
- How is it different?
- Does it show who you would like to be?
- To what extent do you think it is important for your avatar to be a combination of who you are and who you want to be?
- What does your avatar say about you?

- What do the colors in your avatar represent and why did you choose them?
- What does your avatar not tell others about you?
- What important information does it leave out?
- Are there things about who you are that cannot be represented in this avatar?
- How important it is for something like an avatar to be an accurate representation for you are, or what you stand for?
- If your avatar were going to be used as your profile picture on Facebook for a period of time, what things would you consider important in making it?
- Would you use your avatar as your profile picture on Facebook?
- What do you think are the differences between avatars as profile pictures versus real photographs as profile pictures?
- And which do you prefer using?
- What you think your current profile picture says about you?
- Can you comment on how creating an avatar might give you more, or less freedom to express you are than a photograph might?
- How important is it for you to be able to represent yourself accurately in your profile pictures for Facebook?
- Does posting an avatar as a profile picture say you aren't cool? You are cool?

These questions might be addressed to students individually or through journaling activities. However, in order to make the exercise collaborative and participatory, it makes more sense to ask students to meet in a blog space to discuss their responses. As the girls in my study did, such an opportunity can lead to a deeper understanding of how identity is constructed on an individual level and to how limited and limiting our representations are at times. Using the above suggestions as guiding questions, students should be left to develop their conversations without too much interference.

Within the common curricular goal of citizenship, curriculums often invite educators to develop a critical understanding of self within a broader context of citizenship. Lacan's (2000) notion of the self as fragmented, partially fictional and/or mythical, always incomplete, and under the direct hegemonic influence of society's dominant discourses may be challenging. Since autobiographical writing (in whatever form it may take) cannot ever be complete, educators can begin their discussions by asking students to confront the notion that their representations are necessarily and always incomplete, not to mention shaped by the language available to them through the program that allowed them to construct their avatar. The notion of incompleteness may be troubling for students and educators who have been raised within a structuralist pedagogical frame that demands answers of right and wrong in order to be accountable. However, this notion of incompleteness provides an opportunity to create a bridge to a more complex understanding of what it means to selectively include or exclude various aspects of self according to the anticipated audience. Such an engagement with the fundamental English concept of purpose and audience again provides adequate justification for the avatars being in an English classroom.

Do New Literacies Belong in English Class?

Whether it is positioned as a new literacy practice or as a social discursive practice, making an avatar as a personal, visual representation was not something that just anybody could do twenty years ago. Being able to use this kind of representative image on all outgoing forms of communication was simply not technically feasible—except perhaps at the level of a monogrammed letterhead or wax seal. Before any of this discussion can begin, however, it is imperative that I pause to position avatar design in a context that does not allow it to become merely "old wine in a new bottle" (Lankshear and Knobel, 2006). I can thank Michele Knobel for reminding me how important it is to make this distinction. Introducing new technologies to old practices does not constitute a new literacy practice. Put more plainly, new technologies used for purposes of literacy education do not necessarily mean that new literacy practices are being employed. Just because we are using computers or "smartboards" in our classrooms does not mean that we are using new literacy practices. Nor does engagement with new technology necessarily mean that students are "developing, critiquing, analyzing, or even being technically proficient with new literacies" (p. 55).

Lankshear and Knobel have reminded us that "school routines are highly regular forms of practice that are intimately linked to what we call the 'deep grammar' of elements of schooling" (p. 55). Such deep grammar of schooling constructs "learning as teacher-directed" and 'curricular' in the sense that it imposes officially sanctioned curriculum, which bases its information on texts as sources of information. Within such pervasive understanding, education presumes that the world is accessed via the text and the written word. Such deep grammars assume that knowledge exists as a privileged domain, luckily there are those who also understand that knowledge is far more than that which is held solely by educators and their books, rather it is also constructed and created in the spaces where students meet. Davis, Sumara and Luce- Kapler (2008) tell us that

> Knowledge is not some sort of object that is locked inside a head or that is lying around in pools out in the world; rather that knowledge is embodied (there must be an actor) and situated (there must be a context for the action). Bodies know, and that's what makes them part of grander knowing bodies. Knowledge, then, is about relationship. (p. 66)

Beaujolais nouveau

Recalling the description of new literacy practices from chapter one that describes them as interactive, collaborative, technology enabled—the kind of work conducted on blogs, web pages, fan fictions, and video remixes—the potential to move the work of the old, first mindset classroom to one that embraces a new literacy realm within an English language arts class is not such a leap after all. If we allow ourselves to take the personal response narratives of the past and allow them to evolve into a Web 2.0 mindset, we might find students writing fan fictions about the stories they read in school. Or we might encourage them to create blogs in order to discuss issues of social justice and identity as they relate to the material they have read and/or created. Students might be encouraged to work collaboratively to construct original and collaborative work in the increasingly popular genres of a graphic novel or anime. However, instead of relying strictly on print text for the writing of each of these activities, we might invite a multimodal genre of writing, instead. By keeping in mind my previous discussion regarding the importance of the visual image in English, educators might embrace the expanded definition of writing to encourage visual writing as well as the traditionally print centered writing.

Thomas (2007) reminds us that fan fictions have evolved from the pulp magazine *Fanzines* traditions of the 1930s. The increasing popularity of fan fictions are likely due, in large part, to the technology that allows fans to meet in online virtual spaces to share thoughts about their favorite pieces of literature. Beyond typical fan sites, fan fictions give rise to stories that not only extend the original narratives and sometimes mimic them in form and style, but they also invite a sort of collaboration, which is part of what makes them Web 2.0 stuff. Evolving from the original (sometimes canonical) works, new narratives arise as they bring together the original familiar characters with characters and settings from other stories and even with newly created characters, settings and plot developments. Mugglenet.com is an example of a fan fiction site that was especially popular leading up to the release of the final installment of the *Harry Potter* series in the summer of 2007. While there, fans speculated about how the final book might look, and many took a crack at writing their own pieces of the story as they would like to see it.

Besides acting as a virtual collective, what fan fiction sites also provide is a place for critical feedback on the writing process and for the drawing of details from the original texts. While this form of "copying" may not find its way into traditional pedagogical practices English classes, Davis et al., (2008) suggest that it might not be such a bad idea. If we think historically about the methods that have been used to teach the great artists and artisans across disciplines of painting, sculpture, song writing and dance (to name only a few), many have benefited from the intensive training and schooling by masters. Even elite athletes train with master coaches where they can learn to copy the styles and techniques of the greats. In the case of fan fiction sites, such mimicking offers more than a place to copy the style and form of literature that has an established success, and that has received critical acclaim. It also has the potential to be a big business.

As many of my innovative pedagogical ideas do, the idea for the following activity came to me while I was teaching a course called "Teaching Young Adult Literature" to a group of pre-service teachers at Memorial University. The retiring director of the Curriculum and Materials Centre there is Alison Mews. She has been pointing me in the direction of wonderful new books for several years. This summer she introduced me to a hear-t breaking novel *Life on the Refrigerator Door: Notes Between a Mother and Daughter* by A. Kuipers (2007). It is the story about the relationship between Claire, a lively fifteen-year-old girl and her impossibly busy single mother. Their lives are rushing in different directions and they keep missing one another. In order to stay in touch, they catch up by leaving quick notes for each other on the refrigerator door. What is remarkable about this story is how the narrative is developed through the back-story, or by what is not said. The back and forth nature of the notes lends itself to a kind of group writing project that reminded me of the kind of Web 2.0 mindset or new ethos stuff espoused by Lankshear and Knobel. Asking students to extend the narrative form from *Life on the Refrigerator Door*, students are invited to post virtual notes in a blog space designed to replicate the refrigerator door. In this exercise students not only learn the art of telling by not telling by copying the epistolary style of the writing, they are also asked to post avatars with each note as a visual form of writing. Remember the rule is that anything that can be represented in the visual realm must be.

In exercises where I have asked high school students to write visually, there is an initial discomfort as they learn to navigate a direction that runs counter to much of what they have been asked to do in English classes of the past. After all, it is not often you hear an English teacher utter things like: "no descriptive words allowed!" But they quickly learn the power of the image, as they strike out words from their draft narratives that can be depicted in visual form.

If we allow the notion of writing fan fiction to collide with the increasing popularity of graphic novels and amine, the potential for even more interesting work presents itself. The students I teach as pre-service teachers are excited about the prospects of introducing their high school students to graphic novels as a legitimate form of literature. They point to Bill Willingham who has created *Fables,* a wonderful collection of graphic novels which is finding success not unlike of the *Sandman* series (by Neil Gaiman). By working in the tradition of fractured fairytales, Willingham combines story lines and characters from classic fiction (like George Orwell's *Animal Farm*, for example) as he weaves a narrative that relies heavily on both literary and visual allusions. Students might also be invited to try a more complex collective project that involves mashing several of their novels with characters from movies and popular culture. In this case, the students are encouraged to include themselves into the narrative, by using their avatars to represent themselves.

Students who have seen the *Shrek* trilogy in theatres or on DVD will be familiar with fractured fairytales. The trilogy comically combines Arthurian legends, Disney princess stories, Mother Goose characters and stories from the Brothers Grimm together with their individual histories, rich characteristics and personas. When they combine together in the *Shrek* stories, they move out of their traditional confines and often take on characteristics that are counter to the traditional ones they had been assigned. The *Shrek* movies, and the *Fables* and *Sandman* graphic novels allow a model to recombine either one or several characters, plotlines and settings. If we allow students to take this notion one step further by using WeeMees to build their characters and a fan fiction to be written, not merely using print text but creating avatars to accompany the text. The rule might be that anything that can be represented visually should not be found in the print text or in the avatar's speech bubbles.

Finally, in *Engaging Minds* (second edition), Davis et al., (2008) offer a writing activity that begins with a bag of buttons. The idea behind the activity is to provide context and a personal connection with an object that will become the physical stimulus to a narrative. The teacher begins by dumping a bag of assorted buttons on a table and asks the students to carefully select one that they find interesting. The exercise begins quite traditionally. Students are asked to imagine an article of clothing that once sported this button and then quickly write a vivid description of the article of clothing. From there, the teacher instructs the students to describe the person wearing the article of clothing. At this point the teacher provides a visual image which the students must incorporate as the setting. Layers of description are added to the student writing until the teacher asks students to pair up and with only a minute to do so, they must figure out a way that their characters can meet. On its own, this is a wonderfully collaborative exercise. However, taking it to the Web 2.0 mindset, the potential for new literacy is exciting. The kind of collective and participatory culture that develops in a fan fiction space leads to endless possibilities for the way the narratives might unfold. Adding another dimension by including an avatar in lieu of a physical description, students might create a kind of collaborative visual representation.

Conclusion

Any curriculum that espouses personal development, citizenship, and technology must also realize that denying the validity of the very forms of communication and meaning making that our students use in everyday spaces will only serve to further drive a wedge between them and us. New and expanded ways of reading, writing and representing the world bring new ways of understanding the world (Lankshear and Knobel, 2006, 2003). With ever-evolving methods of digital communication available to students, conventional forms of meaning making are being abandoned by youth in favor of new socially recognized forms (Lankshear and Knobel, 2006). Reluctance to embrace everyday literacy practices can be seen in light of a similar reluctance by educators to allow texts from popular culture into their classrooms where traditional practices shun such forms of literacy as lowbrow and unimportant (Coiro et al., 2008). Allowing such expressions in and of themselves may not be seen as significant in terms of their pedagogical contributions, but when we consider their effects of identity, individuality, agency and group belonging, their effects are staggering.

The literature supports giving critical attention to the influence of electronically mediated texts in our classrooms. We also know the profound pedagogical influence of images and sounds, particularly for youth (Buckingham, 2003; Gee, 1990, 2003; Giroux et al., 2000). Yet, the literature also demonstrates that such a commitment to the everyday literacy practices (particularly involving images and sounds) remains wanting (Alvermann, et al., 1999; Coiro et. al., 2008; Dolby, 2003; Kelly, 1997; Morgan, 1998, 2000; Torres and Mercado, 2007). Educators would have no trouble finding that their classrooms are filled with digitally savvy students. Even so, their own pedagogical footprint continues to be that of "linear-thinking technologically stymied instructors" (Jones-Kavalier and Flannigan, 2006, p. 10).

Even with the societal shift from page to screen, particularly within the realm of popular culture, I do not foresee the book becoming an antiquated relic like the vinyl record or 8-track tape. I am not advocating an all-out abandonment of traditional book literacies, or even of canon-based literature in the English language arts classroom. This is not a call for a book-burning ceremony to signal the shift from the book to the screen. Nor am I suggesting that traditional print literacies should be abandoned in favor of a complex online version of Mr. Potato Head. But I am suggesting that writing and the dissemination of ideas are no longer restricted to the page and the written word. Images, in their multimodal still and moving forms have the power to create and shape our perceptions, embed themselves in our individual and collective psyches, and contribute to how we understand notions of identity and belonging. It is not the actual creating of autobiographical avatars that makes them significant inclusions to an English pedagogy, it is in the analysis of how they were created, in the consideration of what was said and what was left out, in what students wanted to say but could not and what they were forced to say instead. It is also the potential they have to contribute to new literacy practices that can bridge traditional English pedagogies to those with a forward reach.

What makes these exercises significant is that they provide a space to merge a new and everyday literacy practice—not far removed from something that students might engage with in their spare time, with a rigorous analysis of self and identity. Rarely enough do we as educators ask students who they are, who they think they are, or who they would like others to think they are. From what we know about teenage identity, belonging and acceptance are among the most often-cited concerns of youth. As the divide between real world and school continues to widen what could be better than finding an exercise to bridge the gap? The literature to support the benefits of getting to know our students is vast. This literature also sheds light on what might be possible when students are encouraged to engage in an exercise of autobiographical writing/representing in an attempt to trouble the social construction of self within a quest for different perspectives.

For teachers, being able to acknowledge the experiences of their students and take seriously their individual voices means refusing to slip into the familiar celebration of personal response narratives, no matter how comfortable or well intended that approach may be. Even though media culture implicitly assumes (or encodes) society's hegemonic ideology where messages are designed to reproduce dominant principles, these avatar representations also present a location for ideological struggle between dominant ideology, negotiated codes, or oppositional codes. Examining the limited/limiting discursive practices of manufactured constructions, or (re)presentations of reality within interpretative communities and social networking sites are key to understanding knowledge creation and the experiences of youth culture. Allowing students the power to construct their own visual identities *and then* asking them to engage in a critical discourse around the manner of their construction as they foray into a new literacy practice may provide a pivotal location through which to view the social construction of identity. Allowing for a playful discursive practice to enter into the classroom, teachers welcome serious ideological analysis of these and other texts. As I have said before, the transformational possibilities resulting from this kind of self-exploratory writing rests in the writer's ability to examine "the culturally mediated themes and implications for social justice" (Shore, 2004, p. 78). Or it might lead it a consideration of how autobiography, especially in its visual manifestation, might provide a means to understand the constructed nature of the sources, structures, and frames of reference that shape our students' understanding of themselves and others, and ultimately connect the macro with the micro (Livingstone, 1998; Morley, 1993).

Only when self-writing exercises such as these find their way into regular classroom practices and valid and valuable pedagogical practices will educators have an opportunity to create a hospitable placc for students to understand how their own identity is constructed, located and situated within a broader cultural frame. At a time when youth are most concerned about matters of self and belonging, it makes sense to work with them as they struggle within their complex and often conflicted world. When we focus too much on methods and on standards demanded by the kinds of accountability sought through standardized testing, then we miss the opportunity to connect literacy (in its plurality) to social and cultural change on a broader level. What we need is for critical spaces to be opened up where students can engage in the critical relocating of their stories. Perhaps those spaces can most safely evolve in the form of new literacies, like fan fictions that move beyond regulated texts in a manner that is recursively elaborative, where identities can be collaboratively explored and tried on, and where words and images can work in tandem to create meaning. Perhaps in this way, a curriculum that makes claims about its role in the constitution of identity, of self and others can actually do just that. Perhaps such new literacies can provide the bridge that finally joins foundational claims of curriculum that intends to celebrate personal development, individuality and issues of social justice while simultaneously serving to devalue the experience of its students by using evaluative procedures that by design are set to exclude the cultural experience of some students. If student experiences and identities are meant to really matter, then let them show us who they think they are in a multimodal language that they are already using.

Furthermore, we know that students not only learn in multiple and differentiated ways ranging from the visual, the metaphorical, and kinesthetic (to name a few), and that they have multiple and differentiated strengths in terms of how they can represent their responses (whether it be, for example, with words, in song, or with movement), yet from behind our placards celebrating notions of inclusive education, we demand that students be judged on what they know based on how they write.

Engaging in the excavation of complex layers of sedimented knowledge is complex and time-consuming work, and it is certainly not for the faint of heart, however, it is rewarding and meaningful work. Not only does it allow students to experiment in visual semiotic forms of meaning making that they are already good at, it asks them to work with a subject they are intimately familiar with and expert in (themselves). The questions that dig layers below the veneer of physical representation and outward appearance shed light on how constructed realities have been borne out in the representation of self. In a kind of literacy espoused by Kellner and Share (2007) the self-reflective work done with autobiographical avatar design allows for a critique of ideology, and it welcomes the kind of analysis that questions "the politics of representation" and the "crucial dimensions of gender, race, class, and sexuality" (p. 8). For those in marginalized groups, new technologies and new literacy practices can provide a means for them to find a voice and claim agency. For those members of the dominant group, on the other hand, this form of critical media literacy "offers an opportunity to engage with the social realities that the majority of the world are expressing" (p. 9). The question that remains is whether educators will be brave enough to break with the traditional pedagogies and not only ask students: who do you think you are but critically explore the vital political space they attempt to claim in their constructed responses.

Note

---

[1] The anatomy bell ringer exam is a standard exam format that asks students to identify specific and minute parts of the human anatomy within a timed format where students have only seconds before the bell rings and signals them to move to the next body part. The bell ringer exam is a stressful prerequisite part of many medical fields.

References

Aapola, S., Gonick, M., and Harris, A. (2005). *Young femininity: Girlhood, power and social change.* New York: Palgrave Macmillan.

Agger, B. (2004). *The virtual self.* Malden, MA: Blackwell.

Alvermann, D. and Hagood, M. (2000). Critical media literacy: Research, theory, and practice in 'new times'." *The Journal of Educational Research, 93*(3), 193-205.

———., Moon, J. S., Hagood, M. C. (1999). *Popular culture in the classroom.* Chicago: International Reading Association.

———. (Ed.), (2002). *Adolescents and literacies in a digital world.* New York: Peter Lang.

Ball, S., Kenny, A., and Gardiner, D. (1990). Literacy, politics and the teaching of English. In I. Goodson and P. Medway (Eds.). (pp. 47-86), *Bringing English to order.* London: Falmer Press.

Barrell, B., and Hammett, R. (2002). Introduction, In R. Hammett and B. Barrell (Eds.). *Digital expressions: Media literacy and English language arts* (pp. 11-19). Calgary: Detselig Enterprises Ltd.

Barthes, R. (1994) The death of the author. (pp. 166-170). In D. Graddol and O. Boyd-Barrett (Eds.), *Media texts: Authors and readers.* Clevedon: Open University Press.

Barthes, R. (1993). The rhetoric of the image. In A. Gray and J. McGuigan (Eds.) *Studying culture: An introductory reader* (pp. 15-27). London: Edward Arnold.

———. (1989). *Mythologies*, Trans . Annette Lavers. New York: Noonday Press.

———. (1977). *Image, music, text.* London: Fontana Press.

Berlak, A. C. (2004). Confrontation and pedagogy, cultural secrets, trauma, and emotion in anti-oppressive pedagogies. In M. Boler (ed.), *Dramatic dialogue in education: troubling speech, disturbing silence* (pp. 123-158). New York: Peter Lang.

Berlin, J. A. (1992). Poststructuralism, cultural studies and the composition classroom: Postmodern theory in practice. *Rhetoric Review, 11*(1), 16-33.

Best, S. and Kellner, D. (2003). Contemporary youth and the postmodern adventure. *The Review of Education, Pedagogy, and Cultural Studies, 25* (75-93).

Blake, N., Smeyers, P., Smith, R., and Standish, P. (1998). *Thinking again: Education after postmodernism.* Westport, CT: Bergin and Garvey.

Bloustien, G. (2003). *Girl making: A cross-cultural ethnography on the procesess of growing up female.* New York: Berghahn Books.

Boler, M. (2004). All speech is not free: The ethics of "affirmative action pedagogy." In M. Boler (Ed.), *Democratic dialogue in education: Troubling speech, disturbing silence* (pp. 3-13). New York: Lang.

———. (1999). A pedagogy of discomfort. (pp. 175-203). In *Feeling power: Emotions and education.* New York: Routledge.

Bruckman, A. S. (1993). Gender swapping on the Internet (pp. 317-326). In P. Ludlow (Ed.) *High noon on the electric frontier: Conceptual issues in cyberspace.* Cambridge, MA: The MIT Press.

Bruner, J. (1987). Life as narrative. *Social research, 54*(1), 11-32.

Buckingham, D. (2003). *Media education, Literacy, Learning and contemporary culture.* Cambridge, UK: Polity Press.

Buckingham, D. and Sefton-Green, J. (1994). *Cultural Studies Goes to School.* Pittsburgh: Open University Press.

Burn, A, and Nixon, H. (2005). Editorial: English and the visual: From montage to manga. *English Teaching: Practice and Critique, 4*(1), 1-5.

Bush, H. K. Jr. (1995). Poststructuralism as theory and practice in the English classroom. *ERIC Clearinghouse on Reading, English and Communication Digest #104.*

Butler, J. (1999). *Gender trouble: Feminism and the subversion of identity.* New York: Routledge.

———. (1997). *Excitable speech: A politics of the performative.* New York: Routledge.

———. (1996). Gender as performance. In P. Osborne (Ed.). *A critical sense: Interviews with intellectuals* (pp. 109-126). London: Routledge.

Callow, J. (2005). Literacy and the visual: Broadening our vision. *English Teaching: Practice and Critique. 4*(1), 6-19.

Cassella, R. (1998). The theoretical foundations of cultural studies in education. *Philosophy of Education Society- Online.* Retrieved from http://www.ed.uiuc.edu/eps/PES-Yearbook/1998/casella.html

Clandinin, D. J. (1985). Personal practical knowledge: A study of teachers' classroom images. *Curriculum Inquiry, 15*(3), 361-385.

Clark, L. S. (2005). The constant contact generation. Exploring teen friendship networks online. In S. R. Mazzarella (Ed.). *Girl wide web: Girls, the Internet, and the negotiation of identity* (pp. 203-221). New York: Peter Lang.

Coiro, J., Knobel, M., Lankshear, C., and Leu, D. C. (2008). Central issues in new literacies and new literacies research. In J. Coiro, M. Knobel, C. Lankshear, and D. C. Leu, (Eds.). *Handbook of research on new literacies* (pp. 1-22). Mahwah, NJ: Lawrence Erlbaum Associates.

Connell, R. W. (1987). *Gender and power.* Stanford, CA: Stanford University Press.

Cooper, R. (2007). *Alter ego: Avatars and their creators.* London: Chris Boot Publishing.

Cope, B. & Kalantzis, M. (Eds.). (1999). *Multiliteracies: literacy learning and the design of social futures.* London: Routledge.

Council of Atlantic Ministers of Education and Training. (Sept. 2009). Literacy: Key to Learning and Path to Prosperity – *An Action Plan for Atlantic Canada 2009-201. Retrieved from http://www.camet-camef.ca/images/eng/docs/Literacy-Key%20to%20Learning.pdf*

Cruickshank, K. (2006). *Teenagers, literacy and school: Researching in multilingual contexts.* London: Routledge.

Currie, D. H. and Kelly, D. M. (2006). "I'm going to crush you like a bug." Understanding girls' agency and empowerment. In Y. Jiwani, C. Steenbergen and C. Mitchell, (Eds.). *Girlhood, redefining the limits* (pp. 155-172). Montreal: Black Rose Books.

Davies, B. (1991). The concept of agency: A feminist poststructural analysis. *Social Analysis, 30,* 42-53.

Davis, B., Sumara, D. and Luce-Kapler, R. (2008). *Engaging Minds: Changing Teaching in Complex Times (Second Edition).* New York: Routledge.

Doel, M. and Clark, D. (1999). Virtual worlds: Simulation, suppletion, s(ed)uction, and simulacra. In M. Crang, P. Crang and J. May (Eds.), *Virtual geographies: Bodies, space, and regulations* (pp. 261-83), London: Routledge.

Dolby, N. (2003, Fall). Popular culture and democratic practice. *Harvard Educational Review, 73*(3), 258-284.

Driscoll, C. (2002). *Girls: Feminine adolescence in popular culture and cultural theory.* New York: Columbia University Press.

During, S. (Ed.). (1999). Introduction (pp. 1-28). *The cultural studies reader* (2nd Ed.). New York: Routledge.

Eisner, E. (1994). *Cognition and the curriculum reconsidered.* (2nd ed.). New York: Teachers College Press.

Fine, M., Weis, L., Weseen, S., & Wong, L. (2003). For whom? Qulaitative research, representations, and social responsibilities. In N. K. Denzin & Y. S. Lincoln (Eds.), *The landscape of qualitative research: Theories and issues* (2nd ed., pp. 167-207). Thousand Oaks, CA: Sage.

Fiske, J. (1992). Cultural studies and the culture of everyday life. In Grossberg, L., Nelson, C., and Treichler, P. (Eds.). (1992). *Cultural studies.* London: Routledge.

———. (1989). *Understanding popular culture.* Boston: Unwin Hyman.

Foucault, M. (1999). Space, power, and knowledge. (pp. 134-141). In S. During (Ed.). *The cultural studies reader* (2nd Ed.). New York: Routledge.

———. (1977). What is an author? In D. F. Bouchard (Ed.). *Language, counter-memory, practice: Selected essays and interviews (pp. 115-138).* Ithaca: Cornell University Press.

———. (1967). Of Other Spaces. Heterotopias. [Online]. Available: http://foucault.info/documents/heteroTopia/foucault.heteroTopia.en.html

Foundation for the Atlantic Canada English Language Arts Curriculum. (1996). Halifax: Department of Education and Culture, Government of Nova Scotia.

Freire, P. (1970). *A Pedagogy of the Oppressed.* New York: Seabury.

Gee, J. P. (2003). *What do videogames have to teach us about learning and literacy*? New York: Palgrave Macmillan.

———. (1996). *Social Linguistics and Literacies,* 2nd edition. London: Falmer.

———. (1990). *Social linguistics and literacies.* London: Falmer Press.

———. (1987). What is literacy? *Teaching and Learning, 2,* 3-11.

Giroux, H. (1999). *The mouse that roared: Disney and the end of innocence.* Lanham, MD: Rowman and Littlefield Publishers, Inc.

———. (1998). *Channel surfing: Racism, the media, and the deconstruction of today's youth.* New York: St. Martin's Griffin.

———. (1994). Doing cultural studies: Youth and the challenge of pedagogy. *Harvard Educational Review, 64*(3), 278-308.

———., Shumway, D., Smith, P., Sosnoski, J. (2000). The need for cultural studies: Resisting intellectuals and oppositional public spheres. Retrieved from http://theory.eserver.org/need.html

Goffman, E. (1974). On face-work: An analysis of ritual elements in social interaction. In B. G. Blount (ed.), *Language, culture and society: A book of readings* (pp. 224-249). Cambridge, MA: Winthrop Publishers Inc.

———. (1959). *The presentation of self in everyday life.* New York: Anchor.

Graff, H. (1979). *The literacy myth: Literacy and social structure in the nineteenth century city.* New York: Academic Press.

Graham, R. J. (1991). *Reading and writing the self: Autobiography in education curriculum.* New York: Teachers College Press.

Gunter, B., Oates, C., and Blades, M. (2004). *Advertising to Children on TV: Content, Impact, and regulation.* Lawrence Erlbaum Associates: Mahwah, NJ.

Hagood, M. (2008). Intersections of popular culture, identities, and new literacies research. (pp. 531-551). In J. Coiro, M. Knobel, C. Lankshear, D. Leu (Eds.). *Handbook of research on new literacies***.** Mahwah, NJ: Lawrence Erlbaum Associates.

Hall, S. (2000). Who needs "identity"? In, P. DuGay, J. Evans, and P. Redman (Eds.). *Identity:A reader.* (pp. 15-30). London: Sage.

———. (1999). Cultural studies and its theoretical legacies. In S. During (Ed.), *The cultural studies reader* (2nd ed.) (pp. 97-109). New York: Routledge.

———. (1993). The television discourse—encoding and decoding. (pp. 28-34). In A. Gray and J. McGuigan (Eds.) *Studying Culture: an introductory reader.* London: Edward Arnold.

Haraway, D. (1991). "Cyborg manifesto": Science, Technology and socialist feminism in the late twentieth century. (pp. 475-496). In A. Jones (Ed). *The feminism and visual culture reader.* London: Routledge.

Harris, A. (Ed.). (2004). *All about the girl: Culture, power and identity.* New York: Routledge.

———. (2003). *Future girl: Young women in the twenty-first century.* New York: Routledge.

Harry, J. C. (2005). A Burkean analysis of a television promotional advertisement. In Smith, S. Moriarty, G. Barbatsis, and K. Kenny (Eds.). *Handbook of visual communication: Theory, methods and media* (pp. 539-551). Mahwah, NJ: Lawrence Ealbaum.

Hartley, M. (Jan. 2, 2009). 2009: The Big ideas. *The Globe and Mail.* Retrieved from http://www.theglobeandmail.com/news/technology/science/article964051.e

Heath, S. B. (1983). *Ways with words: Language, life and work in communities and classrooms.* Cambridge: Cambridge University Press.

Hirsch, E. D. Jr. (1987). *Cultural literacy: What every American needs to know.* Boston, MA: Houghton Mifflin.

Hoggart, R. (1957). *The uses of literacy.* Harmondsworth: Penguin.

———. (1961). *English for maturity.* Cambridge: Cambridge University Press.

hooks, b. (2003). *Teaching Community: A pedagogy of hope.* Routledge.

———. (1994). *Teaching to transgress: Education as the practice of freedom.* New York: Routledge.

Houston, B. (2004). Dramatic dialogue: who takes responsibility. In M. Boler (Ed.), *Democratic dialogue in education: Troubling speech, disturbing silence* (pp. 105-120). New York: Peter Lang.

Jackson, K. (April 12, 2007). The avatars of style. Once limited to smiley faces, web personas now reflect sophisticated fashion choices. *The Boston Globe.* Retrieved from http://www.boston.com/yourlife/fashion/articles/2007/04/12/the_avatars_of_style/?page=1

Johnson, R. (1986-1987). What is cultural studies anyway? *Social Text: Theory/Culture/Ideology, 16*, 38-80.

Jones-Kavalier, B. and Flannigan, S. L. (2006, Nov.). Connecting the digital dots: Literacy of the 21st century. *Educause Quarterly,* 8-10.

Kafai, Y., Fields, D., and Cook, M. (2007) Your second selves: Resources, agency, and constraints in avatar designs and identity play in a tween virtual world. Situated play, *Proceedings of DiGRA 2007 Conference.*

Kalmer, B. (2001). Reading the personal: A critical writing pedagogy. Adelaide: AATE/Interface.

Kang, H. and Yang, H. (2006). The visual characteristics of avatars in computer-mediated communication: Comparison of Internet Relay Chat and Instant Messenger as of 2003. *International Journal of Human-Computer Studies (64)* 1173-1183.

Kellner, D. (2000). New technologies/new literacies: reconstructing education for the new millennium. *Teaching Education, 11*(3), 245-265.

———. and Share, J. (2007). Critical media literacy, democracy, and the reconstruction of education. (pp. 3-23). In D. Macedo and S. Steinberg (Eds.). *Media literacy.* New York: Peter Lang.

Kelly, D., Pomerantz, S, Currie, D. (2005). Skater girlhood and emphasized femininity: 'you can't land an ollie properly in heels', Gender and *Education, 17*(3), 129-148.

Kelly, U. (1997). *Schooling desire: Literacy, cultural politics and pedagogy.* New York: Routledge.

Kenway, J., and Bullen, E. (2001). *Consuming children: Education—entertainment—advertising.* Buckingham: Open University Press.

Kincheloe, J. (2005). *Critical constructivism: A primer* .New York: Peter Lang.

Kinsella, M. (2009). Personal email communication.

Kist, W. (2005). *New literacies in action: Teaching and learning in multiple media.* New York: Teachers College Press.

———. (2000). Beginning to create the new literacy classroom: What does the new literacy look like? *Journal of Adolescent and Adult Literacy, 43*(8), 710-718.

Klein, N. (2002). *No Logo.* New York: Picador.

Knobel, M. (1999). Everyday literacies: Students, discourses and social practices. New York: Peter Lang.

Kolko, B. E. (1999). Representing bodies in virtual space: The rhetoric of avatar design. *The Information Society, 15*, 177-186.

Kress, G. (2005). Pictures from a rocket: English and the semiotic take. *English Teaching: Practice and Critique. 4*(1), 95-105.

———. (2003). *Literacy in the new media age.* London: Routledge.

———. (1997). *Before writing: Rethinking the paths to literacy.* London: Routledge.

———. and van Leeuwen, T. (2006). *Reading images: The grammar of visual design* (2nd ed.). London: Routledge.

———. (1996). *Reading images: The grammar of visual design*, London: Routledge.

Kuipers, A. (2007). *Life on the refrigerator door.* New York: HarperCollins.

Kumashiro, K. K. (2001). 'Posts' perspectives on anti-oppressive education in social studies, English, mathematics and science classrooms. *Educational Researcher, 30*(3) 3-12.

Lacan, J. (2000). The mirror stage. In P. DuGay, J. Evand and P. Redman (Eds.). *Identity: A reader* (pp. 44-50). London: Sage Publications.

Lankshear, C., and Knobel, M. (2006). *New Literacies, everyday practices and classroom Learning (2nd ed.).* New York: McGraw Hill.

———. (2003). *New Literacies, changing knowledge and classroom learning.* Buckingham, England: Open University Press.

———., Gee, J. P., and Knobel, M. (1997). Literacies, texts and difference in the electronic age. (pp. 133-163). In C. Lankshear; J. P. Gee; M. Knobel and C. Searle (Eds.) *Changing literacies.* Philadelphia: Open University Press.

Linn, S. (2000). *Consuming kids: The hostile takeover of childhood.* New York: New Press.

Livingstone, S. (2002). *Young people and new media.* London: Sage.

———. (1998). Audience research at the crossroads, The implied audience in media and cultural theory. *European Journal of Cultural Studies, 1*(2), 193-217.

———., Van Couvering, E., and Thumin, N. (2008). Converging traditions of research on media and information literacies. Disciplinary, cultural and methodological issues. In J. Coiro, M. Knobel, C. Lankshear, & D. C. Leu, (Eds.). *Handbook of research on new literacies* (pp. 103-132). New York: Lawrence Erlbaum Associates.

Luke, A. (May 31, 2007). Dr. Alan Luke: The new literacies. Webcast. *Webcasts For Educators.* Retrieved from http://www.curriculum.org/secretariat/may31.shtml

Luke, C. (2002). Re-crafting media and ICT literacies. In D. A. Alvermann (Ed.), *Adolescents and literacies in a digital world* (pp. 132-146). New York: Peter Lang.

———. (1997). Media literacy and cultural studies In S. Muspratt, A. Luke and P. Freebody (Eds.). *Constructing critical literacies: Teaching and learning textual practice.* Sydney: Allen and Unwin.

———. (1994). Feminist pedagogy and critical media literacy. *Journal of Communication, 18*(2), 30-47.

Mahon, M. (1992). *Foucault's Nietzschean genealogy: Truth, Power, and the subject.* New York: State University of New York Press.

Mazzarella, S. R. (2005). Introduction, It's a girl wide web. In S. R. Mazzarella, (Ed.). *Girl wide web: Girls, the Internet, and the negotiation of identity (pp. 1-12).* New York: Peter Lang.

———. and Pecora, N. O. (Eds.). (1999). *Growing up girls: popular culture and the construction of identity.* New York: Peter Lang.

McLaren, P. (2007). *Life in schools: An introduction to critical pedagogy in the foundations of education, 5th Ed.* Boston: Pearson.

McRobbie, A. (2005). *The uses of cultural studies.* London: Sage.

———. (1994). *Postmodernism and popular culture.* London: Routledge.

Morgan, R. (2000). Uncertain relations: English and cultural studies, In B. R. C. Barrell and R. F. Hammett (Eds.), *Advocating change.* Toronto: Irwin Publishing.

———. (1995). Television, space, education: rethinking relations between schools and media. *Discourse: studies in the cultural politics of education, 16*(1), 39-57.

Morley. D. (1981). The "Nationwide audience" –A critical postscript. *Screen Education, 39*(Summer), 3-14.

———. (1992). *Television, Audiences and Cultural Studies.* London: Routledge.

———. (1993). Active audience theory: Pendulums and pitfalls, *Journal of Communication 43*(4), 13-19.

Morrison, C. (2009). The Everyday Literacy Practice of Avatar Creation: Creating a Bridge between Curriculum Intent and Practice. *Canadian Journal for New Scholars in Education, 1*(2), 1-9.

New London Group. (1996). A pedagogy of multiliteracies: Designing social futures. *Harvard Educational Review, 66*(1), 60-92.

Nixon, H. (2002). Popular media culture, ICTs and the English language arts curriculum. In R. Hammett & B. Barrell (Eds.). *Digital Expressions: Media literacy and English language arts* (pp. 113-135). Calgary: Detslig Enterprises Ltd.

Palermo, J. (2002). Poststructuralist readings of the pedagogical encounter. New York: Peter Lang.

Peim, N. (1993). *Critical theory and the English teacher: Transforming the subject.* London: Routledge.

Perfect, S. (1984). Ways. *School Arts, 84*(1), 39-42.

Peters, M. (1996). *Poststructuralism, politics and education.* Westport, CT: Bergin and Garvey.

———., and Burbules, N. C. (2004). *Poststructuralism and educational research.* Lanham: Rowman and Littlefield Publishers Inc.

Pirie, B. (1993). *Reshaping High School English.* Urbana: NCTE.

Pomerantz, S. (2006). "Did you see what she was wearing?" The power and politics of schoolgirl style. In Y. Jiwani, C. Steenbergen and C. Mitchell (eds.). *Girlhood, redefining the limits* (pp. 173-190). Montreal: Black Rose Books.

Poyntz, S. R. (2006). Independent media, Youth agency, and the promise of media education. *Canadian Journal of Education, 29*(1), 154-175.

Proudfoot, S. (23 January, 2009). Our social networks are shrinking. *Leader Post* [Online]. http://www.leaderpost.com/social+networks+shrinking/1211296/story.html

Quinn, R. (2003). A genealogy of media studies. *The Australian Educational Researcher, 30*(1)101-120.

Richardson, L. (1994). Writing a method of inquiry. In N. Denzin and Y. Lincoln (Eds.), *Handbook of qualitative research* (pp. 516-59). Thousand Oaks, CA: Sage.

Robins, K. (1995). Cyberspace and the world we live in. In M. Featherstone & R. Burrows (Eds.), *Cyberspace, cyberbodies, cyberpunk: Cultures of technological embodiment* (pp. 135-156). London: Sage.

Schor, J. (2004). *Born to buy.* New York: Scribner.

Scott, J. (1991, Summer). The evidence of experience. *Critical Inquiry, 17*(4), 773-797.
Scribner, S. and Cole, M. (1981). *The psychology of literacy*. Cambridge, MA: Harvard University Press.

Seiter, E. (1996). Notes on children as a television audience (pp. 131-144). In J. Hay, L. Grossberg & E. Wartella (Eds.), *The audience and its landscape*. Boulder, CO: Westview Press.

Share, L. (2004). Self writing, Sex Ed, and the creation of adolescent identity. *Journal of the Canadian Association for Curriculum Studies, 2*(2), 73-83.

Sprinker, M. (1980). Fictions of the self: The end autobiography. In J. Olney (Ed.), *Autobiography: Essays theoretical and critical* (pp. 73-83). Princeton: Princeton University Press.

Stack, M., and Kelly, D. M. (2006). Popular media, education, and resistance. *Canadian Journal of Education, 29*(1), 5-29.

Street, B. (1998). New literacies in theory and practice. What are the implications for language in education? *Linguistics and Education, 10*(1), 1-24.

———. (1985). *Social literacies: Critical approaches to literacy development, ethnography, and education.* New York: Longman.

———. (1984). *Literacy in theory and practice.* Cambridge: Cambridge University Press.

———. (Ed.). (2005*). Literacies across educational contexts: mediating learning and teaching*. Philadelphia: Caslon Publishing.

Steinberg, S. and Kincheloe, J. (Eds.). (1997). *Kinderculture: The corporate construction of childhood.* Boulder, CO: Westview Press.

Stern, S. T. (2007). *Instant identity, adolescent girls and the world of instant messaging*. New York: Peter Lang.

Thomas, A. (2007). *Youth online: Identity and literacy in the digital age*. New York: Peter Lang.

———. (2004). Digital literacies and the Cybergirl. *E-learning, 1*(3), 358-382.

Thoman, E., and Jolls, T. (2004). Media literacy—A national priority for a changing world. *American Behavioral Scientist*, *48*(1), 18-29.

Tierney, W. G. and Dilley, P. (1992). Constructing knowledge: Educational research and gay and lesbian studies. In W. F. Pinar (Ed.). *Queer theory in education.* Mahwah; NJ: Lawrence Erlbaum.

Torres, M. N., and Mercado, M. D. (2007). The need for critical media literacy in teacher education core curricula. In D. Macedo and S. Steinberg (Eds.), *Media literacy: A reader* (pp. 537-558). New York: Peter Lang.

Trend, D. (Fall, 2003). Merchants of death: Media violence and American empire. *Harvard Educational Review, 73*(3), 285-308.

———. (1997). *Cultural democracy, politics, media new technology*. New York: SUNTY
Turkle, S. (2005). *The second self: Computers and the human spirit*. (20th anniversary edition). Cambridge, MA: MIT Press.

Turkle, S. (1995). *Life on the screen: Identity in the age of the Internet*. New York: Simon and Schuster.

Tyner, K. (1998). *Literacy in a digital world.* Mahwah, NJ: Lawrence Erlbaum Associates.

Ulmer, G. (1994). *Heuretics: The logic of invention.* Baltimore: Johns Hopkins University Press.

Valentine G., and Holloway, S. L. (2002). Cyberkids? Exploring children's identities and social networks in on-line and off-line worlds. *Annals of the Association of American Geographers, 92* (2) 302-319.

Walkerdine, V. (1997). *Daddy's girl: Young girls and popular culture.* London: Macmillan.

WeeWorld.com. (2009). WeeWorld Company Info, Retrieved from http://www.weeworld.com/about/news_item.aspx?archive=yesand NewsID=35

Willinsky, J, (2000). A history not yet past: When then is here? In B. R. C. Barrell and R. F. Hammett (Eds.), *Advocating change.* Toronto: Irwin Publishing.

———. (1998). *Learning to divide the world: Education at empire's end.* Minneapolis: University of Minneapolis Press.

———. (1987). The seldom-spoken roots of the curriculum. Romanticism and the new literacy. *Curriculum Inquiry, 17*(3), 267-291).

Williams, R. (1958). *Culture and Society: 1780—1950.* Harmondsworth: Penguin

Willis, P. (1990). *Common culture.* Boulder, CO: Westview Press.

Yagelski, R. P. (2000). *Literacy matters, writing and reading the social self.* New York: Teachers College Press.

Index

new literacies ¶ AND DIGITAL EPISTEMOLOGIES

Colin Lankshear, Michele Knobel, & Michael Peters

General Editors

New literacies and new knowledges are being invented “in the streets” as people from all walks of life wrestle with new technologies, shifting values, changing institutions, and new structures of personality and temperament emerging in a global informational age. These new literacies and ways of knowing remain absent from classrooms. Many education administrators, teachers, teacher educators, and academics seem largely unaware of them. Others actively oppose them. Yet, they increasingly shape the engagements and worlds of young people in societies like our own. The *New Literacies and Digital Epistemologies* series will explore this terrain with a view to informing educational theory and practice in constructively critical ways.

For further information about the series and submitting manuscripts, please contact:

Michele Knobel & Colin Lankshear
Montclair State University
Dept. of Education and Human Services
3173 University Hall
Montclair, NJ 07043
michele@coatepec.net